SANDSTONE

SEDUCTION

---

*Rivers and Lovers,
Canyons and Friends*

ALSO BY KATIE LEE

All My Rivers Are Gone: A Journey of Discovery Through Glen Canyon

Katie Lee

SANDSTONE
SEDUCTION

---

*Rivers and Lovers,
Canyons and Friends*

Introduction by **Ellen Meloy**

BOWER
HOUSE

DENVER

Special thanks to Northern Arizona University whose Special Collections and Archives houses the Katie Lee Collection, which Lee donated to SCA over the course of many years.

www.BowerHouseBooks.com

Cover design by Margaret McCullough
Cover painting by Serena Supplee
Photographs provided by the author

Printed in Canada

Library of Congress Control Number: 2021935007

Paperback ISBN: 978-1-917895-13-2
Ebook ISBN: 978-1-917895-14-9

10 9 8 7 6 5 4 3 2 1

Contents

For Joey . . .
the Aussified Dutchman

Acknowledgments

I ACKNOWLEDGE THAT I DID ALL THIS BY MYSELF without a bit of help from anyone at anytime—no other suggestions, comments, or ideas went into this meat grinder-outer of words. They are all my own, fitted together by me and this small machine on a big table in the bowels of my house; sometimes late at night, sometimes late afternoon, never in the morning. Mornings are reserved for getting on the Ameche (telephone to you). Then, I ask the machine, "What's next?" (Well ... yes, the machine did help in a very small way, but that doesn't count.)

"What's next," it told me, "is 'Acknowledgments.'"

"What are they?" I asked.

"Those are folks 'out of the blue' who have encouraged, praised, questioned, criticized, suggested, even entered your stories to make them better. No doubt you have forgotten some—maybe quite a few—but you'll have to deal with that yourself; after all, it's your ballgame—'scuse me, word game."

"But I did this without any ..."

"Like hell!" it lettered.

So, while I waited, it began to spit these people out. I've no idea why in this particular order; just a whim, I suppose, of the Robot mentality.

WAY BACK BEFORE THIS LATEST ERUPTION OF WORDS, and before her own book, *The Heartcore Alternative*, was completed, Nancy Jacques slipped me a piece of sage: "... you need a title that hints at the mystery of this complex and extremely significant relationship." *She's* the one who named the story "Bittersweet Bridges Uncrossed," not me.

Her dear husband, Dave Wegner, supports me in everything I do, whether I do it well or not; and when my science gets slippery, he sticks it to the wall with facts and figures, jokes, and homemade beer.

My Spanish was always tweeky at best—except when I *sang* it. Therefore my faithful friend, Bruce Berger, corrected spellings and dared recall a Baja incident that had slipped my mind, prompting me to add yet another.

Larry Lindahl, designer of my friend Tad Nichol's book, *Glen Canyon: Images of a Lost World*—from which the introduction has been reprinted here in slightly altered form—read several essays and made hesitant comments, as if he might be tiptoeing through a patch of prickly pear. If so, he left fruit behind that I savored.

My favorite, most honest publication—in the face of years of backbiting politics, steamroller industrial tourism, bullshit, unfriendly neighbors, and a few friendlies—is the *Canyon Country Zephyr*, owned and edited by Jim Stiles, a courageous and sensitive soul. He has published a couple of these yarns, for which I feel both honored and grateful. Along with treasured friends like Ken and Jane Sleight and the dear buzzard, Ed Abbey, Jim is one who does not hesitate to say what he thinks is wrong or right, sweet or acidic, about my efforts.

Another publication that often prints my scattered words is *Mountain Gazette*, a bimonthly mag that was resurrected from a shallow grave a few years ago by John Fayhee. Unique among editors, he doesn't whittle your work down to a silhouette; he prints the entire image.

Richard Martin, known on the river as "Ricardo," works diligently on the finger machine as well as the oars. He is the founding president of the *Grand Canyon Private Boaters Association*, as well as editor/publisher of its quarterly, *The Waiting List*. Best of all, he is a dear friend who reads and often pastes my whimsy into his rag. Beyond the call of many duties, he will come and punch out my temperamental "machine" when it throws a tantrum. If not for Ricardo, the damn thing wouldn't speak to me at all!

Merlin Wheeler and Kent Frost, two disparate souls, years apart, love the canyon country in the same way and treat it accordingly.

Between them, they taught this novice the subtle tricks of sticking to slickrock—both figuratively and spiritually. Kent appears here in one of the narratives—albeit slightly disguised—while Merlin, for real or in shadow, accompanies me on every hike.

Leonard Schneider popped out of the blue after fifty years of my not hearing a word from or about him. Only the memory was strong enough to write a line or two about him in the Hollywood tale several months *before* his call. When we met again he sharpened my memory about some scenes with our mutual old friend Burl Ives.

As always, Diane Rapaport, sister-friend and business manager, holds things together for me when they start flying apart. She's the one who will sit down and listen to the reading of every yarn, tell the truth about it, then bounce my objections back to me until they cease to exist.

I am twice blessed—second book—to have more of a family relationship with my publishers than a business one; half my laughs for the year come from a staff that stays in touch even when there's not much ado. At the home of Johnson Books, publisher Mira Perrizo and editor Stephen Topping vibrate with encouragement when this poor writer wears a Dunce's Cap instead of a Creative Crown, while Robert Sheldon wanders far and wide to get the word out and Stephanie White holds the fort for orders with phone in hand and a gentle voice. Serena Supplee—wowee—again the cover painting! Debra Topping, the clean cover design.

I'm really thrice blessed. Were it not for my old friend and former agent Carl Brandt of the staunch New York firm Brandt & Brandt, I would never have been introduced to JB: "Regional presses ... are doing the good work that used to be done by the old line firms. There is a good editor, Stephen Topping, at Johnson Books in Boulder who recently left the Random House group and thus has the right kind of experience. Love, Carl."

And ... well ... I suppose, u-uh, to be kind, The Machine.

—K. L.

Foreword

Ellen Meloy

THE WOMEN WHO LIVE on the red-desert rivers of the American Southwest are helplessly, hopelessly bound to them. Women thus helplessly bound cannot explain their attachment without incinerating everything within a sixty-mile radius. Your scorched eyebrows would forever and beyond all doubt convince you that women understand slickrock and might, in a heartbeat, take it as a lover over any man.

Katie Lee's lover was Glen Canyon in Arizona-Utah, a wild paradise of curvaceous sandstone cut by a ribbon of Colorado River. In *All My Rivers Are Gone* she described that unabashedly passionate affair, from her first river trip through Glen in 1954 to her anguish when, a decade later, the U.S. Bureau of Reclamation dammed the Colorado and buried over 200 miles of canyon beneath Lake Powell. For Katie Lee, a successful singer-songwriter who held her own against the Hollywood pulverizer in the fifties and sixties, that sandstone desert was intoxication, sanctuary, and, in its loss, despair.

The river marked Katie, marked her flesh, her music, and her activism on behalf of wild places (think baby-blue-eyed, five-foot-four flamethrower). But there are other things about Katie that we can know and she should tell: how she took her path to that lost river and where she has been since. The stories in *Sandstone Seduction* invite us into this wider, always intimate terrain.

In a time (1940s) and place (Tucson, Arizona) that was still small-town raw and as rough as a hairbrushed javelina, Katie's father teaches her how to swim, shoot, and skin rabbits. From her mother she learns how to sing and count—to count, she says, "numbers *and* money, a sense of living within your means."

At eighteen, in tandem with two equally restless and unchained brother-friends, she sows what would become a lifelong fidelity to the native music of *la frontera*, the Mexico-U.S. borderlands of dust, beer, bougainvillea, and guitar ballads of the Nogales brothels, "the places where I learned most of my good Mexican songs."

She sings to a Santa Catalina Mountains moon and a Sunset Strip club crowd. Knots a cottonwood leaf stem with her tongue. Tries out a roadside "wig bubble" (wild idea) on a number of dust-drowned drivers of the Baja 1000 road race. Crawls out from poor judgment, near hypothermia, and a dangerous canyon with her hide and humility intact. Bids farewell to passed-on friends and lovers with brokenhearted anguish or a self-designed catharsis, shared with grieving neighbors—hell, shared with the whole town—as a wild bicycle ride down its main street, buck naked.

⚜

WITH KATIE, grunting up a hill on a remote piece of coast in Baja California. Sun low on the aquamarine sea. Frigate birds strafing our heads. Cholla spines in our butts. Katie in aqua-blue T-shirt and hot-pink capri tights. Me in insubordinate hair, motley cotton, and river sandals with soles that ski on the granular soil, threatening to land me in the cholla again. Atop the hill, words about lost canyons and lost friends, rivers traveled, rivers dammed, deserts hiked. Atop the hill, two crunchy native westerners with a hip flask and ants in our pants talk about the fate of the planet. As soon as we return from Mexico, we vow, we will *fix the world*.

Too dreamy, too enslaved by imagination, I am not a good world fixer. The mouth of despair gobbles me up. But Katie ... Katie has been awed, angry, and active for more than six decades now. If there is despair, it comes in flashes that she quickly diverts to music and motion and memories that are never (publicly) dead weights of sorrow and nostalgia. But that lightning glimpse may reveal the price Katie has paid for a life unlike that of most of the women of her generation. Skinner of rabbits. Singer of borderland ballads. Hollywood starlet. River runner. Canyoneer. Ski-town bohemian. Baja *vagabundo*.

A Puritan's worst headache. Outrageous, outspoken, she is so far ahead of her time we are still catching up.

Wordless, we sit through the sunset and into the rising dark. Pelicans slip home on invisible thermals above the surf. The air turns indigo. A jagged sierra rises behind us and stars send us their light. There is lime on our tongues and salt on our lips, even this far from the sea.

ME: Katie?

KATIE: Yes?

ME: Katie, I just realized that you're the exact same age as my mother.

KATIE: (A great big snort of tequila-out-the-nose laughter.)

ME: Katie?

KATIE: (She is rolling on the ground, clutching her sides.)

ME: Katie, I just realized that you're *nothing* like my mother.

⁂

KATIE ONCE SAID that her books "don't get writ fast"—for *Ten Thousand Goddam Cattle* she spent ten years rescuing a fat compendium of cowboy songs from near oblivion—but they get writ. In *Sandstone Seduction* she writes with fists to the wall and flesh to that river-cut slickrock, where her lover still lives. She remembers what it was like to live and breathe before we were entombed in plastic and concrete, greed and speed. Her own stories make her desperately homesick at home, and from that passion we all are moved.

By now Katie's pen and guitar have reached at least two new generations, thank the river gods, because someone has to wake us up out of our techno-stupor, and it is right that it is the still-crystalline voice of a writer-folksinger who remains rock-hard true to the harsh land and sun-bitten people of the Southwest.

Of the sustenance that rivers and deserts have given her, Katie wrote, "These scenes are mine to keep—a gift like no other gift I've ever owned." We are grateful that her gift lies within these pages, too.

Tucson Trilogy

Catmoon

THICK DROPS OF BLOOD, barely discernible on pine needles, finally gave Juan a clue to the big cat's unusual behavior. Glistening faintly, they were tough to see, even under a glaring moon—unless you had his hawk-eyes. Rojo lay belly-down in a fringe of light and shadow, as if a bolt of lightning had struck and charred him to the spot, his arm in an odd position overhead, holding the rifle, palm up against the steep incline, stock under his cheek. He had slipped on the needles and that's where he fell.

By rights he should have bought it.

We'd been lucky the whole day, dodging the game warden, old Blue Thorpe. Saw him heading toward Tucson while we were having a beer at Oracle Inn, which meant he'd probably just come off the control road up Mt. Lemmon and would be checking tags at Oracle Junction. It was the last day of deer season. We hadn't made our annual kill—unheard of in our circle of sharpshooters—and in about three hours it would be dark. Our pride must be considered. Not to worry—tonight there was a full moon. Pride, of course, allowed as how "as bright as day" *was* day. In 1941, at eight thousand feet you could see to dissect a gnat.

The trunk of the Olds coupe held a washtub full of ice and bottled beer, thick T-bones, butter and bacon, potatoes, and a bottle of rum. Going up on the 3:30 to 4:30 control would put us at the cabin before dark and leave plenty of time to chop wood, build fires in the fireplace and cookstove, eat, and load before the moon bashed through the pines, bounced off the lake, and lit the game trail.

THE CABIN. Our first shelter ever. Proof to me now that even then we were starting to soften up. After years of riverbeds, dunes, rock ledges, animal trails, wherever night hit us, Rojo, Juan, and I camped. The point being, once outdoors, stay outdoors.

A year or so before at Bear Wallow in a thunderstorm that was practicing for a Dracula movie, we still hadn't got a fire going by 9:00 and had started to grump at each other and mutter about going down the mountain. Somebody suggested driving to Soldier's Camp at least, to see if one of the cabins with a covered porch might be undrizzled enough to throw our bedrolls down and get out of this crap for the night.

Found one! Whole cabin, floor caved in, roof bashed down at one corner, window out, and door jammed shut. But there was a dry fireplace with wood stacked beside it, enough even for the ancient cookstove in the kitchen.

Within minutes our inch-and-a-half-thick T-bones sizzled in the big iron skillet and potatoes fried in the Dutch oven—sounds that harmonized with rain on a tin roof and drippings on the floor. The enticing aroma of crippled young steer, charred, barely hot through, grappled with the knockout odor of wood pussy. She had come up through the floorboards while we were gnawing on the bones, sniffed around the stove and our boots, acting like the goddam landlady. Maybe she was. Anyhow, we named her Stinky and threw our bones out the back door, indicating she was to eat outside since the new tenants had moved in.

Mattresses from log-framed bunks we'd hauled to the floor to spread out our sleeping bags—me in the middle with my .22; Rojo with a .38 Colt and flashlight; Juan with a 30.06 and the javelina gun, the 44.40. You'd have thought we were going to be attacked by rhinos, the bloody arsenal we carried, but there were real bear and real puma up there then. And, oh yeah, I had a 12-gauge shotgun I used to pack along, if my shoulder could take it from the time before.

That vitreous night, the night of finding the cabin, lives stubbornly in my mind awaiting duplication. It can't happen, of course, and trying to describe it produces the glazed-eye effect in folks who

Katie   Juan

didn't live in Tucson before the war. Others have no place or memory to compare.

The storm passed over. The moon beat us on the head. I remember rainbow colors in drops that glistened on pine needles and fell like comets, straight down or arched by the breeze. The green was *not* sheathed over with silver light, it was *green*—deep, pure green. Beside the ponderosas the old paint on the log cabin roof was chartreuse. We'd been eating, drinking, laughing, wrestling, playing guitar, and singing, but this shut us up, this clarity. We had walked around the cabin smelling the swollen earth, breathing the green air, tasting the piney wood; a night of pure crystal that could've broken with any increased vibration. I remember that we were most tired but couldn't sleep—not inside anyway. We pulled our rolls out beneath that coruscating moon, and she voodooed us back under the sagging porch roof, tossed and turned us, until she grew long shadows and slid over the crest near dawn. That was the only time in all my nights outside I couldn't sleep under a hot moon ... maybe it was some kind of initiation.

What we knew for certain on waking was that we had to *have* that cabin. Somehow it had to be ours, or at least accessible to us. And damned if it didn't happen. Rojo's old man got a Forest Service lease on the place and started fixing it up that September. By hunting season she was shored and waterproofed and pretty much ours.

⚜

ON THIS LATE FALL HUNT, we finished our beer at Oracle, roller-coastered the foothills, and skidded the Olds past the mines and up the switchbacks to the control by 4:20. Usually we doddled, stopping to flush quail or dove for dinner, skeet-shooting our beer bottles, and watering the cacti. But tonight, no farting around—our reputations, remember? The moon would start its ride up over the Rincons when the sun made cardboard cutouts of the Tucsons. By then those steaks had to drip, rise up, and walk to us!

We came past the old sawmill as the sun left the treetops, and were pleased to note that nobody occupied the lean-tos and that Bear Wallow was bare. No cars and no bodies at Soldier's Camp either. *Qué bueno!* Old Blue was long gone. Summerhaven (where we wouldn't be caught dead) was more than two miles away and down in the holler. We had the mountain to ourselves.

"Rojo, I smelled cat in Bear Wallow."

"No, you didn't, Spook. You smelled skunk."

Juan, our quiet member, said, "It was cat, I think."

"I can tell cat from skunk any day, *hombre*. What can a smoke-consuming puffer like you smell? Nuthin'. Right, Juan?"

Grin.

"So okay, you smelled 'em, you didn't see 'em."

"Don't mind if I do. Just don't want him prowling around *tonight* spooking the deer."

Juan said, "Wind'll change after dark. The deer come down off Spencer. Cat'll most likely go back toward Bigelow, the way he came."

"Funny, though," I said, "as many times as we've camped down there we've never smelled 'em before."

Rojo thumbed his glasses up the bridge of his nose. "Hey, don't worry, *muchacha*, they don't eat redheads, blondes, and brunettes. Even if they're hungry."

"They eat deer."

We unpacked the car and trucked our gear across a repaired foot-bridge up to the cabin. For some reason I didn't feel like hanging over the cookstove just yet, so I left the guys building fires and went back down to the ravine.

The air had crisped up considerable. Dusk almost sprinted into dark as ol' Sol's track approached the turn—I pulled up the hood of my hunting jacket and jammed my hands deep into the pockets. No snow yet, but frost would form tonight.

Then, without the slightest warning, I started to cry.

From the time I was fourteen, through university and into my first marriage, I kept a diary: daily entries, explicit in what they *didn't* say about whatever person was in my life then and there, but throbbing with a pulse of mountains and desert. Entry after entry declares a near-fanatic love of the Catalinas, describes sunsets and moon times, evinces how we *hated* the cities—I didn't even live in the city—how we hated to come back down, go inside. Those pages fairly scream disgust with any alteration or invasion of our sanctum: "Who is *that*? How'd *this* get here? Where'd *they* come from?" As if nobody else had the right to walk around. Mom used to call us the "three musketeers." Hell, she should have dubbed us the "three misanthropeers."

My tears were too young then to be falling for anyone but my piti-ful self, but I'd like to believe they were little warning cells built into my genes, cueing me for a million fights in the future, telling me that if I sat back watching the machine roll over every thing, place, and person I loved, I was no more than a glut bug. But let's level. I didn't have a clue how the machine worked, or that it couldn't be stopped or even slowed down with any definitive results. "FUJIGM!" we said—in army parlance meaning Fuck-You-Jack-I-Got-Mine—but we didn't have it for long and what little we managed to salvage came hard. Ultimately, we zigged when the machine zagged, a game of hide-and-seek involving passionate hatred and love.

So I cried for the inevitable.

War was breathing down the canyon. They'd both be leaving me here. They'd be back, I'd be gone. We'd all come back, all changed, even the mountains. It never entered our minds that the very *air* would alter their contour. Sure, we knew there'd be more cabins, more roads. The Prison Road up the front flanks had already started, but the reason they stood out like the giants they were, growing right out of our backyards, even though they were fifteen miles away, was that the glasslike air magnified them. I lived near Saguaro National Monument, watched them through day and night. I knew what the Catalinas—mountains of my name—could do. And say.

Early morning. A sun easing over a saddle in the Rincons spattered pink over their razorback ridges. A higher sun softened them to mauve, folding front and back ranges in an embrace. Mid-morning paled them to a dusty blue. By noon the granites turned to white blotches as the mountain danced in heat waves, with no shadows creasing the canyons and the jagged half-drawn scar of the Prison Road stitched upward like some gigantic surgical repair. Only then did the whole mass flatten out under the weight of too much light. But when the sun dropped to the rockiest, rugged end, offsetting those blooded fangs with dense purple and driving Ventura Canyon deep into her groin, Las Catalinas became articulate—a summons we couldn't resist.

I heard Juan's low birdcall from the cabin as a light beam spit out across the ravine, searching. I answered—beam went out, and before I was able to dry my tears on a sleeve, started smiling. In the dense dark, below the footbridge I could see Stinky parading her family, three little Smellies, their black and white backs like worms wiggling through the brush.

"Hey, Spook, where ya been?" Rojo hands me a rum toddy. "We're most hungry."

"I been cryin', that's where I been. Think I'll probably be there some more before you guys are gone. So what?"

"Ah, *muchacha* ..."

"Juan, I'm gonna beat this old barn owl up so bad tonight he'll wish he'd joined the Foreign Legion!" Rojo's and my wrestling matches, taken over from my brother years ago, kept the libido in control, kept us compadres who never coupled. Though it was a form of love, I suppose.

I cooked. We scarfed it, cleaned up the kitchen, and started oiling and loading the guns.

"Wasn't it late when the deer came down last time, Juan, around midnight?" I asked.

"Close to, but it wasn't a full moon. We should be all set b'fore 10:00. They ain't always creatures of fixed habits. For all we know they could be there now."

"Hell's bells, you guys, everybody in Arizona with even a cap pistol's been after 'em for weeks. We're not gonna see any venison tonight. Betcha."

"Betcha! They all run up here for protection—off-limits like," Rojo assured me, but he didn't sound so sure.

I allowed as how that's what the pussycat was doing in Bear Wallow, trying to get "off-limits" from the Lee brothers and their slobbering hounds.

Juan rammed some oiled flannel down the barrel of his 30.06, saying, "I don't much like the way those guys hunt, with the dogs and all. Professionals or not, I think it stinks."

"*I* don't much like the way some people think we're related either," I say.

Rojo: "I don't at *all* like animals treed and shot at close range with a damn cannon!"

Moonlight crawled toward the ravine in front of the cabin. I took a handful of shells for the 30.06, loaded up, and stepped out onto the porch. A breeze came down the ravine, off Spencer toward the lake, like Juan said it would. We should move now, slowly, and most quiet. The plan was to stay in dense shadows on the lake's south end, where we could see part of a game trail that angled down to the water. Some months ago we'd watched a big buck lead his harem down that trail. If they *were* creatures of habit, he might do it again tonight, just for us.

Moccasin Juan poked his head 'round the corner of the cabin, spooking me. "You ready, Annie Oakley? T'night's your night. Girls first. We best go."

Pines are susurrant in the wind or roaring like a surf, but tonight was another of those glassy nights—only cold this time with ice crystals—and when the needles moved in the downdrafts, they sang like strings on a harp. The air was brittle, yet it held testimony to the musky, dew-sweet fragrance of fall.

We moved slowly down the draw, single file from tree to tree, our boots pressing (with an occasional slip) against the insular coat of leaves the earth puts on before its winter down. A fallen ponderosa a few feet from shoreline made us a grandstand seat. Here we sat and waited.

Half an hour.

Moonlight swam through a gap in the trees onto the lake's far side, its reflection faintly defining what had been in shadow. Sachet kittens were everywhere, six or seven of them sniffing at our boots, climbing over the end of our sitting log, poking each other about. We hardly moved.

Another half hour.

My feet were numb, my hands the same, my nose frozen. As I raised my hands to cover it, I saw something move through the trees uphill. A minute or so later we heard his call. A twig snapped and he came into view. That same magnificent six-point buck!

My trigger finger suddenly had hives.

Inch by inch he moved, stopping, turning that huge rack, scenting, leading the does down, about a hundred yards away now, antlers flickering under moonlight. I put the rifle to my shoulder and slowly stood to sight him in. Steady ... got him locked ... took the big breath to hold it and begin the squeeze ...

Juan reached over and lowered the barrel.

"Shhh ... wait," he whispered. "We just remembered we left a log sticking out of the fireplace. It could get to the floor, so we better go back b'fore the cabin burns down."

Rojo had already turned and was walking away.

"This is some kinda trick, dammit! I had him sighted in. Shit!"

"No it ain't, Katie, and quit swearin'."

Still in whisper mode, I said it again. "Why didn't you let me shoot him and *then* go back? You guys are up to something. Damn your eyes!" I could see Rojo yards ahead moving quietly, but fast, so I took it Juan was serious, jammed the rifle under my arm, and followed. Dammit again! How could they be so dumb?

Rojo rounded a clump of low scrub where I lost sight of him, heading, I knew, for a trail beside a rocky outcrop leading to the cabin. Since it was obvious he'd get there first, why were we hurrying? Why didn't he just go and leave us there? I slowed my pace to turn and tell Juan what I thought of their massive stupidity, but before I got a word out ...

A heart-stopping, feral scream broke the crystal night. And then a loud thump, as something heavy hit.

My temples turned to ice. I froze. Juan raced by, almost knocking me over, but knocking a heartbeat back into me, so that I dug in and followed. Got to the clearing in time to see a scrambling ball of fur unwind and dig four giant paws into the ground, shucking pine needles out like a harvester. Within seconds the lion gained purchase against the mountain and streaked out of sight, some of the needles he flicked up hitting me and Juan.

"*Hay-soo!*" he rasped.

"Where's Rojo?" I hollered. "Whereizee ..." But the words weren't out before I saw him plastered there against the hill at the edge of moonlight.

As Juan knelt beside him, Rojo rolled over, sat up shaking his head, feeling the ground for his glasses, and babbling through his adrenaline rush. "What the hell is this, Africa? What's goin' on up here? That bastard came right outta the sky. He like to parted my hair!"

"Hmmmm ... don't eat redheads," I mused sweetly, teeth chattering. "Smells like he's been here all week just waiting for you." His scent, still floating in the clearing, was almost dense enough to see.

Meanwhile, our more serious member, not into making jokes until he had the answers he wanted, searched the ground for clues.

Unprecedented for a lion to jump a man in this country and scream while he's doing it. For the animal to even be in the area was abnormal. Juan picked up a bunch of needles and held them out to us, a dark shine under the moon.

"It's blood. He's been hurt. Somebody took a half-assed shot at him and didn't quite miss."

"Quit swearin', Johnny," I quipped. "Well, the poor thing can have my venison. If he doesn't die he's gonna need it."

THE CABIN DIDN'T BURN DOWN. But the log *was* burning slowly toward the wooden floor. We didn't sleep outside that night.

While we were eating breakfast the next morning, there came a bang on the door. When Rojo swung it open, there stood Blue Thorpe.

We asked him in for coffee, but he was in a bit of a rush. Then he saw all the shooting hardware leaning against the wall and wanted us to know that deer season was over, and there weren't a whole lot of rabbits up here. Also, it might be better if we didn't prowl around the trails because there was a lion, probably wounded, on the loose somewhere between here and Summerhaven, and the Lees would be here soon to track it down and kill it. Had we heard or seen anything unusual while we were out last night?

"Out?"

"Last night?"

"We just took a walk down by the ..." Juan jabbed me from behind.

"Never saw or heard a thing," said Rojo, "but it sure was a beauty of a moonlight night."

"I know," said Blue, and walked away.

Casas del Noche

Bunches of people over the years have asked me where I learned all my good Mexican songs. Most of the time they didn't get a completely honest answer. So these are the facts, ma'am—as we are wont to say, "the true bite of the gila monster."

ON A HOT SONORAN SUMMER AFTERNOON, 'long about 1940, Enrique was leading our pack down Obregon Street. Rojo, Juan, and I had a quart of Carta Blanca in each hand and the kids, Hector and Maria, were right behind. Hector had the guitar. The plan was for Enrique, whose mother ran the government-subsidized whore-house over on Canal Street, to take us to a new "kloob" later. First, more music, song, beer, more *cantinas y casas del noche.*

Enrique was a mystery—he could have been anywhere from thirty to fifty. He was graying at the temples and in his neatly trimmed Ronald Coleman mustache. Under caterpillar-thick lashes, his dark brown irises floated panned gold. You wanted to keep staring into them. A sinister-looking scar covered his left cheekbone and from somewhere deep below gravity came that extraordinary voice which escaped in a kind of whispery rasp, betraying a blend of local tobaccos, Waterfill & Frazier, tequila, mescal, and alcohol *puro*. God knows about his past. His present looked hairy enough to me. He was never without a fresh cut, black eye, or bunged-up limb. I'm sure he knew where to get anything anybody could want in Nogales, but all we cared about was hootch, beer, and music.

Enrique probably wasn't a pimp because he hardly ever had any money, never wore fancy new clothes, never owned a car that we knew about, and wasted a lot of good pimping time with us. He took on new life when we came to Nogales—as our guide (knew every shopkeeper, vender, bartender, mariachi, and tortilla slapper in town); our bargain finder, taxi getter (when we didn't bring the car across); our entrepreneur, and somehow a friend of the local *jefes*. He'd found Hector and Maria for us—could have been the kids' manager, but he acted more like their uncle.

I reckoned his most valuable asset was that of protector. My Tucson companions seemed not to share this reckon—they were convinced he was planning to sell me into white slavery and was just playing it cool. If Rojo hadn't spoken good Border Spanish and understood a lot more than he let on, Enrique would probably have been our interpreter as well—not too good in view of their suspicions. I knew enough to get by and could fool the locals into thinking I understood as they whipped through their tongue with the speed of light. But we all could sing in Spanish and Rojo could also play the hell out of a guitar. This got us into, and fortunately out of, the kind of places where a trio of young smart-ass *sin verquenzas* could ordinarily expect trouble—the Nogales brothels, the places where I learned most of my good Mexican songs.

Hector and Maria were about fourteen and twelve then, before the war, and holy Christ how they could sing! We'd hit the border on a Saturday or Sunday afternoon, send out the word for Enrique, and wait at La Caverna bar over on Elias Street, playing *silla calor*

Enrique

Los Hermanos
Camacho le descan
Un Feliz año Nuevo,
1942

Maria and Hector

(hot seat) with whoever was sitting in the booth wired with the old Ford coil—the button was behind the bar and we knew the bartender. Pretty soon our friend would amble in and we'd go off to find the *muchachos*. They went everywhere with us and sang the whole night for fifty cents. I remember after the war we bitched a lot because tourism hit Nogales like a tidal bore, bringing the brother/sister act another set of values, so they charged us ten cents a song after that.

How did we get so lucky? None of this tacky *"Rancho Grande–Jalisco–Cielito Lindo–La Paloma"* stuff, no — good songs like *"Hace un Año," "La Barca de Oro," "La Feria de las Flores," "Destino," "Mi Ranchita," "Traigo Mi Quarenta y Cinco!," "La Panchita," "Adios Mi Chaparrita."* Always *"Adios Mi Chaparrita,"* no matter when we parted, drunk or sober (hardly ever sober), in a cantina or the middle of the street, together we sang *"No llores por tu Pancho, que si se va del rancho, muy pronto volveras, aye, que, ca-rye!"*

Back then — 1940 — if you didn't hang out at La Caverna, you could hear mariachis playing great Mexican music in those obscure little cantinas off and away from the main drag. The fact that over half of them were cathouses didn't hurt the music a bit. Actually, it helped because the girls were partial to songs of faraway places and tender sentiment. Enrique knew all the best spots.

The girls hung out at the bar or sat at the tables, mariachis wandered in and out, and the bartender put nickels in the jukebox whenever there was a lull. We'd come with our entourage, take over one end of the bar or a corner of the room, order Carta Blanca or Dos Equis, play guitar, sing with the kids, and dance. The girls would gather around Juan, who'd blush all colors through his smile, and Rojo would untwine tender arms from around his neck from time to time, saying something like *"Ya me no tientes, chiquita,"* or, *"Sabes que tengo novia … posible mas tarde."* They'd laugh, look puzzled or petulant, and go to Enrique for the reason Rojo didn't want to go to the room with them. It seemed Enrique was like a brother to them.

They didn't quite know what to make of me. But after I sang a few songs with the wandering troubadours, or Hector and Maria, they learned to call me by my Spanish name, Catalina, accepting me in terms of song — *la gringa cancionera* — and not the competition. Sometimes the girls would get so distracted singing with us, or so caught up in the music, that they forgot to go to work. Like the night — insensitive slobs that we were — we had the effrontery to sing Augustin Lara's *"Cada Noche un Amor"* in one of the cantinas.

At the end, with all the *putas* and even the bartender joining in, there wasn't a dry eye in the house, and certainly nobody wanted to go back to business. That's when Enrique had to get us the hell out of there.

⊱⊰

THIS LATE AFTERNOON, a summer sun honed in on Mexican pink, turquoise, and yellow walls that were streaked with the territorial markings of both man and beast. The acrid smell fairly crackled in the heat as it mingled with open doorways, delivering a nostalgic bordertown potpourri of sweet heavy tobacco, beer with real hops, cilantro, chile, leather cured in cow piss, *carbon* (charred ironwood), and an occasional whiff of marijuana.

Enrique stepped into the shadow of a two-foot archway and disappeared. We followed through a cool hallway and turned a corner into a ramada-type enclosure looking out on a watered-down square of dirt floor. Bougainvillea splattered a ten-foot wall, then spilled into the open sky. A woman and a girl were tending steaming pots over a carbon fire beneath a ramada. A child, no more than seven, was intently forming corn tortillas.

"*Qué tal, mamacita?*" Enrique asked, encircling her waist—she was not his "little mother," it's what he called every woman in Nogales over fifty—with his other arm he brought the child to him, huskied some rapid Spanish, and pushed him toward the door.

"*Comidas*," our guide said to us, "you guys gotta eat. We got a long night in front of us. Besides, the *muchachos* are hongry, even if you ain't."

Five minutes later the child returned—not at all like your general run of *mañana*—with a pint of tequila in a paper bag. From I'll never know where appeared six cold bottles of Dos Equis, soda pop for the kids bilious enough to camouflage green tree frogs, and huge plates of *machaca* tacos—crisp, juicy with salsa, and *hot!*

We dove in.

When we hit the street again, it was dark. We sang and played our way south up the side streets off Obregon. Wherever light streaked out the doors and archways onto the sidewalk, someone was usually inside playing an instrument or singing. This part of town belonged then to the people of Nogales. It wasn't full of hawkers and ticky-tacky trinkets, nor was it paved. Music floated on the damp and dusty air; the night blossomed, burst in bloom, and then faded.

Sometime, somewhere—reason unknown—I switched to *tequila con limon*, a libation of some magnitude. For me it has all the subtleties of a blackjack and will produce a temperature somewhere around 103. The stuff never seemed to bother Rojo much, Enrique not at all, and Juan didn't drink it, or much of anything else, but just stood around keeping a close eye on everything, smiling his wonderful smile, and singing. *He* was the driver.

Enrique said it was time to go to the new "kloob," but we couldn't take the kids, too late, and besides we couldn't all get in the car. It was quite a ways out of town. We dropped them off at the *mercado* and went south; only way you can go, really. Like the ribs of a canoe, the side streets rise from the railroad tracks, flat for a bit on the bottom, then sharply up the hills on both sides. The boat-shaped valley opens up for a distance through the middle before it narrows again on the road heading toward Magdalena. To the upward bend in one of these high ribs we drove, and stopped.

I looked up at this Casa del Noche from the bottom of a cement staircase that looked like the ascent to Machu Picchu. Arriving at the top, I speculated momentarily about how many *borrachearos* had been rolled, tumbled, thrown, or had just plain fallen down the whole flight and lived to tell the tale. Inside, we heard laughing, girls squealing, the guitars and *guitarrones* booming out over the pandemonium. They were playing one of Juan's favorites, "*El Hijo Desobediente.*"

By the time we wandered past *los cuartos de las putas*, down the wide hallway into the cantina, Rojo had a guitar, I had some maracas, Juan had a girl on each arm, and we were all singing. The room was awash in the heady odors of *cerveza*, cigars, cigarettes, and stale Tabu. Boot heels banged the floor or grated across the rough boards, bracelets jingled, glasses and bottles clinked, pesos hit the bar with the ring of real silver.

I had another *tequila con limon*. Why not?

We picked a big round table as near the hallway to the outside as possible—to get what little fresh air entered the place—and started swapping songs with the mariachis while the girls stood around in a changing circle. They'd listen awhile or sing with us, have a drink now and then (that green frog stuff), slip off to the *cuartos* for a bit, then come back dragging their customers over to join us. Everybody buying everyone else "anodder won."

I was singing, Rojo playing and translating as I sang, "Spanish Is the Loving Tongue"—the room had quieted down considerably for this lovely border song. Then Enrique gave a signal from the bar that I took to mean, "*Bastante, chiquita,* intermission. Don' let the mood get heavy or we godda take a walk."

Two or three Enriques were giving me this signal.

I don't remember much more about that lively night, but according to those in a conscious state, I wandered out of sight onto the balcony with Enrique sometime during the dancing and singing and Rojo didn't see me go. But hawk-eyed Juan did. There was a cement parapet around the balcony about hip-high that you could sit on, and I do have faint recall about wanting to cool off, so I suppose that's where I went. Was I sitting there talking to our protector? The next day, Juan unwound the early morning hours for me.

His sight line from the door of the cantina just caught us on the parapet, but he was twenty feet away. There was only one dim light on the balcony. No, it wasn't red. He said I stood at the outer corner talking to Enrique for about ten minutes, then walked toward the head of the stairs. At the end of the parapet, the blackjack in the tequila descended. Like a Mack Sennett comedy, I stiffened, rocked back on my heels, and headed for the bottom of Machu Picchu. The last I heard was a piercing whistle that momentarily turned my head away from the stairs.

Oblivion.

Rojo verified that Juan whistled, dug his boots into the floorboards, and shot to the head of that staircase faster than the dart from a blowgun. He caught me just as I went over the edge from the *third* step down! Rojo, right behind, caught my feet, and together with Enrique taking the best part (they said), carried my dead weight from those Andean heights to the car.

The only night in our redneck career that I was unable to sing "*Adios Mi Chaparrita*" on leaving fair Nogales.

Juan for the Road

> *Make me no grave within that quiet place*
> *Where friends shall sadly view the grassy mound,*
> *Politely solemn for a little space,*
> *As though the spirit slept beneath the ground.*
>
> *Far trails await me; valleys vast and still,*
> *Vistas undreamed of, canyon-guarded streams,*
> *Lowland and range, fair meadow flower-girt hill,*
> *Forests enchanted, filled with magic dreams.*

MID-JUNE AND SHE'S ALREADY GODDAM HOT.

The look on the face of the Casa Grande service station attendant as I stand under his hose, inaugurating my Desert Rat Cooling System with a head-to-sneakers drenching, proves that he's a dude from some other place who hasn't yet figured a way around the heat situation. I squish into my cool-seat, point toward the Florence turnoff, and leave him staring blankly after me, money dripping in his hand.

Driving now along the Pioneer Parkway, I see Palo Verde rising green and lacy above puddles of yellow fallen blossoms, and thundershowers that crowd the west ridge of the Santa Catalinas trail their long blue beards over the crest to snag on the foothills. The Bird and I cruise River Road, avoid the city, and head for the home ranch out east of town. Where the carved wooden Tierra Linda sign points the way, we turn onto a winding desert trail, deeply incised, high-centered, clean. Sand rakes the bell housing, instantly touching a nostalgic nerve: cacti and trees remember me, caliche dust rills up to greet my nose, old voices call my name, *Paisano* sprints across the road, and I say, "Hi, fellas, I'm home."

The Bird burbles to a stop beneath the carport.

Passing under the long porch arches, I unlock the big hand-carved doors, push off my tennies, and step inside. Heat turns off like an arc light in the adobe's cool interior. For a couple of months it's been locked up, the folks away in Greece. I've been gone for three years, but if I were led blindfolded to this place, I'd know the sweet smell of earth this house is made of—earth and pungent mahogany and Mexican tile; scents and surfaces that make up my *querencia*. My homing place.

Caressing the cool tiles with my toes, I walk to the phone and dial.

"Rojo? *Qué tal, hombre?*"

"*Ay, bueno, muchacha!* You just get here?"

"Yeah, you ready to go?"

"Be there in half an hour."

"Got the beer?"

"Whole case."

"For *three* of us?"

"Who's gonna drive when we leave there?"

"Juan. Who else?"

In my room I look for old clothes: faded jeans, leather belt with Indian silver buckle, sleeveless cowboy shirt. Under a box of Sabino Canyon driftwood I find my dusty, run-down cowboy boots and on a top shelf the flat-top, sweat-stained Stetson I won from my brother on a bet that I wouldn't walk barefoot through a trail of wet cow shit.

Three years—seems like thirty! Hollywood's a goddam far cry from this elegant desert. I suppose I shouldn't complain. I've managed to peck my way into a few very decent deals. I have running parts on three NBC radio shows—big ones. I appear in this 'n' that movie, on this 'n' that television show, have a weekend live show at Cabaret Concert Theater, where I'm a director/producer as well as folksinger/comedian/dancer, whatever.

At 4:00 I hear Rojo's tires popping the gravel on the drive before he skids to a stop. He beeps the horn, like always, blinks behind his glasses, walks bowlegged, and looks the same as always—maybe a few more wrinkles now make up his broad, ready smile. He is short-coupled with round, hard muscles and large hands; golden brows bridge a rough-hewn reddish face beneath a handsome widow's peak of "yaller" wavy hair. Red can be mean with a fist when baited, but gentle with it strumming a guitar. In high school he developed a wide range of skills that he thought to bestow upon me, adding greatly to my advantage in hand-to-hand combat. He coached me in the art of spitting fifteen feet into a stiff wind, which I dutifully managed after two weeks of showering myself. He and Juan taught me to skeet-shoot beer bottles like Annie Oakley; to spin corners and drive

desert roads that would twist knots in a snake; to track; to mark a
trail and cover it; to aim high with the dropsy 44.40 bullet; to know
javelina, deer, and lion smells; and to milk a rattlesnake. He literally
forced me to learn the guitar and about a hundred songs. Wherever
he and I and Juan went, close harmonies followed.

"You got your ax in the car?" I ask.

"What do I need an ax for?"

"Your guitar, ferchrissakes."

Laying another coat of dust on the cacti and greasewood, we skid
the winding gravel trail from Tierra Linda and turn north on Harrison, facing the Catalinas.

The Catalina mountain range—rugged, shadow-pitted, seduc-
tive—came to be our personal property by a kind of mental squat-
ter's rights after we'd sniffed out some of her most secret places. This
possessiveness about places we discover and come to love (the more
inaccessible, the stronger the bond) stretches beyond good sense.
Concerning these mountains, we were clannish and unbearably
smug. There was little we didn't know, or thought we didn't know,
about the animals that lived there, the trees that grew and spread,
the streams that filled her swimming holes and made waterfalls in
her labyrinth of canyons—to say nothing of the obscure trails that
led to all these. And so we jealously guarded our possession and
were enraged if we happened to find someone else there, or even a
trace of someone else having been there. We didn't just see the
Catalinas with our eyes, we felt the old girl on our skins, smelled
her, sucked her stones, chewed her stalks, tasted her waters, knew
her intimately. Which is to say that the mountain all that time was
really teaching us to know ourselves. Only later did we understand
all we knew about her.

Our love affair with the mountain started at Sabino Canyon in
the toothy front range. When the crests were powdered sugar, we
knew a sun-warmed hideaway beside a deep, swirling pool that gur-
gled under a house-sized granite boulder, spun out its foam midstream, and tumbled fifteen feet over another. There were special
rocks that fit us where we lay on our backs to soak up the sun and
white skeletons of sycamore to hold birds in the sky. We scorned

even the little-used trails and made our own, climbing the hardest route directly upstream, swinging like monkeys over falls and dropping cat-footed onto sandbars. In all those years, ten maybe, we could count the times on our fingers that we saw anyone there—a hiker or two on the upper trail, but no one in the canyon down by the stream—and we were there only on weekends, because Rojo worked in his dad's lumberyard and Juan was a lineman for the power company. But on Friday afternoons, when the call of the Catalinas came, we dropped everything and dissolved into nature.

Thimble Rock, on the ridge separating Sabino and Bear Canyons, catches the afternoon light as Rojo turns west to cross town.

"Got to hike up to our old pools in Sabino while I'm here," I say with pleasant recall.

"I wouldn't if I were you." He doesn't look at me.

"Why not?"

"Well, first of all, you have to pay to get in."

"*Pay!* Pay who? I'll be godammed … I'll pay *nobody!*"

"The Forest Service, who try to keep it clean after 100,000 people get through with it every season. Katie, you don't want to see it. The place stinks."

"A hundred thou …"

"Beer cans and garbage, shit and broken bottles in the water. Can't even park your car, it gets stripped. People get shot, raped …"

I blink moisture from my eyes, "But we … you … Juan," I stammer in dismay, "we never saw *anyone!*"

Rojo looks at me and frowns. "Come on, open a couple of beers and just be glad we had the best of it to ourselves."

> *Oh, it's squeak! squeak! squeak!*
> *Hear them stretchin' of the wire*
> *The nester brand is on the land,*
> *I reckon I'll retire.*
> *While progress toots her brassy horn*
> *And makes her motor buzz,*
> *I thank the Lord I wasn't born*
> *No later than I was.*

Three beers later finds us harmonizing on Mexican tearjerkers as we pass between the big stone pillars and stop under a scrawny tree. Rojo takes a case of beer from the car and starts down the path. "Follow me."

There's not much grass in this one yet, it's new. In fact, there's really only desert scrub around and it looks sort of sad. The management has tried for a hedge—oleanders—a few mulberry and pepper trees, but nothing has grown very high. It's nearly 5:00, the sun still a hot yellow blister in the sky, and no one here but us. That's good. I can't picture Juan, who's lived in the same house since he was born, out here in this neighborhood, and I'm curious to find out how he digs suburbia.

"Here he is," says Rojo, bobbing his head to the right.

I walk around the stone to the top of the little mound with a beer in each hand, and sit. "Move over, Juan, we brought you something to wet your whistle. Drink all you want."

"Go easy, *muchacha*. Remember he has to drive."

Tipping the beer can, I watch foam sink into the tawny grass and disappear. "*Saludos, Juan! Y amor! Y pesetas! Y tiempo para gastarlas, y mujeres con muy lindas tetas.*"

Tetas lindas . . . the beautiful breasts of a pretty woman, preferably one in motion, or when she came to rest lying across his arm, or on a bank of sun-warmed pine needles that smelled of Christmas and the rich earth's musk.

> *"I see by your scare-strap that you are a lineman."*
> *These words he did say as I boldly walked by.*
> *"Come sit down beside me and hear my sad story,*
> *I fell off a pole and I know I must die."*
> *Oh, ring the phone lowly and climb the pole slowly,*
> *And check your D-rings when you go aloft.*
> *Keep your hooks sharpened and grease up your scare-strap,*
> *"I'm tellin' you, Katie, that ground ain't so soft."*

"I hear ya, Juan. Jesus! Why didn't you make them take you somewhere up high so's you could have a view, instead of here all scrunched up in this little bitty ol' place? Damn! He's taller'n this, Rojo."

"Hell, yes."

Taller, tanner, younger than we are by seven years. Eyes that look bleached by the sun, so pale and clear blue, shoulders broad as a wheelbarrow (because when he was a kid, Rojo was his idol and Juan lifted weights to emulate him, now he can lift his hero off the ground with one arm). At fifty paces he can count the segments in a bee's eye, and always he smiles, a strong, tight grin over even teeth in his lean face. He could be a double for Clark Kent—there's that clean, square look about him. And his favorite song, "*Juan Charras-quiado,*" he wails out high and paper-thin along the southern Arizona backroads. In the forties when I'd drive to town from Tierra Linda in my little red Model A, I'd hear a shrill whistle followed by the cadenza of a meadowlark's call, look up, and see Juan leaning out of his scare-strap from the top of some utility pole, hooks jammed deep into the wood, waving.

"Why'd you have to fall off that pole, Juan?"

"He didn't fall off. Wouldn't pull a dumb trick like that. The damn pole fell and he was near the top. If you gotta say there's something he shouldn't have done, it was moonlighting for the bunch of schmucks that were erecting the outdoor movie screen." Rojo opens three more beers and blinks hard behind his glasses. "Be glad you weren't here for the dirge they gave him. You'da croaked!"

"Don't tell me about it." I pour for Juan. "Here, *Charrasquiado*, have another, 'n' don't spill it. We don't wanna waste any. Let's toast the mountains of my name. To Las Catalinas!"

… to the Catalinas, the streams and open desert where he'd stand whispering under a sunset because of its near-sacred beauty … singing in the firelight … eating thick, rare steak … testing the fine balance of a good gun in his hand … enjoying the snugness of a snowbound cabin … spinning the Cadillac to Hell's Half Acre, Ruby, Aravaca, Nogales … climbing the trails to Tanque Verde, Mt. Lemmon, up Aravaipa Canyon … up … up … *up* … then suddenly *down*.

The scalding late afternoon sun is still with us, but a slight breeze has risen. I lift my hat to cool my head. Taking another pull at the beer, I stand, then jump up and down. "Feel that, Juan? It's ol' Katie rappin' atcha! Think he knows we're here, *amigo*?"

"'Course he knows. He told me to bring you. Better not stand there too long or he'll rap back." Rojo rolls over laughing. "Oh boy, that'd be great, wouldn't it?"

"And how! Hey, let's sing."

"You gonna take his part?"

"Whaddya mean? Hell no, let 'em take his own part."

A high tenor drawn thin and piercing carries the melody, the only part Juan can stick to, and a yodeling, three-part harmony floats over the stones. The sun gives up some of its heat behind a mesquite and the cicadas buzz electrically.

Red comes to sit beside us, pulling his legs up crossed in front. The sun finally sizzles out behind the Tucson Mountains like a hot iron dipped into a pale green sea. The ground beneath us heaves a sigh. A cactus wren comes to perch on the stone by Juan's head, says a few uncalled-for things, and flits away. From under a mesquite comes the coded message of Gambel's quail—ka-*ka*-ka, ka-*ka*-ka ... Cicadas stop their buzz saws and it becomes very still. Rolling over on my stomach, I try to find a chin to rest in my hands.

I think back and remember why there'd always just been the three of us. Juan wouldn't bring the girls he dated—said they didn't fit.

When they came back from the Middle War, Juan unscathed from the paratroops and Rojo with nine Nazi bullet holes in him, I was married and Rojo was married and Juan was looking for a girl who'd go hunting with him, sing and swim and hike with him, and a lot of other things he'd never find. By the time I was *un*married and off to Hollywood, Juan had got his knot tied, but it didn't last long. By then I think he knew that having a girl like me wasn't all that silky. I'd gotten too independent for them. What artistic talents I had never concerned them much; the important things were spitting, tracking, riding, shooting, and climbing. It wouldn't have done any good to tell them that these fine skills did little to improve my professional image, and they were truly disgusted a year or so back when I'd come home to go deer hunting with them, found a great six-point buck in my sights, and couldn't pull the trigger. But they expected me to shuck it all sooner or later and come back to what they considered cleaner sports. Meanwhile they'd keep the home fires burning.

The first case of beer is gone.

Yup, he can see a sunset pretty good from here. There's a soft turquoise afterglow in the lower sky and the Tucson Mountains rest against that cyclorama in strong, black silhouette. Above them float thin veils of mauve frilled with pink—the kind of sunset Juan called "quiet."

With slow, studied precision, Rojo gets up and walks clear of the stone, steps into the path, and makes a straight, unfaltering line to the car for the other case of iced beer and his guitar, returning the same way. I get up, tilting and weaving somewhat, saying, "Juan, let's go to Sabino and have a swim."

"He can't drive now—had too many. Besides, remember what I told ya about the place. It'll be fulla brats and tourists."

"He kin drive. He kin drive settin' on both hands. C'mon, Juan, let's go swimmin'. We'll run all those goddam EVs [eastern visitors] outta there!"

"How can he go dressed up in that fancy suit, *muchacha*?" Rojo is very serious about this. I stop moving, stare a minute before getting the picture, then squeeze my eyes shut against the thought of him decked out in the sort of uncomfortable duds he always hated.

"Honest to christ, Juan, if I could get in there, I'd rip that straight-jacket off ya!" Making for the headstone, I sit, but it's not like rocks ought to be—very slick—and I fall off.

"Whassamatter, ya frowzy ol' drunk, can'tcha sit up?" Rojo puts the guitar case down on Juan's mound and snaps it open.

"Aw, shuddup and play someting. Since he can't go swimmin' in those stupid clothes an' we can't take him to Nogales in 'em either, we might as well sing and dance here the rest o' the night. I s'pose he can go to a dance in that clostro … fo … cluster-of-obic … shit! outfit."

The guitar rests across Rojo's outstretched legs giving forth the rocking *clip-tee-clop* rhythm of a horse's walk. I try the headstone again, this time with my boot heels hooked firmly in the sod, and sing …

Leanin' on the old top rail
In the big corral,
Lookin' down the twilight trail
For my long lost pal …

How he sang as he sprang
On his old mustang
And rode away ...
Down the track by the shack
He said, "I'll be back
Another day."
Now the moon is shinin' pale
On a lonesome gal ...

I can't make it. Tears grow and spill, roll to my jeans, to the stone, to the ground. Red stops playing and comes over, saying gently, "Maybe it's better he's here, Spook, maybe better'n waiting for some worse things that coulda happened to him. You gotta think of that instead of feelin' sorry for him."

"Hell's bells, I'm not sorry for him, I'm sorry for me b'cause he can't play with us anymore, 'n I'm drunker'n a hoot-owl, 'n sentimental, 'n mad. It's the music. We gotta sing somethin' happy and talk about the funner things we did."

"Your turn." He hands me the guitar. "Gotta go drain the lizard."

"Watchit y' don't whiz on somebody's grave, *hombre*. Juan's got neighbors might think it's disrespectful."

The afterglow has faded and stars begin turning on. Tucson flips her neon switch and from the city several miles away rises a murky pinkish glow. Off in the distance someone farts his exhaust and from the freeway come intermittent revving noises, far enough away to sound almost musical. The guitar strings feel mushy under my groping fingers, but still we manage a three-part harmony on one of our old night-herding songs. We pour Juan his ninth or tenth beer and add our empties to a neat little fence we're making around his mound.

"Hey, Juanito Charrasquiado," I holler, "bet you never been this dead drunk in your life ... er live drunk either."

Rojo leans with his elbows on the stone, peering down. "Betcha can't even stand up."

"We should go shootin' tonight like we useta," I say softly, "suit or no suit."

A dust cloud would swirl around the topless Model A as she careened the curves on the way to Hell's Half Acre, sprouting guns like an arsenal. Her wheels would spin through dry riverbeds; she'd boil up the climbs and crepitate down the hills, cross streams and flats, raking greasewood and smashing cacti like a Sherman tank. Her name was Chee-Chee, and when she hit a good bump, her yellow floor-boards would fly into the air in four sections to be caught by the passengers, or they'd land on the rear seat, exposing the running road beneath. Skidding to a snakish halt, Chee-Chee would spill her company like foam flowing over the top of a beer stein. Juan, Rojo, or I would have seen a ground squirrel, a snake, or maybe a jackrabbit. Before the dust could settle, a volley of shots would boom out in the clean, desert air and whatever had moved, moved no more. On summer nights after a rain, when the smell of wet greasewood rose thickly from the dust-settled earth, we'd head down an old line-road, one on each front fender with a .22, taking potshots at tarantulas that had been flooded from their holes. When jackrabbits or cottontails would freeze in our headlights, they were too easy, just sitting there, so we'd put a hole through their ears, gentle like. Half the time we thought we'd missed because they still wouldn't move, but in the fall, when their meat was fit to eat, we'd go back to that same place and hunt in the early morning or late afternoon like *real* sports. Quite a few of those we skinned and ate had holes in their ears.

I don't know who that person was who did those things in her teens and early twenties, and I've no answers for her even though I vividly remember her deeds and the deeds of her companions. We ate all the game we killed except those poor, hapless creatures we used for target practice with no qualms whatsoever. We never shot buzzards—they were the desert's garbage collectors. Hardly got a feather from a raven—they were too wary and clever, sounding their alarms to everything else around. Beer cans came into use long after we'd skeet-shot a fifty-gallon drum full of bottles. It must have been a total lack of caring or wanting to know the creatures and what they must do to survive in the desert.

Today our wanton destruction appalls me. We were taught to be good hunters, to care for our firearms, to oil and keep them clean, always click the safety, never point them at anything we didn't mean to destroy, never load until trailhead was reached, and never shoot from the car. So why the tarantulas? The ground squirrels? The snakes, centipedes, and scorpions? I was taught to use a gun when I was twelve years old. I kept my family in meat during war rationing and could skin everything from a quail to a deer, but nobody taught me to demolish those poor creatures in my "target practice" sights. Nobody.

Rojo takes Juan's empty, adds it to the fence, and pours him another, saying to me, "I s'pose you wanna take him out to the old line-road."

"Probably. Ya got som'thin' against that too, ya ol' barn owl? Why not? He'd like it."

"But you wouldn't."

"Why the hell not? I always ..."

"B'cause, Spook, some big shit from Chicago bought the land out there and put up a buncha cute little trailer houses, and there ain't so much as a damn cholla for a lizard to hide under. Looks like a scalded pig's ass."

"All *gone*?"

"Bulldozed it off in two days. Whole thing." He shakes his head. "A hundred of us couldn't have done that in two years."

"That's progress," says Juan. "I didn't like it worth a dern, going out there to string the lines."

"Wha'd you say, *amigo*?"

"I said, in two days they ..."

"No, I mean about Juan havin' to string lines out there?"

"I didn't say anything about *that*. How the hell did you know he had to?"

"He just told me."

"Oh, well, yeah ... why not?"

"He also quipped, 'That's progress.' Sounds more like genocide to me."

> *Oh, it's squeak! squeak! squeak!*
> *Close and closer cramps the wire.*
> *There's hardly play to back away*
> *And call a man liar.*

Their house has locks on every door;
Their land is in a crate.
These ain't the plains of God no more,
They're only real estate.

We lie across Juan's little ol' sod shanty roof on our backs, watching a misty waning moon float up from behind the Rincons. The mountains of my name show clearly, both front and back ranges, and along the Prison Road the headlights of some descending car flash from the cool pines of Mt. Lemmon. A silver fence of cans glitters in the pale light. We hear a coyote pack yipping in a nearby arroyo. Rojo, Juan, and I answer in their native tongue and they nearly go crazy talking and yelping to us, until we are hoarse from laughing and howling back. I give one earsplitting cowboy yell and slam the guitar case shut. The ol' barn owl places a full can of beer within Juan's easy reach, takes my empty, and with his, carefully completes the fence around Juan's lot in suburbia.

We start for the car.

I turn and come back to the mound, resting a boot on the footstone for steadies. "I won't see ya again, Juan. I don' like your new house. Ya don't really live here anyway. You're out there on the high trail lookin' things over."

Where dawn, rejoicing, rises from the deep
And life, rejoicing, rises with the dawn:
Mark not the spot upon the sunny steep,
For with the morning light I shall be gone.

For me no sorrow, nor the hopeless tear;
No chant, no prayer, no tender eulogy;
I may be laughing with the gods—while here
You weep alone. Then make no grave for me.

"*Vámonos, Juanito. Andale, pues!*"

The car skids insanely on the turn through the stone pillars. Rojo puts a protective arm around me and blinks. "I tol' ya he had too much to drink."

Bittersweet Bridges Uncrossed

WE NEVER KNOW OUR PARENTS.

Love them, trust them, obey them, live and learn from them, but know them deep inside? I don't think so. After all, how is it possible? Life begins for us with this huge generation gap. My mom, born in 1894, was raised by God-fearing Presbyterian parents in the Victorian age, whereas I, arriving in 1919, fell into the Flapper age. Mom may have followed the flapper styles, a short bob to her naturally wavy blond hair and knee-length dresses like the one I played fashion model in—a drop-waist, rose chiffon, heavy with hand-beaded leaves of purple and green—but if she pictured herself in a Scott Fitzgerald world, it never came through to me. I remember all those boring Sundays, when as a small child I was made to sit in a pew between my parents, wiggling and squirming like some trapped insect, while a big black-winged bee droned from a hive way above, about nothing I understood.

❧

MOTHER HAD A VICTORIAN HANGOVER.

Had this crazy dream about her once—she was in a buggy being towed by a satellite—it didn't make sense to me then, but it does now, considering that she spent her teens in a horse-drawn buggy and lived to see a man zapped to the moon. Quite a leap when you think about it, and I suspect the hangover caused her some deep inner conflict. She rode in that buggy, trying to pull me onboard through my teen years and onward, until her last decade on earth. But I was speeding by with the rumble seat crowd, leaving her in the dust. Or so I thought.

29

How little we know.

My dad was a college football star, very healthy, very handsome, an aviator in World War I—flew Jennies—which made him a romantic figure as well. He taught me to shoot, hunt, swim, handle tools, and take care of myself outdoors. Mom looked after the artistic side. Her health was delicate; she had a beautiful singing voice and had once taught music; she read the classics, took me to the ballet and theater, and taught me to sew a fine seam. So between them, I learned the best of two worlds.

Then the dream bubble popped. 1929. The stock market crashed and we crashed with it.

Up until then, you might say we were a well-to-do family. Dad owned a couple of houses and lots in Tucson, Arizona, a *finca* down in Cuba, and the big fancy home in the Hollywood hills where we were living in '29. He was an architect and a builder, but when the ducks hit the propeller, everything went down the tubes; everything, that is, but the Tucson property.

Well, Daddy just went to pieces, somehow couldn't seem to cope. He'd had a fine business in Hollywood and had worked hard—built some of the first hillside homes off Sunset Boulevard up steep and winding Kings and Queens Roads—but I think he was nonchalant about money. He was an honest, forthright guy, a softie who trusted everybody with a mere handshake; with nothing in writing, he was ripped off time and again. Mother, on the other hand, having solid Swiss-German genes mixed with her Irish, knew how to add and subtract. The next thing I knew, my little brother and I were wedged in between suitcases and boxes in our big Willys-Knight, heading out of Hollywood for Tucson—with mother at the wheel. I was nine years old that fall and my brother had just turned three.

❧❧❧

I DON'T SUPPOSE there are many folks still around who once crossed the ever-shifting Yuma sand dunes on that old boardwalk, but I can tell you it was impressive. Made of lashed-together railroad ties, it was a one-track, ten-mile-long snake, with a wide place every mile that was marked by an old tire on top of a tall pole. A controlled road with certain hours each way. What if a driver came at you between the mileposts? You'd be there yet if you slipped off. By then I was old enough to experience some fear and trepidation—that and the vivid picture of my little brother hanging on to the back door handle of the Willys-Knight, swinging out, and dropping into the dunes. Good thing we were only going about five miles an hour, and a good thing I was watching, because Mom was busy trying to stay on the road and too deaf from all the rattle-de-bang to hear him go, "Whee-e-e-e-!"

Seems to me that was a pretty gung-ho sport for a lady, driving those dunes with two kids, not knowing just where or how she was going to end up. She was indeed a lady—daughter of a founding father of a small Presbyterian town in the Midwest; pretty and protected, a college graduate and teacher; then, in rapid succession, air force wife, housewife, and mother (all with live-in maids); a lady who had never actually *worked* a day in her life. I can imagine now what was going through her head—a lot of fear, worry about her kids, and frustration with her husband's "what'll-we-do-now" attitude. But the thing that most likely kept her from sinking in the dunes, or anywhere else, was her gutsy determination to save the Tucson property.

Luckily she had friends atop the social whirl there—the wives of doctors, lawyers, artists, and businessmen—couples who could help her. Until I was almost two years old, we had lived in the house on Third Street at Stone Avenue, one that escaped the '29 crash, and where she had spent much of her time on the screened-in sunporch resting in bed, recuperating from tuberculosis.

And yes, she did it. Saved a part of it by selling another part and collecting rent that hadn't been collected in months, maybe years. Found herself a job (first woman) in one of the town's big real estate offices, full of macho men who gave her the dregs, rentals only, where she had to split her commissions even after she got her own sales license.

⚶

WE ATE A LOT OF HAMBURGERS that year, before Daddy came back from the coast and Mom had to go to bed again, fighting a recurrence of TB—that time for a whole year—but she beat it down and it never returned. Churchgoing tapered off for sure. Mom couldn't and Daddy wouldn't. While she recouped he designed and built a beautiful house, way-y-y-y out on the outskirts of town in a new subdivision called San Clemente, at Broadway and Alvernon. How they managed, I'll never know, but we moved in and I saw the furniture from the Hollywood house, including the piano, for the first time since we'd left the Yuma dunes behind.

It was one of the most beautifully designed and skillfully constructed Spanish-style homes in all of Tucson—a big leaded-glass, arched window framing the Catalinas and nothing but clean desert between to obstruct the view! Funny, the things a kid will remember. Daddy made beer in the basement of that house, fermenting potato skins, which gave rise to some distressing words from my mother about the smell—especially when the stuff got overripe and bottles began to explode. When they both went to work and left me as caretaker for my little brother, to keep him from pestering me I tucked him under my arm, trucked him a couple of hundred yards away from the house, plunked him, barefoot, down in a sticker patch, and had more than half an hour of tranquillity before he made his way back.

⁂

WHEN I WAS THIRTEEN, Mom and Dad were divorced. And so began the years, until the end of the thirties, that we played musical houses. Mom, my brother, and I lived on every street from Lee (not named for us) to Broadway, and most of them from Euclid to Campbell Avenue, not to mention several more outside that perimeter. During the winter months, the big Spanish-style house out in the suburbs rented for $100 to $150 a month. Mom and I, and my brother if he wasn't staying with Dad, would rent a little house in town for $25 a month and have enough, with her commissions and a bit of child support, to get by. Then we'd move back to the Spanish house and wait for the next round. This went on all through my high school and part of my university years. They not only helped me through my higher education, but somehow they managed to throw in private piano lessons, dancing, and dramatic lessons along the way. I say "they," yet I suspect I owe the artistic part to my mother's nickel.

Was she living a dream through me that she was never able to realize for herself? I wonder.

After my parents separated, the Victorian thing in my mother bubbled to the surface like the foam in that exploding beer. I suppose it had always been there, but tempered considerably by my Daddy's devil-may-care attitude. Now she ragged me about staying out too late, watching my language, running with people beneath my stature—what the hell was my stature? She acted as if something secretive was happening and complained about my not studying hard in school. I suppose every mother becomes antsy when her daughter passes puberty—those *are* the tricky years—but we were very close at that time, often taken for sisters. Yet when I turned the tables and wanted some answers, was curious about her dates and what she did, she'd mum up, cut me off, making me feel left out of something I should have been in on. She'd say, "You don't need to know all those details. I keep my own counsel."

About a year after the divorce, her "counsel" broke tether and slipped through the fence.

She came home late one afternoon, threw herself down on the bed, and sobbed as if her heart would break. I'd seen her wipe away tears before, but this was different. At first I thought she was sick, or had been in an accident and was all shook up about it, but between sobs, she blubbered into the pillow, "Never trust them ... never, never trust them."

"Who, Mom? Never ... who?"

"Men! Never trust the bastards."

I was so shocked to hear her use the word "bastard," I nearly fell off the bed. "Oh damn" was as far as she ever got into the cussing vocabulary. It took me half an hour to get the whole story, and by then I was ready to cry with her.

She'd gone to inspect a house with one of the big real estate moguls. When they got to the master bedroom, "the bastard" threw her down on the bed and tried to rape her. She dug her heels into him, kicking, scratching, fighting, biting, whatever she could, but she

wasn't a strong woman and was about to lose the battle when she remembered a strategy some friend had told her about, and used it. She
started laughing, laughing hysterically probably, but laughing.

Well, the big man's dick went down like the Hindenberg. Mom
grabbed her purse, ran to her car, shaking and crying, and barely made
it home without having a wreck. Years later on a summer night in the
moonlit desert, I found myself under a muscle-bound rodeo buffalo,
pinned against a gearshift and virtually helpless, when I thought to use
her technique. I laughed. It worked. I grabbed the keys and ran home.

MOTHER WAS A GOOD-LOOKER. She had natural blond wavy hair,
a high forehead, light blue eyes, a slightly aquiline nose—said when
she was bathing me, I suddenly jumped up and broke her nose with
my hard head. Her teeth were a toothpaste ad, her figure small and
neat. But her salient feature was eyebrows. In an era of Jean Harlow
plucked arches, hers were railroad tracks. Once in my teen years I
said, "Mom, we have to do something about your eyebrows." So I
began plucking and painting to give them a lift. Why she even let me
try, I don't know. The result ruined her whole face and made her
look like a blond geisha. Yet this smart-ass, taking a course in stage
makeup at the time, told her she now looked *much better*. With an
air of great tolerance, she gazed in the mirror and muttered, "Thank
you, dear, but I think I prefer my own."

My brother and I would often stop by my dad's house, sometimes
stay with him on weekends, or go hunting up in the foothills.
Through a mist of fleeting impressions my daddy comes out smiling—he had a wonderful smile—and nearly always the same. But
the shock, in that day and age, of my mother divorcing him must
have left him bewildered and, I'm sure, angry. (He went on, several
years later, to live with another woman quite openly, or defiantly,
before he married her and moved away.) My impression is that it
wasn't so much anger at my mother as it was with "that fast crowd
she runs with." He wasn't one for subtlety or pretense—too honest
and straightforward for their kind of sophistication. Not an art lover,
he was in over his head, I think, and felt merely tolerated.

Mom

Mother, the odd woman, became part of Tucson's artsy whirl. She was no dummy, quite capable of holding her own with the rest of that bunch. Surely she had an affair or two or three in those years after her divorce. Why not? But would she bridge the gap, confide in me, tell me what her heart was saying? No way.

Wait up. What about Brownie?

How could I forget a man of such stature—intellectually and physically? He was a fairly well-known author, gentle and kind, and had a tracheostomy. I remember the medicinal odor of his fastidious-ness, the snow-white linen handkerchief he always carried, and the clean softness of his big hands. Because of the hole in his throat and the need to hold his finger over it when he spoke, I never pictured him and my mother in any sort of romantic embrace. We're talking "romance" like a teenager drowning in her own hormones, heedless of the fact that her mother could be floating in the same lagoon.

Brownie traveled to Illinois with us the summer I was sixteen, and on the way stopped at Taos Pueblo in New Mexico to introduce Mom to his friends, Tony and Mabel Dodge Luhan. I climbed around the pueblo's rooftops and was bored as only a self-centered squirt can be, never imagining what Brownie's nurturing of mother's artistic soul must have meant to her. When we reached the home of her birth, I stayed with my aunt and granddad while Mom took "Mr. Brown" to Chicago. He was on his way to Europe, and I think the end of the affair. When she left, there were shock waves in that old Presbyterian house that even *I* felt. I rallied to her defense by pretending to go to bed, then creeping down the stairs to listen to my old-maid aunt's accusations, splattered with stinging "She-she-she's," and the words "divorced, married, and not married," as she cannily revved up my granddad's indignation, his softer voice complying with "No, we can't" and "Never."

Three days later when she came back, I was sure they would kick us out, but my uncle stepped in somewhere and calmed the waters, at least until we were ready to go home. I heard her crying in the night and saw her red-eyed and unhappy during the day. To my surprise, this time she actually told me she missed Brownie. I remember the song "Red Sails in the Sunset," the tears it brought to her eyes, and the letters they wrote. After that, there were few times when I was taken into the confines of her heart.

⚜

CAME THE MID-FORTIES, Mom's real estate savvy began to pay off with the kind of property she would buy, design a house for, and have Daddy build it. A very fine house, you understand, no cheap crap—a house we'd live in for four or five years, until the trees got big enough for shade—then when the market was right, she'd sell it for a bundle and start the process all over again. She and Daddy conjured up about eight homes, all on ten- to twenty-acre plots out east of town—most of which received full-page spreads in the Tucson papers. Along with her business sense she had the eye of a decorator and the talent of an artist; a unique sense for blending Victorian and southwestern motifs where everything was in balance and nothing seemed out of place. The beauty of her singing voice must have moved into her hands because she carved all her own doors in varied and difficult patterns. Her subjects seemed to come alive and move with the grain in the wood.

ALONG ABOUT THE MIDDLE of my junior year at the U of A, she started dating this paunchy little Greek restaurateur—and nobody else. He was a nice enough man, had an infectious laugh, and they had a good time together. But when she began acting more than a little serious about him, it was my turn to question "stature." To me he didn't seem quite up to her snuff. Again, she wouldn't discuss the relationship with me; always discreet, my mom, but I wasn't stupid, she had to be sleeping with him, somewhere. That was okay with me; I figured she deserved all the happiness she could corral, what with her fragile health and the monumental job she'd done all through the Depression.

Bill, the restaurant man, received a very lucrative offer to manage the famous Brown Derby restaurant in Hollywood. Mom threw in the towel, and they went to California and got married. November 28, 1939, she said.

Then *bang!* Pearl Harbor.

I went to work for the war effort at Davis Monthan Field, married a shavetail in '42, got pregnant, had a son, got divorced in 1945. Mom and Bill came back to Tucson and Bill started a new restaurant downtown.

Carved door panel

Mom designed another Spanish ranch—style house for the property they bought way out on the outskirts of town, and Daddy built it for them; this time at Harrison Road and Broadway—the old outskirts were inskirts by then. My son, Ron, and I and my brother lived there from time to time, but we didn't like it much. She stiffened up even more about my behavior—at age twenty-eight, mind you!—and Bill began tossing in his two bits when he should have kept the change.

The summer of '48, I split for the big time to pursue a career in the movies, radio, and the new spook, TV. There, I discovered how the other half lived, and quickly outgrew the ingrown Republican politics in Mom's house. The gap between mother and daughter widened and became even broader in the fifties when I left Tinseltown, hit the road singing folksongs for a decade, and had this serendipitous meeting with a paradise in southeastern Utah, where the Colorado River insinuated itself peacefully through an Eden called Glen Canyon. A place where I traded the fast pace of performing for a quiet, one-on-one exchange with Mother Nature—a time and place to relax, observe, meditate, and discover who I really was.

Meanwhile, back at the ranch, Mother and Bill were campaigning for Barry Goldwater who was eager to dam my river and drown the two-hundred-mile paradise that had literally saved my life. It's a wonder we were even speaking, and probably a good thing I was only there for brief interludes. Even then, she would *not* get off her Victorian plinth. Was it just a habit she couldn't break? Did she never realize how arbitrary she was to call me (now in my late thirties) immoral because I sat up until 2 A.M. talking with an old river buddy I'd not seen for a year? I recall some asinine statement that it was her house and I wasn't to behave like that.

"Like what, ferchrissake, Mother? Did you think we were fucking? He's old enough to be my father."

"Don't you use that language around here, Kathryn," she hissed. *Kathryn* being the key word for naughty-naughty.

The gap became a chasm no bridge could span. I didn't return to the ranch for more than a year.

The fifties left another gap in our lives, one far more painful and long-lasting. My little brother was killed in an air force jet accident.

What this did to my mother you can well imagine. As siblings, George and I had grown close, but after going our separate ways we rarely saw each other. He entered the service as a private and was sent to Korea. When he came back to Arizona, he joined the air force, earned his wings, and was sent to England. He was on maneuvers when his jet had a "flame-out," his ejection seat failed, and he died over the White Sands in the English Channel. More than missing his physical presence, I missed picturing him wherever he was; knowing he just wasn't ... there anymore.

For me, life on the road became dollars on a yo-yo—musicians spend most of what they earn just eating and living—so when I badly needed something, I often didn't have the bucks to buy it. Yet, despite all our word battles and political differences, when I was truly in a financial bind, I could count on my mother. I'd always pay her back when I caught up—with interest. All right by me; something she taught me years before when I had loaned her part of a small inheritance I'd received from a relative. She paid me back. With interest.

⚜

CAME THE SIXTIES, Mother and Bill took a trip to Greece where she met his nephew, also named George, a dark-eyed, dark-haired, handsome lad about the same age as my brother, who'd been blue-eyed, with blond wavy hair, and just as handsome. What I knew about that meeting was next to nothing, but I saw it plainly later.

Surrogate son.

They sponsored him, brought him to Tucson, and paid his tuition at the University of Arizona. Barely able to speak and understand English, George lived on campus, worked for Bill at the café when he wasn't in class, studied far into the night, and somehow struggled through his first year, with Bill yapping at his heels all the way. The poor kid had no money, was paid a pittance for his time in the café, and looked so hollow-eyed and tired most of the time that Mom feared for his health. Bill, having made his way as an immigrant struggling for a foothold in New York, was going to see that this nephew didn't have it any easier than he had. He was resistant to the kid's smallest needs, and totally blind to his larger ones. Had

I been living anywhere near them, or stayed for longer than a few days at a time, I would have sensed more than what my mother let show. She was worried for the boy and obviously on his side. But that's all I knew ... then.

⚜

I SLIPPED QUIETLY "off the road" and moved to Aspen, Colorado, singing for the music students in summer, the skiers in winter. Mom came up a couple of times with Bill, then when he died in '64, she came without him. By then, a sucking, slobbering monster called Powell Reservoir had swallowed whole my Colorado River, and along with it, the sanctuary of Glen Canyon.

In looking for a similar place of refuge, which I never found, a friend and I took on Baja California. Though completely different, it eased the pain of loss—being quite wild then and mostly unpaved.

We left Aspen in a loaded Jeep Commando the spring of '68; spent two months camping on "the track" all the way to the Baja Sur tip, back to the La Paz ferry, up the Mexican mainland, and finally to Mom's in Tucson. There we regaled her with stories of our journey, and the next day introduced her to a fascinating man we'd met on the "track" who just happened to live in Tucson and who just happened to be *interested* in her daughter, who just happened *not* to be interested in him.

Brandy, the just-happened man, came to the ranch forewarned about my mother's Victorian tick, and darned if she didn't take to him like an Arizona flash flood. Five months later, when I told her I'd changed my mind and *was* interested, and was going down to Baja again *with him*, her attitude altered from flash flood to slow ocean roll, and whipping into her old form she told me, "I have reservations about that."

At the risk of starting another brawl about "morals," I didn't say— "Tough shit, Mama. I'm forty-nine years old and think I can handle it." I told her that Brandy was due to die of emphysema in about three years; that he was a Marine Corps vet whose affliction was caused by a plane accident of the corps's making, and didn't she think he deserved whatever joy, companionship, or love that came his way?

IT WAS OCTOBER. Brandy and I were about eighty miles south of La Paz, Baja California, on a lovely, lonely moonlit beach, and quite drunk on Jinebra. We'd nearly drowned laughing, as we watched ourselves making love in an iridescent Sea of Cortez, our bodies outlined in dancing lights, with fireworks exploding in the wake of our fusing.

Later, snug and drowsy in our bedroll, he solemnly proclaimed, "If I should ever ask you to marry me, it's not because I love you all that much. I just want to fuck the government one more time."

"Uhhhh, howzzat again? Meaning what?"

"Well, I'm going to die because of them in the not too far away, and when I do my spouse will get my 'big blue yonder' disability insurance. I don't have a spouse to lay it on."

"Ooooooh. As much as I'm against that ball 'n' chain institution, especially in my profession, it might be a grand idea. I'll think about it."

"I said *if* I should ever ask you. I haven't yet."

"Okay." I let the matter drop and drifted off to sleep.

I was back in Aspen singing six nights a week. It was the early summer of 1969 and I hadn't seen Brandy since his onetime visit, which was way too short. He couldn't cut the elevation.

Two A.M.—I'd just gotten home—the phone rings. Brandy. We chat a minute, then he says, "About that government fuck ..."

"What government fuck?" I couldn't imagine what he meant.

"The one we talked about at La Ribera that night, where you get my disability insurance."

"I get your insurance. How come?"

Patiently, as if he was describing something to a child, he says, "We go somewhere, stand under a paper flower bower, say the right words, and *you* get the insurance."

Lightbulb on! "Brandy, is this a proposal? Like, uh, getting *hitched*?"

"Mm-hmm. You could meet me on July 4 at Fisher Towers by the river and we could take it from there."

Now one thing I knew I was *never* going to do again was get the hell married ... but ... Brandy was a truly exceptional human being; and if nobody, and I meant *nobody*, would ever know about it—a matter of conviction that such formal bonding often contributes to the end of same—I would seriously consider his proposal. Why? Because he was more intelligent, funny, and courageous than anyone I'd ever known, making it impossible for him to die anytime soon. And because I loved him.

I took a deep breath into my future and said, "Okay, I'll meet you there."

After which I was flooded with a euphoric sense of conspiracy. My mother, always on my case about where, when, and whom I dated, camped with, traveled, or heaven forbid slept with, would never know that in keeping with her Victorian vision, I was *legally married*! She'd always "kept her counsel"; I bloody well would keep mine—and at last get even with her.

How little we know.

⚓

AFTER OUR SECRET WEDDING under the paper posies, I folded up shop and moved back to my Arizona roots, a wee town in the Upper Sonoran Desert where he could breathe, sort of—when he wasn't confined to the Vet's Hospital in Tucson or staying in the small inexpensive *casa* we rented in La Paz.

The rest of our time we spent in all parts of Baja California. He knew it like the back of his hand, and in the going and coming we always stopped at Mom's, who had at last come to accept Brandy as my "paramour," and ceased her ragging. Well, almost.

The fall of 1970, I think it was, Brandy was breathing well in La Paz so I drove up the peninsula by myself and, as always, stopped at my mother's. But I stayed longer than usual before going home. She seemed more quiet. Worried about something. Self-sufficient as she was, I thought maybe she was lonely—even in the desert home she had designed and loved. This last one was a real work of art. Gold Mexican tile on the kitchen and dining room floors, a bright orange carpet curving into them from the living room where sliding glass doors looked out across a clean desert to the Catalina Mountains, nothing cluttering the view. Five arches fronted a wide front porch where her carved double doors graced the entrance.

She sat in the comfy upholstered chair (which I still have) and in a hesitant yet determined voice said, "Katie [not Kathryn], there is something I must tell you."

"Sure, Mom, I ..."

"But you must promise me that you won't repeat it to a living soul. I think you'll understand why."

Was she finally and at last going to lead me across the bridge to her own counsel in the inner sanctum? Her voice told me the matter was deadly serious, not just some stray piece of gossip.

"But of course, Mother, if you don't want me to."

She held my eyes, looked down at her hands, took a deep breath, then looked up again and said, "Bill and I were never married."

I wish I had a picture of how my face looked at that moment: a quick shutter release from bafflement-betrayal-disbelief, to amazement at the intrigue, to amusement over how she'd hoodwinked us, and finally admiration that broke into uncontrollable hilarity. I crumbled to the orange carpet and doubled over, holding my stomach and laughing so hard I thought I would be sick.

When I could get my breath, I whooped, "Oh, God, this is too funny for words!"

"I don't think there's anything *funny* about it. I've always been afraid someone might find out."

Still hardly able to speak, I asked, "But why?—for heaven's sake, Mom—why didn't you get married?"

She lifted her chin, set her jaw, and quietly said, "We just didn't get around to it."

And I knew by the tone of voice that her "counsel" had taken over and the door to the sanctum was once again closed.

So was mine.

Initially I could think of nothing but her brazenness and the irony of a situation that resembled a sudden reversal of roles in a slapstick comedy. But on the long drive home, many other thoughts hit the fan. Indignation stood up like a back-lit saguaro when I thought of the times I'd been dressed down (by both of them) for staying out late, spending the night or weekend with someone; how I wasn't allowed to sit up in her home with an old river friend until

2:00, *while she was wallowing in sin with the Greek in the master bedroom!*

Scenes flashed, many of them uncloaking a subtlety I had missed, or dismissed, at the time. Letters that had hinted at more than they said; about Bill not approving of this and that, or that I could have something, but don't mention it to him. And was it *release* I sensed in her letter telling me of his death and not *relief* that comes after months of caring for someone ill? All of which set me pondering. But my dear mother gave no clue. It wasn't until long after she died that justification for not marrying Bill became at least partially clear.

Meanwhile, I carried on happily with my own charade. Brandy, now my husband (an extremely closed-mouth type of guy, or he wouldn't have been), should be allowed a share in Mom's intrigue, right? So I told him. He laughed, of course, and praised her brass, then warned me that what she'd done was so against her true nature that she must have had a damned good reason, and that it probably cost her more than we'd ever know. I was so tickled she'd cut her Victorian garments to shreds with this unlikely deception, I hadn't delved seriously into why she'd done it. But Brandy was right.

⁂

SOME MONTHS LATER I had a gig in Tucson singing at a local club, with room and meals included, so I didn't stay way out on the opposite outskirts of town with my mom. Brandy joined me, a blessing that made my time there feel a lot less like the old road trips. The local rags carried daily announcements of my appearance at said emporium; Mom, ever faithful, came with her friends to wish me well and give me moral support.

One morning she called to see if I'd care to drive out for lunch. Brandy answered the phone, chatted with her a spell, and handed it over. After restating the invitation, her tone flattened like a run-over chipmunk and out came the old "Kathryn" (egad, what have I done now?), "I don't think it looks well to have Brandy *openly living* with you ..."

"Oh, come on, Mom."

"No, listen to me, you're a public figure now ..."

"Yes, Mother," I said, in my best downtrodden.

"… and I don't think you should parade your private affairs about for all to see."

"Who's seeing? There's nobody here but Brandy and me."

"You know what I mean. At least you should answer your own phone so …"

"Okay, Mother, okay," and I hung up, boiling over to Brandy, "The goddam nerve of her! She's still at it, and after what she told me about her liaison with the Greek sheik."

He calmed me down, Brandy the Brilliant, and told me what to do about it that might cap her Victorian eruptions once and for all—at least about paramours, inamoratos, and other carnal mating. Obediently, I answered the phone from then on so as not to get any more flack.

The next time Mother and I talked—after Brandy had gone south to Mexico—I did the thing.

Light 'n' airily, I told her, "I have a wonderful surprise for you, Mother. Brandy and I are going to get married …"

There was an honest sigh before she answered, "We-l-l, that *is* good news. When?"

"… and we're going to be married by the same minister that married you and Bill."

Blam!

Never, ever, was another word spoken about it. Never another Victorian reprimand. Did the message come home at last? Was it a mean thing to do? Did she, in the final analysis, deserve that? At the time I was sure she did. The packet of giggles I carried around with me was proof enough, because *my* secret was still intact and I intended to savor it.

When Brandy died in La Paz on St. Patrick's Day of '73, I came home with two broken wings. Even though he lived two years beyond the doctor's prediction, I wasn't prepared to lose him. And when I told Mother we'd been married since 1968, she just shook her head and smiled, nodded, and said, "I guess I deserved that."

Were we even? Not by a long shot.

I didn't enjoy the telling half as much as I thought I would. Sinking into my thick skull was the realization that her secret had lain heavily

on her heart, whereas mine was like a little firecracker favor at a party.
The bitter and the sweet had become one. It wasn't funny anymore.

≈✿❀✿≈

When I reminded her that I, her one and only daughter, had
none of her carvings, she went to work on three Philippine mahogany panels for my front door: storyboards of my favorite western
folksong. Horses figured in many of her panels, running in the wind,
whirling through fire, always in motion. Mine had to stand still with
their "reins a'draggin'," according to the song.

"I can't carve horses standing still."

I had ceased getting mad at her when she said goofy things like
that. She couldn't draw and always took what pleased her from
magazines, or wherever, put it on a grid of squares, and blew it up
to the size she needed for the panel. How she made them look like
she alone had invented them, then made them *live* in the wood, I'll
never know.

"Sure you can, Mom. I'll send you a picture of horses standing with
their reins dragging, or just standing, and you add the reins. Okay?"

"I can't do it."

She did them—all three—with a coyote, a waterfall, a cantina and
a town with agave, yucca and trees, and cowboys standing beside a
well named Old Dolores, inside an adobe wall with an arched gate
that read "HELL" backwards.

The Victorian was eighty years old and still keeping a lock on her
private feelings. But the fact that she had let out the one big secret
didn't keep me from suspecting there might be a few more, or that
someone else had found the key to unlocking them. But who?
Nearly all her close friends had died, and those remaining certainly
didn't inspire that kind of confidence, not in *my* mother. Certainly
not her sister; they barely spoke or wrote to one another.

Wait …

George! George, the surrogate son, living in New York. Someone she cared about. Had she tried to maneuver around Bill to help
and protect the kid when her paramour-in-disguise made the going
too rough? I might have thought to ask if my curiosity hadn't been

Carved door

so dulled by her counsel keeping, but the question flitted by like a
migratory bird and didn't return until the following winter.

That winter she up and died, without asking me.

Telling me, oh yes, "Next time I have to go to that hospital, I am
not coming back," but not asking me if it would be okay.

So she left me with this great mystery about her private life and secret thoughts, which I'm sure we would have found great comfort,
even joy, in sharing. My fault, without a doubt. Something in my
open-book personality kept her from loosening up, frightened her.
She didn't want her private affairs strewn about. I was too open, too
flagrant, for her discretion. Too much like my dad, maybe? The Victorian in her may have *done*, but it didn't *tell*. And now, too late, I
understand the way her friends saw her, trusted her, loved her. The
Victorian part was her charm. The fact that it hid whatever else was
underneath must have added a touch of mystery to that charm.

George came to the memorial service at Third Street (now University) and Stone Avenue. The *same house* she had saved in the thirties.
It had been added to and was now Long's Funeral Home. Talk about
full circle! In the parlor that had once been our living room, we sat
with her friends while Travis sang her favorite songs. I simply could
not do it then, though I know she would have wanted me to. Later,
out in the desert where she'd built her homes, I cried and sang
drunkenly under a half moon to my Victorian, with a backup chorus
of many coyotes. Of that she would have approved.

Thank God, George stayed for a few days.

At last we had some time to get to know each other, a time for me
to hear about his first difficult years in our country and the special
relationship he'd had with my mother. I cried; so did he. I was so
glad, so joyful, to know that she'd been able, at least partly, to soothe
the wound of my brother's death by fostering this sensitive, caring
young man who thought the world of her.

Should I tell him?

Maybe he already knew. What could it hurt? They were gone now.

"You're kidding!" George was floored. She hadn't told him or
even hinted at such a thing. But in his memory, incidents began to
surface that gave it credence.

"You know, Bill hated you," he said. "He once called you a whore."

"He what?" I howled with laughter. "Why, that hypocrite! And just what does his layin' up with my mother make him?"

"Greek Orthodox, that's what," said George.

"Ohhhh, I see." Up from confused waters, pure and pink as Venus on the Half Shell, came answers to my mother's no-marriage.

Bill's first wife had died, so he was freed by the church to marry again. Well, I knew my mom, the Presbyterian—Victorian be damned—would never submit to a marriage that required her to accept any other faith. But the most painful revelation came next.

"There's something else too," he said. "She called me at the Hall one night, sounding desperate, asking me to meet her downstairs. I was studying for finals and really beat, but she was almost crying, and I guess you know I would do anything for her. We drove around for about an hour, most of the time talking about you and me. She was terrified that she would die before Bill, that he'd take everything and leave you nothing."

"George, I never wanted my mom's money."

"Maybe not, but she sure didn't want him to have it. She said he'd been talking about sending me back to Greece even before I graduated if I didn't help more at the café."

"That son-of-a-bitch. What was his game? Christ almighty, it was *her* money that kept him afloat. And what's wrong with a will? She could leave her money to anyone she wanted to."

"I don't know." He broke off, thinking. .

We both were silent, trying to get into her head, trying to understand the anguish that plagued her.

Then George said, "Maybe, maybe, because she wouldn't marry in the Catholic church and he had to, Bill told her he'd spill the beans if ..."

"... if she didn't leave it to him," I concluded. "I'll bet that's it! Even with a common-law marriage she could have made a will."

George nodded. "That makes sense. Your mother was a real discreet lady. She wouldn't have wanted that sort of thing tossed around among her friends."

She wouldn't have, that's true, but we'll never know the whole story—we were guessing. She kept her big secret until years after Bill died, when her circle of friends was nearly gone. She would know that I could never keep such a convoluted tale under wraps, no matter what I promised her. But if this story never sees print and if the family Bible isn't buried with me, some historian, some genealogist, is going to come across a most confusing entry.

In it there are pages for Births, Marriages, and Deaths—no such thing as divorces—but my mother added those on the Marriages page. To the very last she tried cover her tracks ... and blew it. As for me, she only broadens my smile.

MARRIAGES
What God hath joined together let not man put asunder
Ruth Naomi Detwiler Lee of Aledo, Illinois and
Zanna Park Lee—married July 16, 1918 in Aledo, Ill.
[in my aunt's hand—everything below in mother's]
Ruth Detwiler Lee and Zanna Park Lee divorced,
January 7, 1933 at Tucson, Arizona.

Then:

Ruth Detwiler Lee and Basil Vozack of Greece,
naturalized American Citizen, married Nov. 28, 1939
in Los Angeles, California.

Next, an entry for my first marriage and divorce, the marriage of my brother, and below that a last entry that looks hurriedly done— maybe to show someone?—and forgetting the entry above. The 8 is scratched over with either a 7 or a 9 for the day of the year. It reads:

Basil G. Vozack and Ruth D. Lee married
November 29, 1938.

The Victorian.
 The Discreet Lady.
  My mother.
   The Rebel!

Hol-l-lywood!

WE USED TO CALL HER "THE WHISPERER." I hadn't heard her
or anything about her for years. Then, a night not long ago at a
friend's house for dinner—forgetting in what strange full circles our
lives often turn—there she was, her provocative shyness floating
through the amplifiers in pastel silk tones. And the backing, the
arrangements, the distinctive style of her instrumentalists: where had
I heard them before? I read the CD jacket and smiled in wonder-
ment—Howie Roberts, guitar; Red Callendar, bass—the same musicians who backed me on my albums, *Songs of Couch and Consultation* and *Spicy Songs for Cool Knights*, in the late fifties. On the
melody line, The Whisperer carried me back to Johnny Walsh's
Deauville Supper Club, where she stood beside the piano—her first
professional gig ever—in a formfitting gown of soft blue, wavy
blond hair tumbling to her shoulders, the mike so close to her full
mouth she looked to be eating it.

Julie London.

It was circa 1956, after Johnny had moved his popular Café Gala
Club from the Sunset Strip down to La Cienega, renamed it, and
made it more intimate. I had worked for him at the old club the fall
of 1951, billed with such fabulous entertainers as Dorothy Dandridge, Bobby Short, and the much-loved piano team Edie and
Rack, though how this Arizona Cactus Flower—just a little ol'
folksinger, ferchrissake—even got close to such high-altitude performers is hard for me to believe to this day. I was a kind of odd-
ball—not part of the dirty sandal group, loaded down with beads,
tattoos and flowers in my hair—I wore sparkly full skirts and low-
cut blouses behind my guitar. Still, those heavies were superb song

and piano stylists. They were Stars! If I was a folksong stylist, I didn't know it at the time. Nor did I know why Johnny hired me.

Didn't know then, before the full circle.

As Julie's now famous voice wafted through the speakers, I even remembered why I was at the Deauville that night. Johnny had asked me to come by and tell him what I thought of his new singer. Seems that Bobby Troupe had told him about Julie and asked him to give her a try at his club. I'd been out of town for a couple of years working coffeehouses all over the country, and he must have thought I'd gained some knowledge about singers in general. Oy! What a mistake. To the letter, I recall my smart-assed remark: "Well, she can't sing, Johnny, but she's purdy."

Julie ended her first showbiz gig at the Deauville six months later! In high contrast, my first solo nightclub job at Johnny's Café Gala lasted four weeks. I'd sung pop music with bands, with pianos in cocktail lounges in the summertime to help put myself through university, but never before as my own guitarist, singing the songs I really cared about. It simply blew my mind to be on the same billing—albeit at the bottom—with this handsome, debonair cabaret owner and performer who had had a spectacular career in fancy Parisian and other European bistros, singing sophisticated show tunes to the most sophisticated audiences in the world.

He stood in the curve of the grand piano, impeccably dressed in a black silk suit and tie, white pleated shirt, the spotlight accenting his wavy, silver hair. A large linen handkerchief was his signature. As the song dictated, he'd draw it through his hands, sometimes twist or wring it, tuck it back into his breast pocket, let it dangle to the floor, or pull it back of him, using it for a rumba sash. Johnny was a class act.

To further surprise me, he kept me on for an extended two weeks during the time Dorothy Dandridge was headlining his show. Dear god, what a gorgeous female! And what a lovely voice she had. (Later, when she starred with Harry Belafonte in the 1954 film *Carmen Jones*, I walked out of the theater in disgust. The producers had dubbed other voices in for theirs and made them lip-sync the whole score!)

Katie at Downstairs at the Upstairs (New York)

Dressing rooms in most clubs were notorious for being cramped, badly lit, and not too clean. Not at the Gala. There were actually two, one for men, one for women. I shared the room with Dorothy, and we changed costumes for every show—three a night. Her gowns were something to drool over—slinky, but very tasteful, and of course they fit her like wallpaper. When we closed the show, she gave me one of them! It was awhile before I could poke, push, and buckle my parts into certain places in that dress. Of course I never wore it onstage, and in the end I had to pass it on to a friend who could come out of it not looking like an accordion.

One night a couple of friends, Johnny's accompanist and I, decided to go to the Coconut Grove after our show. We were all in the girl's dressing room, Dorothy at the mirror taking off her makeup, when I said, "Come with us, Dorothy. Benny Goodman's playing."

Looking in the mirror at me, she asked, "Where did you say you were going?"

"The Grove. I've got some money for a change, so has Dave—between us we can hack the cover charge."

She turned around, looked up at me like I was some kind of fossil, made a sound between a laugh and a snort, and said, "Well, I can't go."

I felt let-down, because to be honest, I was hoping to be part of that beautiful lady's entourage. I begged her, "Please come. Goodman will probably want you to get up on the stand and …"

"Katie. They won't let me in the Coconut Grove. I'm a black woman, remember?"

I froze. Anger, hatred, and shame burned from my toes to my head; when the heat hit my eyes they spilled in tears. I cried, "My God, Dorothy, Lionel Hampton is playing vibes. What are you saying?" as it dawned on me, for the first time in real life, in this real world, exactly what she was saying.

"Lionel is on the stage, baby," she offered quietly and patiently to the small child at her shoulder. "I could be there if I was on the stage, but they don't let me sit with you white folks."

I think it was the "you" that got me. At that moment I wanted to be anything but the Caucasian asshole I felt like, so I copped out with "Not here at the Gala. Johnny's not like that. He's been all over Europe. He wouldn't …"

"I know, baby. That's why I'm here. Now you guys go on, forget all this. Have yourselves a ball."

No way.

I told my friends "So long" and drove down Sunset Boulevard with reality lying like a stone in place of my heart, wondering how many times the lovely Dorothy Dandridge had had to go through that ugly scene. Instead of the Grove, I stopped at Wright's Ice Cream Parlour and spent my cover charge on a huge hot fudge sundae. Black on white!

I RENTED ROOMS all over Hollywood those first few years—
Beverly Hills, North Hollywood, Burbank, Pasadena—working at
day jobs, doing bit parts in movies, radio, and television—living
mostly on fifteen to twenty dollars a week. When things got better,
I leased a little apartment a block from the Hollywood Bowl. From
there I had quick and easy access, in my little Ford convertible, to
most of the studios and casting offices.

But the big payoff was the Bowl—didn't buy tickets for more
than two performances in three years—just walked a block, crossed
Highland, went up the hill and sat on the grass. Other nights it was
great to lie in bed and listen to symphonies, big-name bands, or
operas. It was a small town then; traffic didn't drown out every other
sound—not even the nightingale that started up at midnight in the
big magnolia across the street. Loudest goddam bird I ever heard. I
got so mad at it one night I took my .22 Remington rifle, went out
in my nightie, and tried to shoot it. I didn't, of course, but at least it
shut up for about a week.

≈≈❧≈≈

WHEN SOME FEATHER-HEADED REVIEWER makes the comment that
I'm "name-dropping" by mentioning the people in Hollywood who
were instrumental in helping me up the ladder toward whatever
small acclaim I achieved, I wonder if they'd be happier if I mentioned Jack Sprat, Joe Whozit, or my mommie. The players whose
names get "dropped" happen to be the people who knew what I did
best and tried to help. They'd once been where I was and understood that a little nudge in the right direction, an introduction to the
right person, could do a lot more than haunting casting offices all
week. When Burl Ives told me, "Even being seen with the right person can help you in this phoney, egocentric town," I wasn't ready to
believe him.

There are plenty of reasons I didn't achieve fame. I didn't have
the stomach for the harsh, ugly climb up the ladder. Like a blotter,
I soaked up every nuance, every cruel thing said, every lie and evasion.
I broke every halter anybody tried to put on me and balked when
music publishers tried to make me "commercialize" my folksongs.

What I didn't realize was that Hollywood had a mighty low tolerance for imagination, and that the moguls spent tons of money on
scriptwriters for stars like Jack Benny, Fred Allen, and Red Skelton
for one simple reason: to dumb those guys down, keep them in line,
so that each show sounded much like the last. As for me, agents and
managers never knew how to classify what I did—couldn't stamp
me with a label, and showbiz needs labels like snow needs white—
they recognized a talent, but how to use someone who got there too
late to be an ingenue, and too early to be a character actress? I could
also sing and play the guitar. I shouldn't have told them that—it
confused them even further—yet that's how I got my running parts
on NBC radio.

Always have been lucky.

Before I left the little desert town of Tucson, Arizona, to make
my splash (drip) in Hollywood, other friends and fellow artists had
preceded me. I knew Andy White from my acting years with the
Tucson Little Theatre. By the time I got to Tinseltown, he was a
scriptwriter for *The Great Gildersleeve*. Andy wrote me into the
show as The Girl in the Wood with so much nostalgia that it received an unprecedented amount of mail—something like five hundred cards and letters from all over the country—asking who I was
and when I would return to the show.

Well, by public demand, they had to give me a running part: a
come-and-go character in the life of *The Great Gildersleeve*. Only
Gildy wasn't happy. The poor man took it as a threat rather than an
enhancement to his show, and vetoed several of Andy's scripts that
brought back The Girl. That many letters (which he had never received himself) must have scared the hell out of him. As a radio
piece, *The Great G.* was beautifully crafted to make each of the
regulars an intricate part of the Family. The rest of us (and I wasn't
the only one) came and went, the same way a small town is jazzed
up by a newcomer now and then. Hal Perry was the originator of
the Gildersleeve character, but because Hal had asked for more
money, NBC replaced him with a mimic, Willard Waterman. Since
NBC owned the title (*The Great Gildersleeve*), Perry had no leg to
stand on and therefore lost everything in a legal loophole I'm sure

Katie with The Great Gildersleeve

he never expected. It was Waterman I worked with, and he wanted no interference from me or anyone else.

So I learned the ugly part of Hol-l-lywood.

Not to worry. The part with Gildy opened up other NBC shows. I spent a summer on the very popular *Railroad Hour*, billed as a folksinger/guitarist with Gordon MacRae, the fun-loving, smiling singer of pop and show tunes, who was making the movie *Oklahoma!* just thirty miles from my hometown. From Gordie's show, someone heard I'd be good on Ronald and Benita Coleman's *The Halls of Ivy*. There, my role was Glory Golightly, the singing hillbilly wife of the forty-year-old Freshman, Barton Yarborrow. Then came daytime programs: *Roy Rogers, One Man's Family,* and *The*

Walter O'Keefe Show. On fledgling TV, I acted in the *Armchair Detective Series.* On *Helen Parish's Telephone Hour,* I served as actress/singer/guitarist and folk music director.

What I remember most about those early TV shows was that they were all done live—no filming, baby—make a mistake and everybody eats it. NBC had only one or two TV soundstages then. As soon as our show was over, in came Dinah Shore to rehearse and do hers. By staying out of the way, I could watch the whole process— half-hour rehearsal, half-hour show—and I did love Dinah Shore! Even when she was sick with the flu she sailed through rehearsal (and the engraved one) with ease, hundreds of hours of live performances giving her the edge. Stage actors fared better in the new media than either movie or radio performers because memorizing a whole play is second nature to them. With movies it's one scene at a time; with radio, no memory at all—you get to read it.

Recall of the happenings, there in the Halls of NBC on the corner of Sunset and Vine, are priceless.

Here I am, my first *Gildersleeve* rehearsal, a little desert rat with her guitar, sitting on a high stool in front of a thirty-piece orchestra directed by the esteemed Carmen Dragon, trying to look like I did this every day, all the time shivering inside like a cottonwood leaf in a dust storm.

Next thing I know, the whole orchestra is on its feet bowing to me and Carmen is saying, "Want you all to meet Miss Katie Lee. She'll lead us through the song."

Gulp! Oh yeah, sure ... gonna lead ...

"Ready?" Down comes the baton, orchestra plays the intro, and I enter a dream world, carried away by the sound of a thousand strings, violins, flutes, and oboes. After the first couple of lines, I stop playing and singing so I can listen to this enchanting ... ahhhh ... music.

Rap-rap-rap!—the baton—then Mr. Dragon: "Something wrong, Katie? We going too fast for you?"

"Oh, no. I'm sorry. It's ... I've never had a real live orchestra play with me before, and it sounds so lovely, I ... well, I keep listening to you instead of me."

He smiled and told me that was all right, he understood, and said I'd get used to it after a few minutes.

He was wrong there. I never did.

❧

ONE OF THE GORDON MACRAE SHOWS featured Mimi Bonzell, very famous opera star. I was there to be an Irish lass, sing and play an Irish folksong. At rehearsal—we had only one, a couple of hours before they let the audience in for the real show—Miss Bonzell could hardly talk, much less sing. She had a horrible head cold. Surely they'd have to alter the script or get someone else, quick. On her cues, she strolled calmly to the microphone and tore the songs apart, high notes and all—no huskiness, even on the highest. Afterward, I asked her how on earth she did it.

"Oh, you sing over it, dahling. Just open your throat. Forget the resonance and fake it." She then pinched my nose shut, told me to sing, and showed me how it worked. Every word I sang came out with a "b" in front of it.

"You must practice, dear," she insisted. "You'll find it veddy handy in the future."

How right she was!

On the stages of the big sound studios, some show was either in rehearsal under work lights, broadcasting live, or waiting for the audience to enter the theatre. You got used to meeting the stars in the halls, coming in and out of the heavy doors marked *Red Skelton Show, Jack Benny, Fred Allen, Amos & Andy, Baby Snooks,* et al. But when the red light over that door said: BROADCASTING, you sure as hell did not open it!

One afternoon, I'm heading down the hall for some reason or other when I see Mr. Skelton ambling in my direction.

He stops right in front of me and says, "Wel-l-l, yew purdy little thing, where did you come from?"

I was sure he was still in whatever character he'd just left in the studio, and I'd been forewarned about his sometimes—shall we say—*flamboyant* approach to lady strangers. So I played it as cool as I knew how and told him I was rehearsing for the *Roy Rogers Show.*

He threw back his head, opened his mouth and eyes wide, and gasped, "Purdy li'l thang like you in 'ere with that horse-horsey dude? Why, mercy me ..."

Suddenly he looked over my shoulder and froze, slammed into high, and tore down the hallway, skidding past the blinking red BROADCASTING door. He reversed, pulled it open, braced it with his foot while he smoothed down his vest, patted his hat, and walked slowly onto the soundstage.

I heard applause as the door closed behind him.

⚜

I GOT A CALL FROM CENTRAL CASTING to show up on the set of *The Capture*, starring Lew Ayers. Earlier, I'd tried out for a bigger role in the picture, but somebody else was sleeping with someone and I didn't get the part. This would only be a "bit"—maybe two or three days and I'd be sitting around the set most of the time waiting for my scenes to be shot—so I brought my guitar to get some practicing in.

I had never met Lew Ayers, but I knew quite a bit about him. The reason why the new road across the front face of the Catalina Mountains in Tucson was called the Prison Road was that much of the early work was done by a gang of light-security prisoners during the war, when other manpower was scarce. Lew had been a conscientious objector during that war and he'd worked on the road.

When he first arrived, all Tucson knew he was there, but with time everyone forgot about it. I didn't. In fact, we used to take the old road up the back, then drive down the front as far as we could go, in the hope we would meet up with him.

A decade later, there I was, in Hollywood, in a scene with Mr. Lew Ayers, playing a telephone operator at a mine. It seemed such a helluva coincidence, I wondered if I dared mention the past to him. Very likely he wouldn't take it kindly, so I decided not to tread the path that angels fear, sat down behind some flats, and went about my guitar practicing.

Next thing I knew, some of the extras were gathered around, and standing behind them, arms crossed over his chest and smiling, was Lew Ayers. I could make this a really good story and tell you he asked if I knew any prison songs, but he didn't. What I did discover, spending most of the day playing and singing (except when the director boomed "*Quiet, rolling*"), was that he loved folk music. In fact, he played a bit of guitar himself. At first he seemed reserved and a bit standoffish, which most stars are just for self-preservation, but before long, all of that dropped away and he began singing along and asking if I knew this or that song. We talked of mutual friends and acquaintances who appreciated folk music: Eddie Albert (look out, here come the names again), Wendel Corey, Burl Ives, Josh White, Woody Guthrie, and the new group The Weavers. Then, the last day of shooting, he asked the fatal question.

"Where'd you learn all those songs?"

I'd sung everything from sea shanties to cowboy songs, from Scotch-Irish-English ballads to railroad and miner's songs, many that he knew and joined in on. "Learned a bunch off of Burl's early folk records, and most of the western songs from the cowboys where I lived."

"Where was that?" he asked.

I decided angels were sissies, looked him in the eye, and smiling, said, "Nice road you guys built."

"What?" A pause. He sat back, cocked his head, gave me a quizzical look. "Road? What road?"

"Catalina Mountains. Tucson."

For a minute I thought the connection was broken, then quietly he muttered, "I'll be damned," and started laughing.

I told him how we used to go looking for him. He nodded, but he didn't offer anything more about his time up there, nor did I, perceiving it was a very private thing to him. We finished the day with more songs, rehearsing lines and shooting the scene. After we said good-bye, I never saw Lew Ayers again, except in movies where I'd first seen him. Yet, I never drive the Prison Road without thinking about him.

⁂

THE TREBLE CLEF was a nightclub on Melrose Avenue that specialized in blues and jazz. The night my roommate and I went, the attraction was Josh White, a black folksinger. I'd never seen him in live performance, though I'd had his records for ages and was enchanted with his one-and-only guitar style and voice. After his first set, I was so blown away I could hardly move from my chair. How could anyone make their hands dance like that on a stringed instrument? Well, let's face it—most folksingers couldn't. We were knocking on his dressing-room door hardly before he got behind it.

Thus began one of the longest friendships of my career, a friendship so warm, so instructive, so unpolluted by sex or racism that it changed my style of singing and playing and even my thinking. What Joshua had gone through—to be who he was and have the extreme talent that he had—not many could have endured. And, of course, being black, was *still* enduring. The way I looked at it, he had all the qualities I only wished my peers had. He was a well-spoken gentleman, a gentle man, a sincere, unpretentious, giving human being who stirred joy, sadness, and yearning in the hearts of all those who listened. He told great stories and sang great songs—songs that had made up his life in the south, in Europe, in Harlem. "Strange Fruit," "Tol' My Cap'n," "Take This Hammer," "John Henry," "I'm Going to Live This Life I Sing About," "Baby You Know What I Want from You," "I Gave My Love a Cherry," "They Crucified My Lord," "Free & Equal Blues," "Delia's Gone," "Foggy Foggy Dew," "One Meat Ball," "Slats on the Bed Go Blam-tee-blam!," "Black Girl." I can name a hundred of them—from spirituals to down-and-dirty blues—no one ever sang them the way he did.

Late at night after his shows, he and Sam Gary, his bassist and dear friend, would come to our apartment; Josh would sit on a stool, sip scotch, and sing until pale dawn tinged the sky. Sam, usually asleep by then, would be snoring away on the couch. We'd wake him, fix them breakfast, and they'd go back to whichever hotel, motel, or (if fortune smiled) to a friend more than happy to accommodate the color of their skins. Here was the man who, in the early forties, set the stage for the whole folksong movement; the man who paved the way for every folksinger, black or white, to come after him; and in his own country, couldn't get a place to sleep!

Yes, "Joshua fit the battle of Jericho," he surely did.

BURL IVES WAS A BIG MAN, as everyone knows. Yet in spite of his bulk, "fat" was never a word I could put with him. His bones were big, his movements and frame were big, and when he was angry his voice was very big, and a bit midwestern nasal.

What isn't known, or at least not common knowledge, is that he had been a Julliard student and had spent hours singing German Lieder. There's no better way to gain control over your vocal cords. His guitar playing was uncluttered, with very little fancy finger-work; the fancy work was in his phrasing and the way he used it to tell a story, making something that was really complex sound quite simple.

In the late forties and early fifties, Burl was undoubtedly the best known and widely recorded folksinger in the arena. His concert audiences saw him as the big, jolly "Jimmy Crack Corn" man behind a big guitar he made look small, and a clear tenor voice that didn't fit his frame either, yet always fit the song. The trick was, he made the song fit him.

I met him in 1951 or '52, before his leap into international fame in *Cat on a Hot Tin Roof* (1956, before he became Big Daddy to everyone) and an unjolly, disturbed, and angry man.

Many of his friends in the folk field had turned away. They said he'd named names at Mad McCarthy's House Un-American Activities Committee hearings; a committee that targeted all folksingers of the period, to say nothing of actors, screenwriters, authors, any public figure who leaned further to the left than the senator's power-crazed brain would tolerate; a committee that mutilated the careers of some of the finest artists in the country.

The whole ugly business had left a mark on Burl's personality that, according to some of those old friends, hadn't been there before. When prodded, the only thing he said to me was "Be careful," meaning look out where I sang and for whom. But with hindsight, I believe he was transferring the painful loss of his folk fellowships to the general public, whom he saw as not enough, and therefore not enough appreciation for his music.

Well, he got it a few years later with *Cat*, not with his songs.

What I remember about Big Daddy is that he saved my ass several times. Why? I haven't a clue. One of the first things I told him was that I needed his expertise, needed to learn the best way to present my songs; that we were not going to fornicate, that he was going to be my friend. He seemed amused by that, and he said, "All right Kathryn" (the only one, outside my mother, who ever used my given name). When he had spare time, we went to work on my repertoire.

That was the first thing he did.

We'd meet at my friend Lenny's house in Laurel Canyon, have dinner, sit around the big kitchen table with our guitars, drink wine and whiskey, and work sometimes until past midnight. I probably knew more than three hundred songs in those days, and some of them could be mighty boring for a coffeehouse or bistro audience, but he went through that list like shit through a short Portagee, picking songs that would hold an audience's dwindling attention span, as TV moved higher in the public sights and live performers sank to the level of a lizard's belly. As he'd done with his own folk tunes, he might add a verse, or an extension to a chorus, or make up one with more swizzle. He had a knack for turning a drab song into something riotously funny or downright sad, depending on how you sang it. It was a gift he passed on to many aspiring folksingers—more than once I ran into someone who'd received his help in one form or another—the list is probably uncountable, and I know he enjoyed doing it.

At the end of the P's in my folk file he pulled out "Pueblo Boy" and started laughing. "You don't want to sing this. It'll put everybody to sleep—and anyhow, it's 'Pueblo Girl.'"

"I know that. So what? We've changed a lot of genders. It's a nice, nostalgic little song."

"'Tis for me, not for you. I wrote it in ten minutes, sittin' on the can at Columbia Recording Studios. They needed one more short little song to finish up the album and I'd run plumb dry."

The next thing may sound frivolous to some, but let me tell you it's a gift of gold to singers, actors, and public speakers.

I came to Lenny's one night stuffed up like a kid's teddy bear— head, throat, and chest full of green goo. "You need to get the snot out of you," he said, and led me to the bathroom sink, where he mixed a few pinches of salt in a glass half full of warm water and handed it to me. "Pour this in your palm and sniff it slowly—very slowly—up your nose, tilt your head back, and let it drain down your throat, then lean over and blow the rest out of both nostrils at the same time. Do it until the crud is gone and gargle what's left."

I do it.

It goes into my upper sinuses, shoots a pain through my eyes and forehead, sends a hot iron up my nose, and sets me coughing.

"Damn it, I said *gently*. Not like a fucking vacuum cleaner!"

"You did not, you said *slowly. Hak-hak-hak!*"

"Arrrghhh! Gently, slowly, easy-like. Here, let me show you."

With his example and a few more tries I learned it: a way to irrigate your sinuses. To this day it works wonders, show or no show.

※❀❀❀※

'LONG ABOUT SPRING 1953, Hol-l-lywood was starting to give me a big ruckus in my tuckus—people clawing tooth and nail, stepping all over each other, trying to get up that ladder. Seemed like every time I went on a date, I'd have to argue my way out of bed, pay for my dinner with a "feel-me-up" job, or listen the whole evening to some bore's overrated opinion of himself. Sometimes I'd be in rehearsal for a play, join a hootenanny with my folky friends, or perform on weekends at Cabaret Concert Theatre, where I was a member of the production and director staff. But the bulk of nights I spent home alone, inventing guitar arrangements, learning songs—and studying. Once a week I joined other friends in a special Jungian therapy class, where we learned, then put into practice (the hard part), many of the old master's theories.

Then came the event that altered life as I had known it, as well as the direction and purpose that life would serve in the future.

I ran the Colorado River through the Grand Canyon from Lee's Ferry to Pierre's Ferry on June 15, 1953, and following that, through Glen Canyon of the Colorado every year for a month or so for the next ten years—until it was drowned beneath Powell Reservoir.

Those desert wilderness experiences so altered my thinking about show business in general, about myself and my talent, that I questioned why I was trying to climb this stupid ladder to—what? Fame? What the hell was fame but sucking up to a fickle public's attention to the latest fad in the arts? This folksong thing would not go on forever. But I would. It's what I wanted to do and whatever talent I had would allow me to do. Folksinging, especially my kind, was not "big audience" entertainment.

I had rarely written words to songs before I ran the river; mostly I just doctored them to suit myself and wrote music to words already there. After life in the canyons, heartfelt words poured out in song after song about the grandeur of the river, the majesty of the country, the awe and humor of discovery. And toward the end came songs of anger and frustration over the killing of the Colorado River's unique life-giving system—killed behind a mass of politically appointed dams.

Songs of protest. Songs that led me down the road to becoming an activist for my rivers of the Southwest, far, far away from the heavily trafficked highway to fame.

In keeping with this new reality, Burl Ives slowly and persistently urged me into the coffeehouse circuit and out of Hol-l-lywood. He and Lenny loaned me enough money to split for Chicago, where Burl had arranged a press party through his publicist so the media would review my shows and write about me. Within two weeks— November 1954 to be exact—I had a job in one of Chicago's popular nightclubs (headlined by Carmen MacRae no less) and my career as an intimate folksong stylist was launched.

⚜

BUT WHAT OF THE FULL CIRCLE, of Johnny Walsh and his Gala Club?

We jump from the fifties to the seventies, from Hol-l-lywood to a wee mining town perched on the side of a mountain in northern Arizona. I and my third, last, and best husband dine at a restaurant well-known for its fine cuisine. It's a small, intimate place with soft lights and candles, suggesting a Victorian parlor. Seated at another table and facing us is a most distinguished-looking man with a full head of silver hair, who speaks softly and smiles often at his lady companion. He looks familiar, and I spend half the dinner hour trying to remember where I've seen him before. Finally I give up and ask our waitress if she knows him.

"Oh, yes, of course. That's Johnny Walsh," like he was an everyday experience.

My God! What on earth is he doing here? I haven't seen him since the mid-fifties; have no idea when he closed the club, or even if he did; and am certain he's forgotten I ever existed. Braving it, I go to his table, face him, and give the usual lame introduction: "Mr. Walsh, I'm sure you won't remember me from years ago, but my name's Katie ..."

"Katie Lee!" he exclaims before I can even get my whole name out; then he stands, takes my hands in his, and asks, "How are you? You look wonderful."

How true to the gentleman Johnny I knew! If anyone looks great, it's him, almost as if he hasn't changed a hair on his silvery head for the past fifteen years. I never knew how old he was; he was simply ageless. I won't dally with that evening, even though it was one of the more memorable ones in my life; it's enough to say that when he asked me what I was doing there, I turned the question around to him.

"I live here, Katie. My father and his brother were both town physician back in the mining days."

Later that night, sitting beside him on his piano stool—we were half smashed by then—I asked him whatever possessed him to hire me.

"You were good, and folk music was hot stuff."

"Naaah, and two extra weeks, you hadda be outta your mind."

"I'm not known for hiring duds, and besides, you were an Arizona girl. You told me so."

"Then why didn't you tell me you were an Arizona boy?"

"Would you really have wanted to know? Stars in your eyes are better than dust; why spoil my image? And Katie, you were on your way to someplace you weren't even sure of at the time. I just thought giving you a little push might help you decide. Anyhow, I'm not totally an Arizona boy, I was born in St. Ignace, Michigan."

I looked down at the piano keys, recalling how influential he had been in my career as an entertainer. "What a blessing you've been to so many people, Johnny. I'm so glad I've found you again."

Less than a year later we moved to that little town.

We spent some happy times, visiting and partying in his tastefully decorated home, looking at photos of people like Dorothy D., Julie L., Bobby S., and many more he'd helped along the road—to fame?—to wherever they wanted to go.

He gave a concert for the historical society one year, and I got to see him perform one last time, white handkerchief and all. The master of show tunes was still a master, even up to doing my old favorite, "Down in the Depths on the Ninetieth Floor," a real tearjerker about a rich guy in his Bronzini dressing gown, pacing his penthouse floor, mourning his lost love. Only Johnny could cut a corny lyric like that and make it sound believable.

But when he couldn't handle his infirmities by himself, and no one was there for him, he made the decision to go down the mountain to an "elderly whatever," where he had one little room instead of his whole house. The smell of pills, old clothes, and weary souls replaced the smell of fresh flowers on his piano; yet the staff was periodically entertained with his songs, one of which he claimed to be Walter Winchell's favorite request: "Dirty Old Man."

Within a year his breathing became labored and his lush tenor singing voice was gone. When I came to visit—which I knew was not often enough, my excuse being that it pained me so to see him there—he'd have on a clean shirt, his wavy silver hair, which never thinned away, neatly combed back from a widow's peak, and always the famous Johnny Walsh smile promising a good day, if not a wonderful song.

Then one day in March 1988, I came back from a gig to find Johnny gone. Then and only then did I learn his age.

He was ninety-one.

The Race-car Driver

EVERY TIME I OPEN THE CABINET and see, on the inside door, the photograph of a smallish race car, my shoulders hunch and a memory tingles through my frame. The car is in midair, upside-down, wheels flinging mud to the sky, torso of man hanging down, one gloved hand *inches* above the earth, red-and-white board fence on the racetrack rim (over which the car is about to fly), standing impotent and vainglorious beneath the flying vehicle.

How could anyone outlive that scene?

He was just a kid in his twenties then—a lucky kid, I might add—when, according to those who saw him go, the race car rolled once more, topped the fence, and landed on its side, where it skidded into a tree. Broke his hip all to hell. Medics thought he was dead, but his buddy came up and said, "Just give him some oxygen, he'll come around. He's got emphysema."

Brandy. The cat with nine lives.

He was one of my deceased husbands, the dearest one actually. The others were, well, like growing pains, though it may seem heartless to say such things. None of my marriages was a total waste of time; all of them taught me something. But Brandy was like the whipped cream on top of a hot chocolate sundae—he melted too soon.

Shortly after he recovered from that accident, he quit the racetrack gig; he had more inventive ways of almost killing himself, like being a test driver for Ford Motor Company on their Detroit track for ten years. I think he only got hurt a couple of times there. He was nearly buried in a sand dune one night, took a long sailing trip without his oxygen tanks, wrapped his dune buggy (with him in it) around a boulder down in Baja, got caught in the Bahía de La Paz

Brandy, the race-car driver

tides and couldn't start the motor on his ponga but was ultimately
rescued by a lone fisherman. The last three excursions were when *I*
knew him. God only knows how many times he parted St. Peter's
hair before then.

I met Brandy in Bahía de Los Angeles on the Baja California
peninsula, and contrary to what some might think, he was a man
with a *life* wish rather than a death wish. He was fascinated by the
razor's edge and kept coming back to it—talked about how far you
can make yourself go toward that edge and still stay alive, about "the
razor's edge of credulity, the fantastic plateau of elation, the heights
it takes one—acting almost like dope, to keep you going back again
and again for that ultimate sensation." He had an intuitive gene that
kept him alive longer than many of the riders who either couldn't,
wouldn't, forgot to, or didn't know when to back off. Rock
climbers, bush pilots, and competition skiers can tell you about the
edge of the razor. Perhaps they have more time than a millisecond to
think about the edge. Maybe it's slower, maybe not, but Brandy had
a millisecond reaction time built in. It was part of his DNA. He had

it with word pictures too—said things off the top of his head that were beyond invention—that's how I got sucked in. With words.

My first trip down the peninsula with my traveling compadre, Nick-the-Slick, when it was nothing but a two-wheeled dirt track, took nearly two months and 1,500 miles. From mid-April 1968 to mid-June, we dawdled to La Paz and hung out for a week or so at the *palapa* campground owned by Rude Valez, brother of Lupe Valez, the famous movie actress. Having beachcombed most of the Sea of Cortez and half the Pacific Coast, we zigzagged to San José del Cabo and "circumcised the tip" (as Brandy called it), explored our way up the Pacific side to Todos Santos and back to La Paz, then took the ferry to mainland Mazatlán and finally the USA.

Journal Note: May 16, Bahía de Los Angeles

Conversation at the table this morning with the few stray tourists was indeed interesting. This road obviously separates the sheep from the goats, and the people who come here either have something to come for that's of a scientific nature or they are nature lovers to start with and come for the beauty and wildness. A young couple with a baby girl are traveling in a sixteen-foot outboard all along the coast! Jesus, in these tides and storms they've got plenty of guts. An interesting-looking man with red hair, beard, and long-handled moustache, traveling with a teenage, long-haired hippie-looking boy [his son], were talking to a man who's conducting experiments on turtles—I was told last week, in Tucson at the Sonora Desert Museum, that they'd be down here, but I forgot about it—the bearded man made a statement I think I'll steal. Of the turtles, he asked, "They can really abbreviate your fingers, then, if they get a chance?"

Didn't say *snap* them off, *bite* them off, *chomp* them off, but *abbreviate* them. Nick-the-Slick is a writer too; both sets of eyebrows went up at the same time, and without further adieu, we wiggled into the conversation. The rest is history.

⚬⚬⚬

THE BAJA TRIP WAS AN ESCAPE journey for me. Escape from the pain of loss—the drowning of a beautiful river canyon that had become my friend, my sanctuary, my home, and finally my true love. I went in search of a wild place of a different kind to fill the void, a place that would not remind me of that loss. When Nick, who had been with me on my last trip through Glen Canyon and who was now a close and cherished friend, said he would like to go to Baja as well—we would initiate his new Jeep Commando—the perfect solution surfaced and the two of us quickly made plans to split Aspen as soon as the ski lifts closed that spring.

The peninsula was virgin ground to us—a place we looked to for open spaces as yet unpaved, unpeopled, unpolluted, undammed, and undeveloped—*tierra* for new adventures and encounters with a culture that differed from our own. Nick spoke very good Spanish. I played guitar and sang the hell out of it but couldn't speak it without getting lost in the forest of verbs and undergrowth of tenses. Because I was raised near the border I had the pronunciation down pat, and that caused another problem. Hearing their accent correctly—what words I knew—the *paisanos* assumed I was fluent and rattled it off so damn fast I only half understood what they were saying. I exhausted the phrase "*Mas despacio, señor. No entiendo quando usted habla muy rapido*" and got along okay, but more often than not, Nick had to pull me out of the confusion I got myself and everyone else into.

There was another reason I needed an escape journey. A longtime love affair had finally come to the end of its tether and I wanted absolute freedom from the smothering, cloying clutch of it. Free air, wind, desert, wide sky, sand and sea, and *hands off me* seemed to be the answer. Friends, acquaintances—fine. No lovers need apply.

Brandy entered our lives in disguise.

His clever choice of words and phrases, his photographic memory, his "hipness," shall we say; his in-depth knowledge of jazz (Turk Murphy, the jazz trombonist who owned Earthquake McGoons in San Francisco, was his close friend, as well as the banjoist Clancy Hayes and the rest of the band) belied the facts that he did time in a VA hospital every month or so; had terminal emphysema with three years to live, if he was lucky; and that he was crazy, as all race-car drivers surely are. Yet, as I see it now, terminally ill lovers of life are crazy *not* to do it while they have it. So for five years, not just three, Brandy played Russian roulette with St. Peter. *Doing it!*

Being a student of the history and culture as well made him a true Baja aficionado. Up and down, through, over and around the territory he'd been many times, in as many different vehicles; probably the only thing he hadn't ridden, driven, or reconstructed was a motor-cycle. Toting his oxygen tanks, he'd even run the Baja 1000 Race a few years back and placed somewhere in the ranks. Therefore, when Nick and I met up with Brandy and Ken, his son, at Bahía de Los Angeles, it seemed odd that Ken had never seen Baja from any angle and had never driven anything but a surfboard until a few days prior to our meeting.

Ken earned his own razor edge the hard way—no testing of the waters. Up to then, Brandy had towed the dune buggy behind his VW bus, El Toro Volador. At the bottom of those steep and nasty cuestas beyond Puertecitos, he'd handed it over to Ken, offered a few minimal instructions, and told him to mount. Ken told me of his terror long after the happening and all I can say is, Brandy's lucky Ken survived what could have been a six to eight hundred–foot *adios!* Did he know the boy would? Questionable—but his dad's genes after all.

Nick-the-Slick and I got a raw taste of this car fetish on our first exploratory trip—trailing them, losing them, finding them, hiding from them, looking and waiting for them—first one car, then the other. We began to question our "luck"—meeting up with someone who knew the peninsula so well—missed the tingle and delight of discovering things and places for ourselves. Being led to them de-stroyed some of the uniqueness and mystery that explorers know are half the fascination of roaming new territory. Still, connecting with Brandy and friends was also unique; he mentioned several sce-nic camping spots that we could easily have missed. Should we stick or split? We'd kissed off more than one gringo on the way down, why not him? What, after all, was the strange attraction to this hurry-up-and-wait critter?

Katie in the dune buggy

Abbreviate! finally won over *Now-where-the-fuck-has-he-gone?*
So we put up with the fetish and latched on to the intellect to learn
more—not necessarily more about Baja, but about the critter. I'm
amazed we survived his stubborn, repetitive goof-ups as we zigzagged down the peninsula; a disjointed, landlocked trimaran on
twelve wheels, all going in different directions at different times.
Tooling into La Paz, looking, we thought they were ahead. Backfir-
ing into La Paz, waiting, they thought we were behind.

Probably the only things Brandy and I had in common were our
love of music and our marriages, twice removed—mine, long ago;
his last, more recent. The reason Ken had not been trained in the
fine art of car-care was that he'd lived with his mom all through his
teenage years. Dorothy and Brandy had also produced three daughters—a form of over-birth worse than Ed Abbey's—with Helen,

Brandy in the dune buggy

wife number two, he had none, bless the saints. Once, I asked him, "Don't you know what makes them?" He said, "You undo that little golden screw in her navel and they just drop out like a slot machine. If you're lucky you get ..."

"Forgeddit! Sorry I asked."

***

THAT I WOULD DO ANOTHER whole Baja trip with Mr. B. in October '68 attests to his unquestionable magnetism and to the amount of liquid on my brain. He was like a combination lock I could never open in time to save myself. Even though I had thought we couldn't get fucked up too much with only *one* car—the dune buggy, this time—he proved me wrong. Whatever made him believe this little girl, just a guitar-strumming folksinger, could pull

him out of all the tangles he got into? His smarts, that's what. He
knew more than I did, and he'd *show* me how to change a tire (six
this time), get the wood, cook, make the bed, and rub his ... back.
What that all boiled down to was he'd met his match, and I'd met
mine. I had never been so pissed with a human in my lifetime, nor
laughed so hard for so long over our immediate and about-to-be
life scenario.

Journal Note: November 5, Salt Flats of Laguna San Ignacio

*The race started this morning, so we planned to get to San Ignacio
before they do—heading for Becky's over the coast route through
the face powder, sand, and salt flats. This place is so desolate with
the coast wind howling; poor sputtering Jaibita* [the buggy] *choked
up with fine silt, sand, salt, mud, and dust—Brandy too, his face
mask not doing the job. But of course we don't get anywhere near
SI tonight. There are about twenty-five miles of pure face powder
in foot-deep ruts to negotiate. How we keep from hanging up is
beyond me—and of course, throttle trouble in the middle of this
moonscape. As the sun gets lower, the landscape becomes more
dismal and the spook bushes produce the eerie effect of some
monster trying to escape from under a blanket ... the thing stuck
under a wad of molasses—grotesque—a word for the trees and
the rest of the ride today!*

*Just at dark we make the salt flats that harbor the next pit
stop. No one's come through yet, but they are ready. They feed
us huge steaks and baked spuds! We have a drink and Mr. B.
decides to sack out a hundred yards or so from the crew and
their equipment.*

"Doesn't it matter to you if we get run over?"

"We won't. They'll see the pit lights and head right for them."

*There are few places in Baja that I don't find interesting, and
this one sure added to the variety! Great place to sleep if you don't
mind 250 race cars coming at you in the middle of the night, in a
dead heat. Interesting place to meet James Garner—he came in
about 10:30—could hardly see his face it was so full of polvo.*

Interesting place for a charade.

When Brandy can't sleep, his imagination goes into orbit. He runs the whole reel through his head and gets inspired to involve others in his scenario so *everybody* can have a good time. As a racer zooms in, he rolls over and blares in my ear: "MizKittyLu, I've a great idea. We can't sleep, we might as well have some fun."

"Not tonight, Brandy, some flake could shine their lights on us."

"Exactly, but not at what you're thinking."

"When did *you* not?"

"Now. First time. Hear me. Long-haul racers begin to hallucinate after this many hours of intense driving—over rough terrain especially. I've seen lotta impossible things out there myself, and I've listened and talked with other drivers about their wig bubbles."

"No wiggier than yours, I'm sure," says I, thinking, this one's going to be a lulu.

"Up the road a couple miles, before they get to this stop, there's a tall rounded boulder and some spook trees on a curve, just before the track heads out onto the pan. I know, because I've been there ... and ... I was just thinking ..."

"Please don't do that, Mr. Brandy. It's always dangerous."

"This won't be dangerous. This'll be fun! We can drive up there ..."

"*We?*"

"Oh, yeah. You're the centerpiece."

"Shit-oh-dear! Of course, when was I not?"

"Drive up there, pull Jaibita out of sight, the Brown Skin Native Girl climbs on the rock, just as she is, stands there in all her purity ..."

"In all her *what?*"

"Her *nada*, her *purisima*—and when the guy comes 'round the curve his headlights sweep over her—making his hallucinations, his day, his night, his life, complete."

"What if he stops to take a really good look?"

"He won't. He's in a *race*. Trust me."

"Trust you? I know better than that, Brandy."

"They'll talk about what they saw, or thought they saw, when they get here to the pit stop. They will in La Paz, too, I know they will. And the crew is going to repeat what they heard when we have breakfast with them in the morning. Be a blast!"

We belly-laughed all the way home. At least three drivers had had the same hallucination! Did they ever compare notes? Or find out they'd been had?

⁂

BECAUSE BRANDY COULD NOT BREATHE the rarefied air of high elevations, after our marriage in July '69 I moved from Aspen (which was going to hell in a high-priced handbasket) to Sedona, Arizona— before it got crystallized. From our honeymoon hogan in that once quiet cow town we watched the steady drag-chain death of the piñon/juniper forest at the foot of Grey Mountain and made love on the veranda to the nightly songs of the coyotes—before they were poisoned out. We dune-buggied the redrock backcountry where he could drive and I could hike out to get help when he got us impaled on the sandstone spires, or a clutch gave out, or a wheel fell off, or a tie rod came loose, or whatever. I hiked to the top of Grey Mountain several times; Brandy could not. He sat in the shade and wrote what we in the doggerel business call doggerel:

The Loving Plot That I Have Wrot

She mounted his flanks
she clambered his shanks
she admired his brow
it was grey

She crawled up his shoulder
and got even bolder
I tell you, she's wild
in her play

His slope it did please her
his beauty did seize her
but mountains are lucky
that way

Now me, I'm much tamer
and I don't really blame her
for finding my challenge
quite bland

But with patience I'll lead her
'til she finds love has freed her
and turns to me just as
I planned.

Also penned wild and wise sayings …

You've got such a lovely goddam ass, I'd like to bite it, get lockjaw, and have you tow me through town right past the post office.

A new groom sleeps clean.

There's nothing like a deck screw to hold you down.

Farcical—a bicycle used for traveling long distances.

If you can't be right, be wrong noisily and you'll confuse a lot of people.

"But …" he said, thoughtfully, watching a passing *derrière.*

Knowing that I would not wear a wedding ring, he had Carlos Diaz fashion a gold band encircling a black heart of jet that hung from a gold chain around my neck, around the band the words *"No tengo mas que darte."* (I have no more to give you.)

⚭

NOW YOU WILL FIND ME in the position of being a good friend to both of Brandy's ex-wives. Strange, unless you know their ex-husband's creative talent for warp-and-weave. I had much to learn. They confided, told me secrets of survival for which I was grateful. Was it because they pitied me, thinking I might be in their shoes one day? Ho-ho. Though they didn't know, I already *was* in their shoes! (Terms of our nuptial knot? *No one was to know—*might spoil my image.) An irresistible object (me) to an immovable force (him) is the way I describe the hitch. When we traveled—together or separately—we stayed with Dorothy or Helen, one in La Jolla, the other in Tucson. Neither had remarried and both were on good terms with him (if not each other) since they no longer had to put up with his craziness. Yes, I had much to learn, among other things that they still loved him—Dorothy in particular, mother of his kids, but she wasn't about to let him get close enough to open her wounds again, though he tried.

"But Dorothy Annie, I just want to hold you and go to sleep. I don't expect anything."

Estupido!

So let's check out the other stupid one—the bouncing ballad singer, MizKittyLu.

I married Brandy because I loved him; because he kept me on a skyhook; because he knew more and was smarter; because of his lizard-quick tongue—don't get ideas, I'm talking mental, not physical—because his blue eyes stared me down; because he loved me. And the glue that bonded all that together? *He made me laugh!*

There was more. His logic: Time after time I gave up in despair of not finding a publisher for the book (*Ten Thousand Goddam Cattle*) I'd been writing since 1958. I would not have finished it without his constant editing, encouragement, wordsmithing (he was a *vocal* thesaurus); his enlightened suggestions (rejected, of course, then modified or used); his goddam nagging me to keep writing.

"I know you hate waste. Think how many hours, days, years you will have wasted putting cowboy songs back with their authors, telling the stories behind these songs that nobody else knows. Think about that when you decide to quit."

His cute little tricks: It is morning. Coffee time. I've put the whistle-kettle on to boil and gone to the bathroom for my morning (uh, 'scuse me while I look this up in the thesaurus) ablutions. I'm washing my face when I hear the teakettle whistle. I grab the towel and run for the stove, turn it off, and pour tepid water into the coffee cone. Shit! It hasn't boiled at all.

Brandy has learned to whistle exactly like the kettle—*just before it boils*. This happens over and again until I learn to wait, to see if it's the real thing, or if he'll run out of breath. Sometimes I wanted to strangle him ... prematurely.

But I'd go to the bedroom where he spent most of the day, to find him propped up on pillows for easier breathing, listening to tapes of his friends playing jazz or penning a letter to the editor over some blatant stupidity that had fired his ire. Sparkling blue eyes—almost turquoise above the green tube that supplied oxygen to his ravaged lungs—would look at me, innocently and childlike, over starched, red handlebar moustache and neatly trimmed beard.

"*Buenos dias*, Bibby Snug [short for Beautiful Brownskin Native Girl]. I just thought of some new names for rock groups: Standing Broad & the Four Jumps, or Jack Acne & the Blemishes. Or how about Wyatt Burp & the Upchuckers?"

"Or, the Pukes," I'd add, and crack up.

Yes, tricks: Our good friend Les, rehabbed from hard drugs, now working at his old vocation as painter and wallpaper hanger, had joined the World Church—as part of his cure, perhaps?—an organization I didn't know much about then and still don't. Anyway, he was ordained to marry up folks who wanted to marry up. Brandy decided he wanted to be in that position as well and got Les to ordain him. Jesus! ('scuse me) what next? I have a photo of him in the "frock" he was to use for this ah ... hitching purpose: black flattop hat, long-sleeved, sincere, caftan-like robe with black boots, damned if he doesn't *look* like a preacher! Why he wanted to marry up people when he could barely marry up himself is beyond me. Or ... maybe that's why. Do unto others as you can't do unto yourself.

❧

WHENEVER I DIDN'T HAVE A GIG, or wasn't in cahoots with the muse, we'd grease it to La Jolla, Big Sur, and San Francisco for our R&R, ending up with Turk at McGoons listening to jazz, to Clancy's banjo, his chatter and songs. I tripped out on their music and Mr. B. loved jazz because it was happy. He'd always wanted to play tuba with the band. What else would a cat with no lungs want to do?

Brandy's Solo

I heard you last night,
singing.
You don't sing too well
or often
breath being quick and dear
as mercury
to you—but notes
tip-toeing to my ear
woke me, and
I turned to hear
your song.
I caught
the tail of Tiger Rag,
I thought,
then, a segue to The
Saints.
I elbowed up, leaned
close to hear,
unbelieving.

Exhaling on the long green hose
of oxygen
to your nose,
your breathing blew
staccato tunes
that would have made
Turk proud to
trombone to.
coming up: Sweet Sue.

Then ...
I was truly mesmerised
by you! Beside the melody,
your heart

(its jaunty beat uncoiling,
chest to throat)
VAH-ROOMPFFT out the bromide
of the band.
With style and flair
you picked the notes
and played
the tuba!

Flip the coin.

Journal Note: Punto Colorado, Baja Sur
[One of our dozen trips to "circumcise the tip"]

Decided to bug it to Santiago—then the day turned into a Brandy
day. That means when I say right, he goes left—when I say down,
it's up—when I say east, it's west—late, no early—no gas, enough,
etc., etc., etc. There was no gas in Santiago because the truck had
been delayed from La Paz. Wasted an hour of daylight going the
wrong way to Miraflores—then from Miraflores to La Ribera on
a road heading south—Ribera is northeast—dark coming, still
going south into a strange canyon. No gas. Wrong way. Meet a
paisano who tells us the road only goes to Rancho Trinidad, up
the arroyo. Brandy doesn't believe him and wants to take the
arroyo to the beach—probably twenty miles away—with no gas.
My foot goes down—NO. We run out, following the paisano's
truck back to the carratera, and use the half gallon in our small
can. The left brake is sticking. Reach the highway with barely
enough gas to Buena Vista. He doesn't like Buena Vista so he
goes past the turnoff to Las Palmas. No gas at Las Palmas,
because they don't want to sell it to us, so back three miles to
Buena Vista. We come to the turnoff; he still doesn't like it and
goes by. Whereupon I scream, "It is the goddam road! Take it!
I've had it, and I've had you. Maybe if you'd shut your mouth

*and shut your eyes and let me drive we'll get to a beach where
we can go to bed!" Now it's really night. No gas at BV—a liter
at Casa Ruis near the edge of town—in the BV hotel bar we
meet Gil* [friend with a nearby ranch] *who will give us gas in
the morning. We sack out down the beach from his place.
Tomorrow, baby, there's gonna be some changes. Another
Brandy ramrodded day and I'll be ready to cut for home!*

❧❧

TOWARD THE END OF OUR SECOND YEAR in Sedona, I about convinced myself that I didn't love this man at all.

I was merely fascinated by his antics, the roulette wheel of what
he'd do next. All those asinine cars in the yard: two dune buggies
(one of which was the Blue Fart he'd traded something else for and
given to me); a goofy four-door Citroën that puffed up and down
like a fat lizard when you got in or out of it; the potbellied VW bus,
El Toro Volado (to fly, explode, or blow up—*volador* has all those
meanings in Spanish); engines and parts strewn around like an over-
used car lot. The only sane vehicle was my very own classic 1955 T-
Bird with removable porthole hardtop, for which I'd constructed a
sensible sling and pulley in the garage to let it up and down. White
Bird was a veritable rose in that punchbowl of turds.

Some of us have energy to burn, and if we can't burn it, one way or
another it turns inward, making us restless and angry. Brandy had all
that energy until the Marine Corps scrambled his lungs. Now he fought
for breath after ten stairs or two blocks of flat walking. He would be in
bed by 8:30 or 9:00. I, on the other hand—having entertained in coffeehouses and bistros most of my adult years, not even going to work until
10 P.M., or to sleep before 3 A.M.—after writing and practicing all day I
was gung ho to be *doing something, going somewhere*. By myself? No.
That's not what I hooked up with Brandy for—to go to a movie alone,
or to dinner, or to the local bar. I never went near gin mills anymore.

So I tried to devise a release.

We had a circular drive at the Sedona house that I began using as
a personal racetrack that I would walk or run around at night—

preferably in the moonlight, porch lights if not—singing, swearing, crying, wondering why and how I got myself entangled with this critter who couldn't play with me anymore. Around and around and around.

Flip the coin again.

Letter: Brandy to Me, August 1, 1971

Ours is a special yet uncomplicated love, much too vital for ordinary workaday people who could not cope with it—hung up as they are with their Thou Shalt Nots and the restrictions and conventions of what they term a "good marriage."

We will soon be far apart and unlikely to see each other for some months. We will be other things—friends, confidants, short term lovers—to other people, but will again and again be together and be able to get inside each other, to walk around looking under rugs, checking the shelves to see what we each collected since the last time together, not afraid to point out cobwebby corners, warmed as two become one again. Together only because of a mutual need and desire to be together, the strength of the bond in the ephemeral ties of mind and emotion.

I have a distaste for discussing such things lest by clinical study the spontaneity and hence the lifeblood of the relationship be lost—it's been my experience that if you allow the convergences to just happen, the firmest foundation results. To push and crowd a relationship into the shape and form you want, or think you want, requires constant effort and eventually one or the other grows weary of working at it.

If, on the other hand, you keep all your sensors working and nerve endings alert for incoming signals you will, if it is meant to be, be drawn into the more intimate relationship.

It is sad but true, however, that such relationships are almost invariably foredoomed, particularly those involving the most vital and creative people. Change and growth is implicit in their make-up, and the mind that was tuned to one wave-length, then, is tuned to another wave-length, now. And in a month, a year,

*five years from now the odds are good that what exists now
will then be only a warm and gentle memory ... and the wistful
thought will run across the mind: "Maybe we could have made
it if only ... "*

That I was in a state of total denial is clear to me now, but not
then. I was blinded by frustration and self-pity, reading only "constant effort," "weary of working at it," "push and crowd into the
shape you want," ignoring that I'd cauterized my nerve endings and
was accepting no signals. I would not admit to a retuning of wave-
lengths, or to anything else that implied Brandy was changing (his
deteriorating health being the cause), that he was going to die, which
of course is what he was trying to tell me and prepare me for.

Blind as a bump on a log (a Brandy malaprop).

The above letter was written at the VA hospital in Tucson, where
they kept him for the better part of a month. Just prior to his leaving, I received the good news that I'd been accepted by the National
Humanities Council for a nine-month tour of the USA. Meanwhile,
I had to vacate the house (they'd sold it out from under us), find a
place to live (not in Sedona—too expensive for a vet's disability
check and my earnings), move everything (his cars to Tucson, our
furniture and belongings to a new place twenty-five miles away and
two thousand feet higher), settle up all bills, pay rent, clean house in
Sedona and the new rental, do all this by myself and be in Princeton,
New Jersey, for rehearsals on the first day of September.

Brandy came "home" to the newly rented house a few days before
I had to catch the plane to Princeton—said he couldn't stay there,
too high. I understood but couldn't do anything about it. He'd explained long ago that when he got too much or too little oxygen, or
the wrong mix, or some new medicine they were guinea-pigging him
on, it could affect his brain, making him respond with odd behavior.
I laughed that one off; he'd been Mr. Odd Behavior from day one!

That night I got a taste of day two. In a wink I became his enemy.
He said I'd made him take pills that were going to kill him. He
wouldn't let me near him—he actually twisted my wrist when I tried
to rub his sore neck. I went to bed sobbing and shaking, in shock, a

little motor that wouldn't turn off buzzing in my solar plexus. I couldn't stop crying. I got up in the middle of the night to find him wide awake, cutting out words from letters and notes with a razor, little scraps of paper all over the table and floor.

"Brandy! What on earth are you doing, luv?"

His blue eyes, darting suspiciously, glared a warning at me. "Never mind. I don't need your help. Go away!" he held up the razor.

Trembling and short of breath, I backed out of the room. Dear God! What had they given him to make him crazy like that? I locked the bedroom door. Now, I was *afraid* of him!

Before I could drag myself from bed the next morning, he'd left for Tucson in the Citroën, the cut-up letters still on the table and floor, along with this note in shaky handwriting:

> *The Steroids, being an adrenal stimulant may give you a big boost, but do you tend to overwork your heart in responding to that rush of adrenaline? Once again I've laid it on the line to advance the forward edge of medical knowledge! What's my medal—my tombstone courtesy of the VA?*

And this:

> *If only I'd met you years ago, we'd probably both be somewhere else by now.*

Less than a week before I had to be in rehearsal, I had a nervous breakdown. I didn't know it then. I didn't understand what was wrong, other than my sorrow over Brandy and what it could do to your body and your will. I took on his symptoms, could hardly breathe, couldn't lift anything heavier than my fork, could not walk to the car and back without sitting down. I wanted to sleep. No way. The little motor in my gut, with its ringing in my ears, never quit for a minute. I was completely exhausted—mentally, physically, and emotionally. I suppose now they'd call it "depression." Whatever, it was a bitch, yet somehow I dragged my bags and guitar, if not my mind, to Princeton on time.

THIRTY-SIX STATES, ninety-eight cities, home five days out of each month to exchange my wardrobe for the next state, and to see Brandy. He was staying with Bob, an old racing buddy in Tucson, when he wasn't on his way up from or down to La Paz, living there in the little shack in back of his friend Tony's house. He'd traded Jaibita (the little crab buggy) for the Plastic Goat—a corrugated Citroën, a jeeplike thing that reminded me of pieces of lanai roofing, only red, not green—said he'd had to *back* it up the cuestas. I spent the Christmas holidays with him in La Paz and was back on the road January 3, 1972. He really had to live at sea level now in order to breathe without constant oxygen. Come March, he was back at the Tucson VA hospital in intensive care. Bob called me in Boston—as far from Brandy as I had ever been on the tour—and I was at the hospital within hours. He didn't die—it was the time he tried to do the sailboat trip without his tanks—a week later he was back at Bob's house and getting ready to head south again in the Plastic Goat.

At the end of May '72 I was freeee!

Tony's shack was way too small, so Brandy found us a nice house on the outskirts of La Paz town; I sublet the one in northern Arizona and came down with all my gear and typewriter, intent on finishing my book, *Ten Thousand Goddam Cattle*. After all, my Roget's Thesaurus was walking and talking again. The hospital there had his prescriptions and doctors still made house calls, as of old, to see him.

Nick-the-Slick came and went. He sat in the dry fishpond under the palm trees, buck-ass, typewriter between his knees, clicking out essays. Daily the two of them would set me up as "straight man," knowing I would bite. Then they'd walk off, hilarious over the punch line, leaving me with egg on my face. I wish I could remember some of that repartee—it came quick as lightning, just like the laughter—after I wiped the egg off. We recircumcised the tip a few more times, Brandy too. We had Sockit-to-me's (our special rum libation) almost every night beside the bay, when sunsets of raging red and orange and green fire fell from the sky onto its rippled surface. Christmas was damp and quietly festive, but we were together with our Mexican and American friends. Helen wrote, I wrote Helen. Dorothy came down once, didn't like it much, and went home. One of their daughters came down, but I *sent* her home, nutty as a peanut farm. She wanted to have her dad committed! Should have been her.

I flew up to do my concerts and finish the film series Brandy had insisted I make (from my not-done-yet manuscript), about two Arizona cowboys before they died. The University of Arizona produced the first and only one, it turned out, before the book was ever published, and *The Last Wagon* won the Cine 1972 Golden Eagle Award for a documentary. All Mr. B.'s doing. For sure I would not have known where to go to get such a thing done, let alone the *cojones* to think I could direct and be a part of the documentary—as was the Blue Fart! In one of the last scenes, to emphasize the rip-up of the West, that dune buggy rides fence. Every time Brandy saw it, his waxed handlebars stuck him in the eyes. He was so pleased!

Do we learn from others to have faith in ourselves? You bet we do. When we see the result of what we've done that we thought was impossible, and are proud of it, do we credit the instigator? Brandy's name is not in the credits, nor do I know how I could have put it there. No one but MizKittyLu knew the moving spirit behind the writing and the idea of documenting it. The book is dedicated to Brandy, but that's not enough. He did not live to see it finished.

In early March of that spring, the La Paz hospital took him in, pumped him up, sent him back, took him in again, and kept him. I went to stay a few nights with him there. You don't want to know about it.

Midnight, March 16, I kissed him, told him I loved him, and left the hospital with instructions to call me if anything changed. At 3 A.M. I bolted upright in bed from a restless sleep. No phone had rung. I reached for the little serape that Brandy often used and brought it to my face.

"Goodbye, my love," I said. "Go well. At long last there'll be no more pain."

Ten minutes later the phone rang. It was St. Patrick's Day.

The Panteón Civil
(La Paz Cemetery)

Inside the Panteón Civil
a thousand Cristos writhe on
Cadillac's of wealthy dead,
a thousand crosses waver blue-hot
in crystal sky,
and heaving earth falls slowly
back in place when
longer shadows gnaw
the gold day down.

My Love, so short a time,
so long a wait.
What did I know of you?
or you of me?
Enough to stack our hands,
pronounce our fate
and be each to the other
what needed each to be.
Yet I would crawl back in
my words and burst the beads
of speech
to hold you in health
and know things I will never know.

White Crested Prickle Poppies
do not dance in desert winds,
they freeze, mutely hold their
dust up to the moon.
and I? ...
I drain the sky of tears inside
the plastic garden
of the Panteón Civil.

His Heart to the Hawks

July 1969

HONEYMOONING IN THE WILDS of southern Utah. We lie on the sand beside an as-yet-undesecrated part of the old Colorado River, making love and reading parts of *Desert Solitaire* to each other.

Next morning, we take a little trip in the car, leave our stuff at camp, and return in the late afternoon with a gift we intend to send to the author, a little piece of wood with a Day-Glo plastic strip tied to it. There's more trash like it down in the bottom of a very deep canyon.

We laugh a lot, read some more Abbey, and marvel that someone finally has put to print the ethics of an activity I've championed since my first run down the Colorado (1953), one that yet has no name. And we marvel that after his one trip down The Glen, he has expressed a depth of feeling similar to mine about that most special place.

Back home we strap the stick to my album, *Folk Songs of the Colorado River*, and ship it off to Organ Pipe National Monument.

September 1969

Dear Miss Lee,
Muchas gracias for the surveyor's stakes. Keep up the Lord's work.
Thanks very much for the Songs of the Colly-Raddy, it's a great
record and I've been playing it about 3 times a day, wallowing
in nostalgia. Come visit if you have a chance, I'd like to hear
you sing these songs live, in person. So don't forget your guitar!
Best regards, Ed Abbey, Ajo, Ariz.

Now the activity has a name: the Lord's work!

Ed and Katie

October 1969

WE GO TO ORGAN PIPE, spend two days and nights with Ed and
third wife Judy, his mom and dad. Wonderful, generous, gracious
folks. Susie is in her crib and Judy is in Tucson during part of our
stay, taking courses at the university.

We sit under the stars. I sing for hours. Ed smokes and listens. What
a listener! They don't make 'em like that anymore. He smiles, and
with that dry wit, offers up the ingenious remarks I have tried for
years to invent about dam builders, greed-heads, and pus brains.
Brandy, my husband, and I hate campgrounds, so Ed tells us about a
road inside the park where nobody will bother us. "Don't blame you,
campgrounds are for birds," he says. "Come back for breakfast."

June 4 1970, Tucson International Airport

BRANDY AND I are just returning from La Paz, Mexico. En route to
claim our baggage, we run into Ed. He looks haggard and worried,
but smiles when he sees us.

"Where you off to, Edwardo?"

"My wife is very sick, don't know what's wrong. She's at her parents' in the East. I'm going back—it sounds serious."

"Oh, Christ, Ed, that's real bad news." My exuberance over seeing him suddenly turns to sorrow when I think about Judy, whom we've seen only once, and the baby, Susie. What a helluva thing it would be if he should lose her. I ask to be kept posted on developments and we drive up home to Sedona in a very depressed mood.

July 1970

Dear Katie,
Thanks for your letter. Judy did not make it. She died early in
the morning, July 4th. Acute leukemia—the poor kid never
had a chance. Sent a copy of your protest letter to the Escalante
Wilderness committee. They want to make sure all such letters
are included in the record.
Best, Ed, North Rim

Ed zigged while I zagged, and it was almost a year before I saw him again. Our notes to each other were about protest meetings, wilderness hearings, how convenient it would be if someone blew up the Glen Canyon Dam, and a mention or two of my manuscript of the "river book" I'd started in 1964 but hadn't been able to finish. (For many reasons: the pain of beauty gone forever, the bitter anger and pure hatred I felt for the people who'd done my river in, and lack of confidence in my writing ability—I couldn't turn the trick.)

"How can you keep the humor, Ed? Goddammit, the whole thing is *sick*, not funny!"

At least he told me never to take a writing course, though I still don't know why.

May 1971, Home from the North Rim

Okay, Edwardo,
Hey, it was nice up there in the cool, watching from your Ivory
Tower. Not since the Glen have I come upon a more poignant
moment than walking up the trail (not knowing you played

anything, let alone the flute!) to hear that completely right and woodsy sound leafing down through the aspen and conifers ... like much-needed rain. I lay there on the porch of the old cabin for a long time, hearing old melodies I used to know, had forgotten, and wondered why I had. Bless you for offering to read my manuscript when you have so many things of your own going [writing *Black Sun* and screwing the local lady park ranger], *but you saw the river like it once was. I lived on the river like it once was, and my life has been changed by its destruction. Don't be easy with me. I'm a severe critic and I expect the same back. Publishers and agents tell me it won't fly, but they don't tell me why. I gotta have reasons. Luv, Kanyon Kate*

August 1971

Dear Katie,
I agree with your agent. Rewrite the book as a straightforward autobiography. Why? Because the truth in this case is more interesting than your fictional version.
Best, Ed

That is *not* what I wanted to hear. I put it in the trunk and walked away, no longer able even to think about it. I wanted to write like Ed Abbey and knew I couldn't, so what was the use?

I did a U.S. tour for the National Humanities Series for a year, then went to live in La Paz with Brandy—the only place he could breathe—and didn't come back to stay in Arizona until he died of emphysema, on St. Pat's Day, '73.

May 1973

Dear Katie,
Sorry to hear about Brandy. I know exactly how you must feel. I'm off to Navajo Mt. And the Escalante Monday, back in about a month. Call me at Aravaipa if you come this way.
Ed

Sometime in August of that year, I show up at Ed's Aravaipa Game Refuge trailer with Bruce Berger in tow (author of *There Was a River*, a journal of his only and my last run down The Glen in '62). We get drunk with Ed and Renee, his fourth wife, and talk long through a coral and deep purple sunset. He signs my hardback copy of *Desert Solitaire*, which first brought us in touch, and chuckles about how and where we read it, accentuating the spray of sun wrinkles that frame his honest eyes. Our talk drifts on into a starlit night beside a juniper fire: about books, loved ones gone, rivers, pricks and princes, and how to put a hole in Glen Canyon Dam—wishful talk, you understand, that ends on a sad note. Ed has had the last confrontation he's willing to risk with rednecks firing their guns in a game refuge and will be gone when we return from our hike. "Look for the lions," he says. "In spite of those assholes, thank God they're still here."

April 1975

Hi Old Lee,
I'm very happy to know you like the MONKEY book. I liked
Berger's story very much, altho I missed the celebrated account
of how you escaped by bosom-suction from the big pothole. Sorry
I can't join you on the Slickhorn hike, but hope to see you at the
Glen Canyon Wilderness hearings in Page (May 14?) or Kanab
(May 15th?).
Love, Ed

Ed had read the incident in my river manuscript, and because we all steal from each other in ways we often know not, *his* invention of the pothole escape turned up in the last book he wrote, *Hayduke Lives*—my escape was *not* by bosom suction!

May 1975, Kanab

I AM THERE. We pass on the stairs at recess. I tell him I've tried to write it out like he does and read it, but I can't compose the thought and stick to it without some vitriol leaking out in an aside and ruining my cool. Actually, cool is not my thing unless I'm singing, and this ain't no gig.

He doesn't berate me for getting emotional like my other wise friends do on occasion, like I berate myself, knowing full well that the way to get a point across is to keep the fact and the frustration separate. He just tells me I should say what I know about the place and its singularity, beauty, and restorative qualities. He insists that I probably know more about it than anyone there and wishes me well.

I try, God knows. I try to impress upon that group how prohibitive the cost, how unnecessary roads in the area will be, but I'm talking to a wall of stone heads and faces, and finally blow it when I hear the old saw: "I wanna be able to take my mother over to the edge of that canyon in a car because she's old and can't walk about like these rich young backpackers, etc., etc."

I'm thinking, "She's lived there all her damned life, right? Why didn't she go see it when she *could* walk? It's been there since the ground was put in. What was she so busy doing? I know, raising a multitude like you? Why don't y'all carry her over there if she's so hot to see it now!" Aw, hell, what's the use.

But you're there Ed, thank God, and you say it right, like always. You say it like you write it.

September 1976

Dear Ed,
… Northland Press says they're jamming for release of my book before
Xmas [Ten Thousand Goddam Cattle: A History of the American
Cowboy in Song, Story and Verse]. *Should be out in November.*
Have you seen the T-shirt "Hayduke Lives?" And I love this:
   Hai'duk (hi-dook), n. Also Hey-duck, -duke, -duc, etc.
(G. hai-duck, heiduck, fr. Hung. Hajdúk, pl. of hajdú brigand).
One of the bandit mountaineers among the Balkan Slaves; also, in
Hungary, one of a class of mercenary foot soldiers who received
privileges of nobility and local independence in 1605. Ain't you
smart! Write.
Love, Katie

October 1976, Moab

Dear Katie,
You're the first—so far as I know—to discover the key to Hayduke's
name. Ain't you smart!
Love, Ed

Actually, it wasn't me, but my smart friend, Bruce, who found it
in the dictionary by accident while looking up something else.

January 1977

MY FIRST BOOK WAS RELEASED in late November, and one of the
first to get a copy was Ed. He sent back a response I still use today.
In fact, he sent it so fast I'm not sure he even read the book. Once,
years later, I intimated that he probably hadn't. That was the one
and only time I ever got the "curmudgeon look" so many others
seemed to know about. He growled, "Certainly I read it." I never
probed further. His quote, 2/15/77: *"You've done a beautiful job—*
exact, comprehensive and witty—and I predict it will become and
remain a basic history of the subject for many years to come. Con-
gratulations"

Early August 1977

Dear Katie,
Come visit. Bring self, guitar, beaucoup vin du Paris. We're up
on Aztec Peak L.O., Tonto N.F., about 20 miles south of Young
off 288. Will be here until October, probably.
Love, Ed & Renee

Late August 1977

I ARRIVE IN THE VW SAFARI about sundown with gallons of the
grape and a hiking buddy. We stay for two days, hiking the mountain,
singing, goofing around. I take his book out to the privy, sit down
on the hole, and have him take a picture of me reading it, then coax
him to take the same seat, reading mine. I don't think he was too
keen on the idea, but he humored me just the same, then inscribed

my copy of *The Monkey Wrench Gang* with these treasured words: "Here's to Katie Lee, artist and fighter, from a friend and admirer. Ed Abbey, Aztec Peak, '77"

September 1983, Jerome

MANY PLACES have been hiked and plenty of rivers run. Sadly, I never got to take a trip with Ed, but we had many talks and met at least twice a year.

The Jerome Historical Society has a film program going, and we want to show *Lonely Are the Brave*, the movie adaptation of Ed's novel *The Brave Cowboy*. I call him to ask his fee for giving a talk before and after the film.

"Hell, Katie, I don't want a fee. When is it? I'd like to see old Jerome again."

"October. You and Clarke can stay in our 'tower.' C'mon, at least let us pay your travel expenses, honorarium, something."

"No, just buy me a drink."

I ask him to send me a photo for the press. "What do you want us to say about you in the releases?" (He hates this kind of thing and I hate asking him.)

Long sigh ... "I'll write it out."

September 18, 1983

Dear Katie,
Here's a photo, as requested. You can say that I'm the author of the Brave Cowboy, Monkey Wrench Gang, Good News, Down the River, Desert Solitaire *and other books. My next book is called* Beyond the Wall *and will appear sometime in Spring '84, Deo volente. What else? well—I live near Oracle, AZ.* [he never lived in Oracle]*, have a wife, children, house, bills to pay, the whole catastrophe, and am looking forward to becoming a mean, nasty, ugly, wise old man.*
Love, Ed

ENOUGH! I never meant to do this, but when I got out his letters, notes, photos—the file—I thought sharing his words with others who cared about him might be a way of showing how much time, patience, and guidance he freely gave to those of us who could use his help.

I've thought of little else but Ed and his family, and have been able to do nothing since his death. I didn't even get to the Tucson wake; my Aussie and I were in Baja when we heard what sounded like rumor, and I flat refused to believe it. The file coughed up a flier from the last time we performed together at an Earth First! rally in Tucson, February 1986, in protest of yet another piece of our desert being chewed up by the bulldozers. The last photos I have of him are with Clarke (his last, best wife, he said) and their new baby, Ben, on their porch in Tucson, Christmas '85. He was sick then, but Clarke couldn't get him to go to the doc.

The knowledge that he was my friend I will carry with great pride. His last written words to me, on the usual postcard, are pinned above my desk, supportive to the last—giving, giving, giving.

June 1988

Dear Katie,
Quote me: "Anyone who loved the living Colorado River
(pre-damnation by the swine who run America) will love these
songs by pioneer Glen Canyoneer Katie Lee."
Love & Luck, Ed Abbey

He hadn't even heard the new cassette.

When you have a talent, not great but good enough, and you seek to make it better, you go to the best there is for advice. You don't fuck around with the mediocre, egocentric in-betweens. Edwardo is the best there is and he took the time to assist me as a writer—something much harder for me than singing. The day of that last photograph, he asked me again about *All My Rivers Are Gone*, the "river book."

"What are you doing with it?"

"Nothing. I can't write it as an autobiography, no matter what you say. Who could give a shit about my life?"

"It's about the canyon, Kate. Lots of people give a shit about Glen because they never saw it. They're beginning to know what they missed."

"I can't write in the first person. I don't know the tricks—too self-conscious."

"Then write an 'autobiographical novel,' whatever that is, but *write* it."

"Easy for you to say. Easy for you to do. I can't."

"Bullshit. Besides, your cow book is in the first person, in case you hadn't noticed."

April 1989

I am more than halfway through, Ed. I think I might make it before the end of the year. Jesus-God! Have you any idea how I thank you? But now I'm talking to the hawks. What a generous heart you have given them! I'll never see a zopilote or an eagle without thinking of you and smiling. If my philosophy of "Pass-it-on" holds up, Ed, there'll be a whole bunch of people with enough of your kind of love for our Southwest to hold back the tide. None may say it as well, mind you, but the desire to act will grow ... Dave Foreman ... Chuck Bowden ... Doug Peacock ...
THE LORD'S WORK ... KEEP UP THE LORD'S WORK!

We all feel a terrible emptiness with you sailing off like that on your own. It's as if someone stole the monuments from Monument Valley. They're gone! My favorite winding fluted canyon has been zipped up, leaving a void. The desert has been wiped clean.

This too will pass.

You are a "Giant Still Among Us." Your last gift—Your heart to the Hawks!* Or, as you'd probably say, "to the buzzards."

April 13, 1989

(*Title from a poem by Robinson Jeffers, "Give Your Heart to the Hawks.")

When Rivers Sing

I HOPE YOU WILL BE LISTENING.

Oh, yes, they sing. And they whisper, and giggle, and warble, and laugh, and burp. They hiss and roar and I'm sure some of them scream. To use the nicer term, they often crepitate. In other words, *they are very much alive*. They talk all the time, from love murmurs to angry protest. The only time they sleep, it is the sleep of the dead behind some grotesque dam; some block of man-made cement that hangs around their joyful necks and shackles them into slavery. Even then their ghosts are restless, angry ghosts—probing, crawling, vaporizing … and, heh-heh … waiting.

In Glen Canyon, when it *was* a canyon and not the foul racetrack reservoir it has become, the Colorado River was laid back in the embrace of more than one hundred beautiful side streams and canyons. There he became a gentle lover. (The River has always been a *he* to me, but we really drop gender here—it's the spirit that counts.) After much teasing and playing around in Cataract and before his wild sex orgy in the Grand Canyon, there, in a glen like its name, is where the River took his time, his R&R, between those high, reverberating canyon walls. And there is where he sang his most entrancing songs … at least to me.

My first trip on that great river was through the Grand Canyon. Since I'd been asked to bring my guitar and sing around the campfire at day's end, I brought with me the songs I knew, the folksongs I sang on radio, in coffeehouses, and in concert. None of them were songs about rivers, especially *this* river, and they didn't sound quite right to me down there in the beginnings of the earth with its deep-throated sounds of power echoing up or down from a rapid. I knew

When rivers sing

a lot of Irish, English, early American ballads, cowboy-and-western songs that were popular in that folk era of the fifties, but when we camped on the mile-long, clean, river-built, untracked beaches (that no longer exist) beside quiet riffles that chortled their chocolate tunes, my songs didn't seem to cut it. So, with the sounds of the River's eccentric melodies in my ear—the new music I'd found there—I wrote some words that fit the place. Did it before I even knew it was done, but sang it to a tune I had borrowed from a popular songwriter friend. Why not to my own tune? It was too soon. I hadn't yet learned how to read the River's special score.

Then I met Glen Canyon.

On a blackout kind of night in the summer of 1954, sitting above the River on a sandstone bench watching stars ride a riffle—watching them slip and bob and couple and split and ride again polygamously, changing mates on the rippled surface—I heard and was able to read that score. Not only the music but the words. It became a matter of the time I spent there, the quietness all around me, no foreign stimuli to bombard me with trivia. There was open space and beauty beyond description to be filled with only my private thoughts and the songs of moving water, but I had to learn the listening process before I could understand his chatter, his moods, his anger, laughter, and whispered secrets. Learning that singular language honed all my other senses to an awareness of, among other things, rhythm.

A rhythmic river! I had never thought of that before.

Through a violent storm, from faraway timpani to crashing lightning and unleashed, thundering waterfalls, there would not only be a change of rhythm but a change of key, and afterward, some of the finest music of all. From the canyon, rather than the River, I could hear notes clear up and down the scale in harmonies, with syncopation—water drops falling into pools of every size and depth, like music played on a xylophone.

As anyone can tell you who has ever been on a river listening to human music—a guitar, flute, violin, harmonica, whatever—it sounds different there than anywhere else. First of all, mostly unnoticed by the novice, is the accompaniment by the River itself; then the enhancement and enlargement of the notes as they pass over, around, and back to the listeners from the canyon walls. But it is the river's accompaniment that is missed when the same song, the same instrument, is played elsewhere. The echo, the feedback, can be addressed with electronics, but *electric* is how it will sound. Never can or will it replace the natural acoustics that resound from the canyon's cathedrals, overhangs, walls, and alcoves. Absent will be the underlying support to the music—subtle, but imperative—the backup musician. The River.

For reasons unexplainable (except that our senses do play in symphony), color, especially in Glen Canyon, added a kind of magic to the music there. A number of musicians I know see color in their minds that isn't right before their eyes. Had I been a composer of symphonies, that canyon would have been the place to transmit vivid color into sound. Even in my simple, folky form of music—I play by ear and hardly know more than twenty chords—after being in The Glen, I could see color in a melody.

The attention I gave to what the River was saying and singing helped me store the vision, the sounds, and the color in my memory, which saved my dear butt time after time from life's many encounters with anger and despair. Dear God, the nights I've spent in supper clubs, coffeehouses, concert halls, and auditoriums with high-tech, state-of-the-art equipment, and never once heard a sound return to me like a river's singing. Standing under the spotlight in full makeup, pantyhose, high heels, and sometimes even a wig if I'd gone swimming that afternoon, befogged in cigar and cigarette smoke as blue and dense as what rose from the stacks of the steel mills in Gary, Indiana, and underlying all, the sludge of stale booze that smelled like a wet moose in rut, I could flash on the memory of my River's music ... hear that underlying throb ... see the vivid color surrounding it, and tease my brain into *being* where that pure earthy melody originated.

After that, I would wait, wait, wait for the day when I would again be on the River.

⚜

I CLOSED MY GIG at the Hungry I in San Francisco, stashed the guitar in my already packed T-Bird, and headed for Reno at 2 in the morning—a great time to drive; smooth, speedy, trafficless—I'd done it before. Many times. Somewhere past Vallejo I pulled to the side of the road, stripped off pantyhose, bra, and black chiffon, wiggled into jeans, and drove hard and fast, still under the stimulus of a performance high. When dawn spread across the Carson Valley plains, I pulled into a motel near Truckee and flaked out for four hours, awoke in early morning sunshine, ate, coffeed heavily, and drove the black ribbon that pulled me toward the River.

As I arrowed toward a horizon of foaming suds, with bottoms of dingy gray about to be dumped on the low hills, I felt like a homing pigeon winging over the wide, familiar desert that holds me and other westerners captive. Through hammering rain that pulled the knockout incense of sage and creosote and wetted silt from the earth, I pushed the Bird past the Great Salty into Green River, Utah, where I slept on Ken Sleight's lawn until dawn.

⚜

DESERTS HUM. Oh, yes. They whistle and toot and click. Rustle, scratch, and thump the tabla. In our western theater of sound, deserts provide the percussion. Under stormy heavens they vibrate the snares across their taught skins, playing strident Sousa marches. Another day, another theater, and we're given soft fripps of the brush across their sounding skins in rhythm with the wind.

Deserts play woodwind sounds through fluted stone, their most captivating sound of all. Like a siren call, it is. Once upon a Glen I stood in a sequestered gracility, an erotic sinuosity, a three-foot-wide, six-hundred-foot-deep fluted canyon, and heard a melody so out of this world I could not capture it again. Couldn't hum it, sing it, or remember any tune — only its gentle persuasion to take me to another place, a place I'd never entered before.

From Ken's lawn toward Hanksville, dry and wet streambeds vein out from the knuckle-raised fists of the San Rafael Swell and Reef that runs south and parallels the Green River above its junction with the Colorado. Red-orange-yellow-pink-buff-purple cliffs clutch at dark green juniper and piñon on top of the reef like lustful fingers tangled in unruly hair.

The drive from there to the River is pure sensation.

Beyond Hanksville, the Summerville formation, like sheaves of rippled wet parchment, crumbles beneath the snow-tipped Henry Mountains to the west, while to the south and east rises the Colorado Plateau. My track paralleled the Dirty Devil River before it plunged into a deep red heart of hobby-knobby chocolate drops that cordoned off the river above Hite — Moenkopi mudstone — a fiery furnace that some called hell. I called it heaven.

Then I braved the unknown.

Not exactly the unknown. I'd come that way more than once with someone else driving the nothing but sand-silt-rut-rock road from Hanksville, around Little Egypt, over the dunes and down North Wash, one of the hundred or more side canyons into The Glen. No bridge spanned those several hundred sinuous miles of river from Ken's to Marble Canyon, Arizona, then. This time I was alone in terrain where I could be up to my crotch in crocodiles before someone came along to pull me and my low-slung '55 T-Bird out of the dunes.

Well, I was damned if I'd go all the way around through Moab, Monticello, Blanding, and down Farley Canyon two hundred more miles to the river. When in doubt, keep moving. So what if there were seventy-five to a hundred crossings of North Wash? I'd do it. Be there by late afternoon. (Take a look at it sometime as you go from New Hite to the Pissing Springs turnoff—yeah, that's what the Mormon cowboys called it before the mapmakers got to it. You'll enter North Wash on an elevated, bitumen highway now and can't see the bottom until you get miles up the canyon.)

Lucky for me, the rain had traveled from the Great Salty down Hanksville way, or I'd be there yet. It doused the dunes enough to harden them for my tricky but triumphant crawl across to the Wash. I plowed, crawled, and burrowed through them, whatever seemed right—I got stuck only a couple of times; a few rocks and my shovel, and the dunes let me go—down to a mostly bedrock streambed where I found a more or less constant trickle left over from what had been a dandy flush of the system some twelve hours earlier.

Fleshy mounds of petrified Navajo dunes poked up on all sides of my vision, hardly discernible from the soft moving ones that had nearly obliterated a good part of the road. Many times I stopped, got out, and listened to the desert, the stream, and the rock. It hummmmmed and moaned and whistled. I would spread my arms, lie down, and press my body into those sensuous curves. I just couldn't pass up a rippled crevasse, a set of Moki steps, or a soft, round bum with potholes up its crack. One ragged hump spit at me as I reached up for a handhold, and beneath an alcove, with cicadas cavorting in a cottonwood by the Wash, I had to cover my ears— they sounded like four hundred six-year-olds practicing the violin!

About fifteen miles from the drop into North Wash I neared the River. Winding down through Navajo, Kayenta, Wingate sandstone, I stopped for the last time between towering Moenkopi bonbons, hardly wide enough for the Bird's passing—to listen for what I knew I would hear. It came up on a breeze of earthy cologne. Murmuring, chortling, laughing, welcoming me home.

The song of my River.

Learning About Rivers

I WAS BORN IN THE SOUTHWEST where a river is a sometime thing, so if it isn't there, you can't write about it. And I didn't.

Instead I watched the dry, sandy beds that occasionally were invaded by "rivers"—with great force and fervor, I might add—removing every anthill, packrat, and bird nest, every old tennis shoe and cowboy boot, even a buried rusty can containing my fortune of nickels, dimes, and pennies—only to conclude, first off, that rivers were thieves.

So much for childhood impressions. Later, no matter the paucity of that liquid, wherever found in the desert—stock tank, horse trough, pothole, stream, or river—the first thing I did was *get in it*. Then and only then would I think about what it meant, what it *was*.

When I at last met the big one, the real one, the Colorado, I was made to understand that rivers are about water: the lifeblood of our planet, a more than magnificent force, an elusive substance, sublime and vital to all living things, a factor to be reckoned with, constantly. Pick a river and you have a subject of infinite variety—mystical, historical, real. And if you listen to it, it will tell you things.

Rivers have a language of amazing clarity with a range of voices like those of good actors. In the space of a few hundred yards, they can make all kinds of wild sounds and people sounds, but they aren't very good at motor noises, jackhammers, or the *beep-beep-beep* of backing-up land-scrapers.

Rivers have distinct personalities that can help you learn who they are: master or slave, healer or killer, sick or healthy. Like people and snowflakes, no two are alike. The only thing they have in common

Learning about rivers Katie's way

is the place they're headed for: a sea, an ocean ... somewhere. "Headed for," I say, but with less assurance of arrival, given our meddling with their stream of consciousness.

To learn about flowers, one studies botany; about ancient cultures, archeology. To learn about rivers, you live beside them; row boats on them; study their moods and currents, their clarity or siltiness; play in them; swim in them; try not to drown.

In Tajikistan I stood beside a river that could tear your toenails off. It was the color of light gray marble and was carrying half of its feral power in glacial moraine from the Parmir Mountains between Afghanistan, China, and Tajikistan. It was *roaring*—no, shrieking, not even in full spring flood—shrieking with laughter because some fools downstream were building a dam that it would chew up and spit out in less than five years.

I didn't learn that river's talk, or how to listen to a river, all by myself. A boatman I knew, whose respect and devotion to "his" river was phenomenal, taught me the secret—taught me that listening can sometimes tell you more about what a river is up to than watching it can.

Sandbanks will surrender to the shameless advances of a river on the rise. A change in the twisting ribbon of current, from one side to the other, can alter its conversation with the bank. Winds can erase the river's slate clean, but if you can still hear the water, it will send you clues.

Rivers are great therapists.

Depending on your needs (if you know them), pick a river, from the bouncy, clear, and bubbly ones to the muddy, wild, and dangerous ones. If you're not a listener, then watch. They are *curious*, probing into every breach and hollow, circling back to catch what they missed. They are *relaxed*, at peace in their thoughtful meanders. They are *determined* and always know where they are going—it's ordained from birth. They are *angry* when stifled in unnatural puddles of regulated outlet not of their choosing. They are *patient*; waiting ... preparing ... for their ultimate release.

Sit and watch for an hour, a day, a week. It's a fascinating pastime. And if you're lucky, you'll find you've learned as much about yourself as you have about the river.

A more than fair exchange, I'd say. Go for it.

My Friend Tad

(Note: This piece was originally written as the Introduction to Tad Nichols's book, *Glen Canyon: Images of a Lost World*, Museum of New Mexico Press, 1999.)

WHEN I THINK ABOUT TAD NICHOLS, most often it has something to do with the Colorado River and Glen Canyon. But the connecting tissue to our becoming good friends is forever lost in our murky memories.

I call him Tadito, E.T., Tadpole, or Professor, and from him I acquired the names and status of pal and chum, which I liked far more than darling or sweetheart because they last longer—in this case, well over fifty years.

When I was presented with the honor of writing an introduction for Tad, I realized I'd already sketched him in my own book, and since he claims the description fits perfectly, I quote some of it here:

> To know Tad Nichols is to love him. As one of my oldest and
> dearest friends, to love him is to know the true meaning of
> frustration. My Irish can really flare up at him until his utter
> defenselessness douses it. I think of him always as born with silver
> spoon in mouth; as never having had to do anything, and therefore
> doing nothing (unless he thinks he's about to miss something, like a
> good time, a new adventure, a photo/movie assignment where he
> can prove out the unique talent that is his behind a camera lens).
> And oh gawd, he is lazy! Says I. Took me some time to realize it's a
> combination of metabolism, preoccupation, and the "absent-minded
> professor" syndrome.

Tad on the river

He stands well over six feet, is lean to skinny with long muscles,
long legs, long arms, and slender fingers, a slightly bowed torso, and
eyebrows so black and thick they look like two caterpillars fighting.
To hike with him, when he's finally ready, willing, and motivated
to move, is to trot ahead, then wait, rather than be stepped on
from behind. If I do elect to stay behind his easy, lanky stride,
sure enough I'll round a bend and run smack into him, because
his fine camera eye will have stopped him mid-step to case the
scene, and there he'll be for no one knows how long. … He knows
a lot about plants and bugs and rocks and constellations and sea
life and, of course, photography. [From *All My Rivers Are Gone*]

Then there's Mary Jane, Tad's wife. M.J. to her close friends. I
call her Tad's Regal Eagle—nearly as tall as he, with somewhat the
same metabolism, her eyes behind binocular lens, identifying

Tad behind the camera

birds. She knows her man better than he thinks. When Tad, Frank Wright, and I made the "We Three" trips in Glen Canyon in the fall of 1955, 1956, and 1957, where many of the photos in this book originated, M.J. didn't come along. She said, "That would make four. It's Tad's trip." I think I know why, now. Despite what I've said above, Tad is a gentleman, and because he's sensitive to his wife he is easily distracted from his work. She probably stayed home because she knew how intent he was on photographing the place.

I sure didn't. I'd often stand next to him and his light meter, ask the exposure and speed, peer into the screen of his Rollei to check composition, question the need for a tripod, and blow his concentration completely.

But, as I've said, to know him is to love him, and I owe Tad more than I'll ever be able to repay because he is the person responsible for bringing me to the river. Although we both loved Glen Canyon mightily, we had individual ways of reacting to it. What I wanted to touch, he wanted to wait for light and shadow to enhance. Tad would see the whole scene, put a frame around a section, and take a perfect photo.

I visualize him now, in the shadow of an overhang, crouched behind his tripod like a frog. Or ambling up a canyon with the fully extended tripod balanced on his shoulder. In fluted canyons (with not an inch of level ground), he'd extend two tripod legs and leave the third one very short, braced against the side wall.

Once, high on a slickrock bench, I found Tad and Frank on their knees, bottoms up, heads to the ground, intently studying something. They were trying to figure out a way to photograph smooth, watermelon-size stones balanced above the slickrock on tiny pillars five or six inches high. Finally, after squirming around on their bellies and leveling their cameras, they made their photos.

Glen Canyon was a place where you didn't just see color and shadow; the light acted upon you physically. No one I know has been able to explain why it differed from light in other beautiful places. Even the Grand Canyon was nothing like it. It was almost as if some mystic force had you in its beam and moved you about into places you'd never think to go on your own. Where the light didn't *send* you, the enticing side canyons *drew* you. We'd walk, crawl, and climb through alternating air currents—warm, cool, hot, moist, dry—into deep twilight; ten steps later we'd be standing in a slash of bright sun beside a vibrant green redbud tree.

The color was intense, radiant *in* a wall, not merely *on* it. Then, as with the turn of a kaleidoscope, the wall would soften to delicate lavender and flesh tones. How? Why? I spent a lot of time trying to figure this out. Tad spent his photographing it. I decided the river was one answer; the way it curved, twisted, and rippled; reflected sky here, masses of green trees or shrubs there; and on the walls and ceilings of alcoves that hung over water were reflected the dancing sequences of sunlight that Frank called "music on the walls." Not to mention moonlight, which turned the river corridor and side canyons into magical places we'd never seen before—no matter that we'd already been there in daylight.

What did moonlight do? It cast a blue scrim over everything, softening the mighty shapes. On our slides, it streaked the sky with star-tracks, washing away detail in some places, theatrically spotlighting others. Pools wore a tinseled rim and all the writing on the river was gone, water smoothed to a solid sheet of molten silver.

I recall one especially lush evening camp at Tad's favorite spot, the bar above Hidden Passage. Just after the sun dropped behind the rim, the sky took on a lemon yellow glow. This usually meant inclement weather on the morrow; meanwhile, what it was doing to the canyon walls, the river's surface, and the lush growth across the river on Music Temple Bar sent E.T. into rapture. He must have shot an entire roll before the light became too reluctant, even for his tripod.

THE FOLLOWING CONVERSATION appeared in *All My Rivers Are Gone*.

Like me, Tad says *this* is the spot. Glen Canyon, this river, has it all.

"Why, Tad-O? What makes it so special?"

He stretches his arms up high, palms up, and almost whispers, "The light, sweetie, look at the *light*. It drives me crazy!"

"That all?"

"No, of course not."

"What then?"

"Oh, well, mmm … you know. The canyons, each one full of surprises, the colors, the clarity. Never seen such a variety of texture and form. The shapes are incredible! And the river, so peaceful and quiet; not like the Grand."

"Why does this place make you *feel* different?"

He stops and looks upriver for a long time, then shaking his head, says, "I don't know, Pal. I really can't tell you why. Maybe it's the silence, the way it pulls you in, the secrets it holds, the ruins. Maybe because it's so … clean, hardly touched. I get a new perspective on photographing things here."

"Everything here seems to be lit from within, huh Professor?"

"That's a great way to put it, sweetie."

"Heh-heh. I got it from you, Tadito."

≈•◦•≈

IT DIDN'T TAKE ME LONG to find there were two things Tad really hated: cold water and Moki steps up a vertical wall. One time in Cathedral Canyon, one of those narrow, deep, ripple-walled canyons where we had to swim through winding trenches of chilling water, he stopped before the third one, tested the surface with his toes, shivered, and moaned, "I simply cannot dip my tool in that cold pool!" But curiosity would nearly always drive him on.

Moki steps were chipped into the cliffs eons ago by the Ancient Ones so they could cross the narrow side canyons and get down to the river. Some could leave you with a certainty that the Anasazi walked on air. Those leading above Music Temple were five hundred feet high, steep, partly eroded, and very hairy. Yet I've seen E.T., with his long legs, go up and down some steps with two or three cameras hanging off him.

Not these!

He stood at the bottom, twiddled his cowlick, looked up, squeezed his eyes shut, and whispered, "Ohhhh, no."

But we got up them all right, and spent the best part of a day above the Temple. We found a true Shangri-la up there with ruins, potholes, trees, and running water.

Back at the top of the Moki steps, the first descent was real easy, not vertical at all, only about thirty feet before the big drop. Tad stopped, sat down, and moaned again.

"You'll be okay, it's not as bad as it looks," Frank said in his gentle way and backed over the ledge.

Tad went next, holding on to my leg, then my ankle, as he negotiated the first few steps. About halfway down he made the mistake of looking over his shoulder instead of between his legs, and froze. He began shaking. Very quietly and gently, Frank talked him down, telling him where to feel for the next step without looking.

When I jumped down beside them above the last easy descent, Tad turned to me in a fury. "Dammit, *you* make me go up these awful places where I don't want to go and scare the shit out of my-self. It's no fun! Why'n hell can't you be satisfied staying on the ground doing your exploring?"

I backed up and blinked. "How's that, again, Professor?"

"I nearly killed myself on those deadly steps just now, all because of you. Bullshit! I don't like it!"

My Irish, along with my Scorpio tail, went up. "You're fulla crap! Why don't you just sit down here on your skinny ass if you don't like it. I don't remember forcing you."

"Like hell. *You* plan this and *you* plan that, and the next thing I know we're hanging on nothing over a five-hundred-foot drop!"

That set me off and running. "You wishy-washy bastard! Who comes to me at the end of every trip and thanks me for his 'little moments of exquisite endurance?'—to quote your own words—and says, 'I'd never have seen this or that if it hadn't been for you?'" I stormed off down the last set of steps.

The next thing I knew, Tad caught up with me, put his arm around my shoulder, and said, "I'm sorry sweetie. I really was just *scared to death*. I didn't mean to take it out on you."

Forgiving was easy, especially on the river.

WE TOOK ANOTHER PHOTOGRAPHER FRIEND of mine to The Glen one year—a professional to the core—and for me it was a real eye-opener to discover how differently each man approached his art.

When we came to one of the most intriguing side canyons of the whole trip, my friend dropped his Hasselblad in the sand. He stopped cold, picked up the camera, and headed back to the boat, saying, "I don't even want to see it if I can't photograph it."

I'll never forget that. He was so unlike Tad, who neither had to nor wanted to photograph everything that enthralled him. He could enjoy the splendid, mysterious aura of the canyon, keeping it in his *mind's* eye, and let the camera go.

In the evening, after dinner, E.T. would act as our dispose-all, eating whatever was lying about. Yet he never gained a pound and never forgot to save a few last bites for the furry fellows.

"Come here, little mousie, eat this, it's good for you." He would wait until his offering was gone or he'd found something in our larder more to their liking.

After sunset, in full moon, or under starlight so intense we could read by it, we'd build up the campfire and I'd bring out my guitar and sing for them, for myself, and to the canyon. Tad, his lanky form propped against his bedroll, firelight dancing on his face, always smoked his pipe. (To this day I will smell that sweet mixture when sitting by other campfires.) On the Mexican songs, he'd join in when he knew the words, and always supply the *carcajadas*. His *Aye-yie-yie! Oooie-ooie-ooie!* would ring through The Glen until the pipe went out, his eyes closed, and his snores rose to replace them.

When we woke him so he could go to bed, he'd always apologize, "Oh-h … umm … sweetie, I'm so sorry," no matter how often I told him I didn't mind singing him to sleep.

I see Tad's photographs more often now that there is renewed interest in and increasing resentment over what was lost when Glen Canyon went under hundreds of feet of dead water behind the dam, killing everything there. Everything but our memories and this legendary collection. These photographs will leave a lasting impression because Tad didn't just *see* the canyon, he felt it deeply and brought it back with him, for us.

Reentry from the Wild Out Yonder

YOU WILL NEVER BE HOMESICK until you have a home.

You will not suffer "reentry syndrome" until you've been out of this world. Until you have touched, seen, become a part of the Other World, heard its call, and felt the magnetic pull to go back *out* of this world and return to Nature's.

Reentry takes many forms, its pulse not the same in each individual, but the greatest manifestation of this syndrome won't be denied. Frustration. The frustration of not being able to explain the Other World to someone who hasn't been there. Where one person will feel ostracized by this disconnection, another will feel aloof and pleased. Some will be angry, some joyous, others thwarted and disgusted with the world they live and work in. Some even feel guilty for having experienced what the others have not and cannot share.

Among this disparate group there is a gaggle of souls whose Other World is the Colorado Plateau, its rivers, sibling canyons, and tributaries; souls who have experienced the pain of reentry over and over again. Both blessed and cursed by this nagging, they nonetheless hold tight to the experience, because no one can take from them the fact that they *have* been there. A thing to covet.

My years in Glen Canyon, before its damming, initiated me into this ambivalent fraternity, and left such a mark on me that I can see, smell, and feel it as if I'd left it only yesterday. Something zooms in to remind me of the place and *zap!* I'm there in an instant. At times that makes me feel like the most fortunate human being on this earth; at other times, the most devastated.

We riverphiles are plagued as soon as we leave the sounds of a living river behind. Since I can't heed the call but two, maybe three, times a year, the stimulus will begin a few days *before* takeout, along with a nagging apprehension: How long before I'll be here again? Soon? Next year? Never? Because of that, I will look more intently at each detail; inhale deeply and store memory of the smells, tracks in sand and mud, temperature of the water in a certain pothole, a seep, a bird nest I saw passing beneath an overhanging limb, a steep set of Moki steps up slickrock; then put it all on save for coping with the mess we call civilization, that world where I do whatever I have to do in order to return to this one. Those last days I won't even recall the magical places I've so recently been—the ruins, waterfalls, cathedrals, fluted canyons, caves, and cataracts—because those places are still part of me and I have a few more hours of discovery to heap on top of them.

Knowing I must get back to work, I will try to think about where I have to be and when. Just simple stuff. Not what I actually have to do, prepare, wait for, or step over. Yet those thoughts will skip from my brain swifter than a bat scooping water from the river. I have trouble remembering where I left my car. Where's my wallet? Am I supposed to meet someone? Are there extra clothes in my trunk? Nothing finds a conclusion. I will even pass off, as if it weren't a fact, that within hours I won't be *here*—here on this river. I just go on living in this Other World as if it's the only world I've ever known.

How do I do that?

I step out of linear time and thinking, away from learned experiences—into dreamtime. For days—weeks if I'm on a long trip—I empty my brain and wash the decks of my mind to live within the moment, the hour, the present. In *this* place. Untutored, my imagination and intuition rise to embrace these exquisite surroundings. I don't calculate or plan, just take it all in, alerting all my senses to respond to Nature and her stimuli; to accept it, become a part of it, and move blissfully along with the flow of the river. I become highly light-sensitive and adjust to shapes and motion rather than ways and means.

It is obvious that we cannot achieve this state in a flash, not until we get our footing, so to speak, in this Other Place. Our hangover from social living prevents it. If we're lucky, given a day or a few hours, we will begin to merge with the terrain and the wildlife already in place, and will not fall from a ledge any more than a coyote from a cliff or a bird from its perch, because the primitive in our nature, what little is left, will lead us. But if we do not go to the Other World prepared to enter as in a dream, without learned information, we will not know it. Worse, it will not speak to us.

More people than you would guess have never reentered — have ended it right there by choice, like Buzz Holmstrom, the first solo boatman down the Green and Colorado Rivers from Wyoming through the Grand Canyon to Reservoir Mead. He couldn't cope with life in cities, even his hometown. Instead he built his houses (boats) and took them to the rivers (his real home). Some of us live half in, half out of that Other World, floating like salsify plumes, drifting, swirling in the air of fakery that surrounds us.

Step lightly.

When your friends have just come off the river or a wilderness hike, give them space. Try not to ask serious questions or expect them to concentrate on a problem. They're still "out there," not at all ready for this brain-battering rivet machine we live in and must deal with. Quite likely they are wishing they were not here with you at all. They are still on a wilderness high that can easily last for days, especially if they want to sustain it.

One way is through songs, if they know some, or have made a few of their own. A song can act like a broken record that keeps running through your head for days. There were times when dreams would let me hold on to the immediacy of my wilderness trip. I found a method to direct, or at least influence, my dreams through concentration, or with photographs; through talking or writing to someone who had been there; and by holding to a mental picture of the place. It didn't always work, yet there were a surprising number of ways to keep that "presence" from fading — and to my great delight, the hint of wilderness would now and then *find me* when least expected.

Along about sunset, I'd sometimes stop wherever and whatever I was doing, waiting for something. What? Then, one late afternoon, standing on a busy hillside street in Hollywood, it connected. I was waiting for the wind to change from upcanyon to down — felt it there in the passing traffic, remembering its brush against my skin. At night if there was static on the radio, I'd hear our campfire crackling, often wake up with my arm asleep from hanging over the bed feeling for the river, the sand, the stream, the sandstone. In dreams I would smell the river's silty, earthy essence and breathe it in deeply. After rowing my own boats, weeks or months later, at odd times and in obscure places, my palms would itch, pulling me back to the river.

We're not crazy, those of us who have these flash dances with wilderness. We've been given the gift of finding a way back to our private zone in the *natural* world, and mostly we don't give a damn if anyone understands our behavior or not. Take note of people who say they have "been there" but have not. They will talk about it long and loudly. Those who have, don't.

I had no reentry problems after my first fast and furious trip in the Grand: four of us in a twenty-one-foot Chris-Craft diesel powerboat, leaving Lee's Ferry June 16, 1953, arriving Pierce's Ferry six days later. I had hardly been gone. Everything went by so fast I didn't have time to focus on anything but staying alive while running every rapid on a river moving at 66,000 cubic feet per second. Back at work, it was nonstop yapping to anyone who would listen—and some who wouldn't—dramatizing the hairiest parts of the journey, the biggest rapids, the narrowest canyons, the wild adrenaline rushes.

But I got no *spirit* of that magnificent place, other than it was un-like any other, bigger than all hell, full of wild water and the softest sand I'd ever felt on lo-n-n-n-n-g, wide, driftwood-piled beaches. (I can be grateful that I wasn't crammed into a motorized pontoon with fifty other dudes who get far less of the canyon's essence now on a five-day *half*-run. Eat your heart out!) But I hadn't really "been there" then, any more than they have now.

My first symptoms broke chrysalis the next year after one float trip on the San Juan and two more in Glen Canyon, each marked by a bewildering loathing to return to work in the *place* where I worked; each successive reentry stronger and longer. Because in The Glen's sensuous, gentle beauty and silence I had time—a soft ticking of the oars—to take a good look at where I was, discover its hidden secrets, and allow the canyon's primitive spirit to spark a memory in my own genes. Only then did I fully understand what I'd been handed. The rarest of privileges. An everlasting gift. A treasure that was going to add limitless depth and meaning to my life. Shape it. Change it.

When we become involved in an intimate relationship with a place, we are asking for the same kind of turmoil, frustration, rapture, devotion, and loss we experience when we fall in love with a person. Actually, if we don't have such a relationship, love, or deep and abiding friendship with the place, we haven't "been there." Been *through* there, you could say—looked at it, but didn't really *see* it. If someone asked you a question about its intimate nature, about the colors, smells, sounds, and feel of the place, would you be able to answer? Did you want to embrace it, know all about it, learn its moods, enjoy touching its parts, feel an emotional contact with the plants-water-earth-sand-rock? Did you feel welcome there, relaxed, at peace? If so, you have "been there" and you will want to return.

When I returned to Grand Canyon in the summer of 1955 for an oar-driven float in the "Cat boats" (the sadirons Norm Nevills designed for two passengers and a boatman, not two "snouts" filled with air), I was familiar with the heart-stopping significance of "being there" as opposed to "been-there-done-that." Adrenaline flowed, but it was no roller coaster ride; it was a lesson in how the earth was put together, how insignificant we are in the overall plan, how little we know and will ever know, and how the best we can do for ourselves, in our little time, is to try to discover who we are, then make the best of it.

❧

CHARLES EGGERT, who made a documentary film in Grand Canyon back in the fifties, *A Canyon Voyage*, explains his reentry phenomenon this way:

> *Maybe it's because the experience is so psychologically personal and ephemeral that it can't really be translated into words.* [After thirty-one days on the river in 1955] *I felt the most profound effect of reentry was in relating to other people once I got back atop*

the earth's crust again. I felt I had been to a place which defied
understanding or describing … that somehow in my soul I held
something which was totally personal and private. … And it is this
awareness of absence in others which is perhaps the most profound
of the "reentry" experience.

BRAD DIMOCK, coauthor of *The Doing of the Thing*, was a Grand
Canyon boatman for many years. He says:

For many of us, reentry is the hardest and most disturbing part of the
river experience. Having just recently discovered (or rediscovered)
an entirely different world, it is wrenchingly difficult to leave it, to
return to the so-called real world. Which, one wonders, is the real
world after all? The more one comes to know and love the River
and the solace it brings to the soul, the more miserable reentry can
be. Those of us who spend our lives on the River experience the
symptoms on an even greater scale. The end-of-the season blues can
be devastating, and worst of all is the time when a boatman must
leave the river entirely for family, health, or fortune. Many of us
never fully reenter, but live out our lives trapped in some limbo, torn
between the pain of parting from the River, and the joy and vision it
has given us to carry through life.

SERENA SUPPLEE, dear friend, artist, and boatwoman, paints the
river and almost literally has the river with her when she leaves.
What's more, she lives near the river and rows its silky, ruffled, bur-
bling, roiling surface at least once a week and often for many weeks
at a time, so to her, reentry should be like cloud dancing—no problem. She often won't finish a painting while she's in the canyon, but
brings it home to work on, which in essence puts her back on the
river. This is true so long as she's painting, but when she stops to
attend to the myriad chores of this world, life becomes oil on water
that can't be homogenized. She grows frustrated and angry over the
way nothing fits into a logical or sincere rhythm and flow, the way
Nature and the river arrange things. She doesn't want to think about
how rough it would be if she didn't have the river to return to.

Other World: Serena sits on The Ledges after dinner, as she has so many wondrous nights, under the glow of an almost full moon. The water is high, rushing and surging under the stratified tables along the water's edge. The wind is warm, the rocks clean, the river restless. An upstream eddy and a downstream current argue in a whirlpool until they disappear beneath the surface. She looks up. Within the orbit of the moon's glow no stars shine, but above the rim they swim in a sea of rich indigo. Strips of angel-hair clouds ride west to east on a high wind over the monoliths. Looking down, almost in a trance, she watches a thin strand of molten silver backlight the cliff, then slide eerily down its edge to burst open upon the river's swirls.

Paints it.

I buy it. Just looking at it calms my spirit.

***

ADAM STERN, a member of the Glen Canyon Institute and a budding writer, noted a particularly difficult reentry following a second meeting with the Green River:

> *The first visit was breathtaking, the return visit was ... breathgiving. But by the time I approached the airport, I felt like my spirit was being squeezed into a snug piece of Tupperware after it had just spent a week expanding in the sun. Sad, because I felt like I was giving up the week's gains.*
>
> *In retrospect, however, I think the long-term benefits justify the pain of reentry. That's why we return to sacred places. The trials and scares we encounter in the wild, as well as the awe, are Good. The experience of living in the real world (Nature's), as opposed to the human construct, grants the ability to separate real problems in your life from imagined ones. This provides perspective to get on with the task of living, if you're brave enough, or to humbly accept your failings if you're not.*
>
> *Be it a sweaty hike up Pyramid Peak in the Adirondacks, a sun-baked scramble up Green River canyon walls, or a mystical float through Glen Canyon, reentry demands a physical return to rank and utter bullshit (comforts of home excepted) but with a spirit strengthened, wisened by the experience, more equipped for living ... maybe.*

What we all mean to say here is, the Other World can show you
ways of doing things compatible with your nature, talents, and peace
of mind, like the river and Glen Canyon did for me. I only wish I
could return the favor, set those rivers free of aneurysms, and let the
lifeblood of our planet flow again!

Humbly I submit a navigational warning about the tricky waters
of reentry:

If you dearly love someone, take them with you. You could enter
Nature's world as a larva and return to this one a ghost moth or a
butterfly—unrecognizable to your mate—or your mate to you.

With what remains of your primitive genes, you could morph
down there, combine with similar forms (read boatman-guide), and
elect to reenter only on specific, altered, mostly unacceptable terms.
That it was The River, the Untamed, Nature's Other World that cap-
tured your imagination and touched your primitive wellsprings
hasn't occurred to you yet.

Navigate.

Journal Note: July 14, 1956, Phantom Ranch

*... SUN WAS GONE when we rowed beneath the suspension bridge.
The eight (passengers) who take it from here are still up on the rim,
coming down tomorrow morning as we go up. Boy, aren't we a
bedraggled-looking crew? I tell you this old canyon makes you live
hard. Too bad everyone can't have the feel of the elements firsthand.
Humans under glass: what a sad thing. In the east they don't even
know what you're talking about, the way of life is so different. Out
in the wide open it's a little better, they spread out, build rooms that
look like living outside—but even then, under glass. So it rains on
you. You get wet at 100 degrees or over, what's that? And there's a
little sand in your bed. Oh, I can think of a lotta people who should
never go without sand in their beds. I can't even lavish sorrow on
those made-up people, because they don't care. They don't know.
And the sun: strong, all day, weathers you up a bit. Devoid of
powder and paint, the face takes on a little character, not just from
the sun but from relaxing into the real you.*

But I'm so glad Gina came with us—such a grand person to have on the trip. She's one of us and understands why we feel as we do about our canyon. I sang for quite awhile tonight, out on the lawn—turned in and thought about civilization tomorrow. Oh, Lord, if only we could be ourselves in that world. But they'd take it all and leave you nothing if you were. So on go the protective covers.

Journal Note: July 15, 1956, Bright Angel Lodge, Rim

WHEN I SAID GOOD-BYE, *I didn't feel very good inside. There they were, those four little white birds* [the Cat boats] *all nosed together on the sand below the bridge. As we ascended, they got smaller and smaller, and I got sadder and sadder, while the river kept calling, calling. I got on the right side of the Packer and had the first mule behind him. This is a verrry smart move. The farther back, the more dust, pardnuh! And for a while I rode his mule, so I had a nice comfortable journey up.*

That evening we dressed for dinner and went to the bar. I didn't want a drink. Russ (one of the passengers) seemed to fall right back into the slipshod phony world with no trouble at all. Gina and I had more to shake off than he did, I reckon—couldn't get with it—didn't want to dance, drink, listen to jukeboxes, do nothing but sit there on the rim and try to keep what was left of the canyon stillness imprinted a little longer. But he was jumpin' and bumpin' and shovin' and suggestin', while I was trying to forget where I was, trying to be down there in the canyon with the rest of them. I was almost rude. I finally gave up and said I was tired. I was—of all the yakkity-yak. And sorry for being so bored, because Russ and Paul are nice fellows, just not able to soak up stillness or know where they've been.

So when the two deer stood in the flood of headlights, frozen in silhouette and fuzzy, I gasped at their beauty and longed for their kind of freedom.

Then the lights went out.

Reentry

The Lesson

THE LITTLE PLANE TILTED SLIGHTLY and the mountaintop reached my nose, glued to the Plexiglas. Straight and level again, the window buzzed against the airflow like a bee checking out my ear, going away, then returning for another look. I placed my forehead against it and looked down.

With our friend Barnstorming Bill, Fletcher and I were flying from Sedona, Arizona, to southeastern Utah in a little Cessna, on the way to a river trip down Glen Canyon. Sunset found us over Monument Valley, looking down on Comb Ridge, earth's backbone, the spine humped up and twisting for many miles across the carmine sands, like a legendary dragon with armored plates aflame. *Tanques*—turquoise water jewels that never were before and might be a long time coming again—reflected a lucid western sky, and the blush of green that lay between the stony ridges was sweet and pristine. For once in a turtle's age, the Navajos would be blessed with a bonanza!

A sight to long remember. After three days of rain, not often seen on our deserts, the human mind is slow to comprehend the rapid transformation from blood rusts to virgin green.

It's a miracle, pure and simple. Where multitudes live in arid cities, none of this is visible; water comes from a pipe, a canal, a reservoir. It's shocking to realize how few people know what an aquifer is, much less *if* or *where* one might be. They haven't the faintest notion where the "elixir of life" originates, don't think about it, and don't really care, *just so long as it's there*. To them water is forever and everywhere. Not in *this* desert! It comes teasingly, or not at all, and is damn stingy with itself. No rain falls for a year, no aquifers fill, no streams trickle. Big rivers evaporate and stink behind huge, ill-conceived dams, and where they are allowed to flow, the poor things shrink down into their sandy bottoms looking for a way home.

I turned to speak to Fletch, who was as fascinated with what lay below as I, but elected not to try expressing my thoughts over the ratcheting of the plane's engine.

We flew around Navajo Mountain and along the Colorado River to Hite, Utah, where we would start our trip two days hence; flew over canyons we'd hiked many times before, and I felt a surge of emotion that took me a few minutes to qualify. It was like seeing a famous actor onstage whom I knew intimately, not just as someone famous, but the *real* person; knew his whims and foibles, his good and bad sides, knew what others *didn't* know, and it left me with a smug sense of gratification. After awhile, such impudence appalled me.

I didn't know a minuscule of what I wanted to know, or even should have known about what was down there—even after all our exploration. As the side canyons squirmed between the great sandstone domes and my eyes searched the alcoves and pools, my love for all those hidden mysteries grew by fathoms.

I would much rather fly over a place *after* I've come to know it intimately from the ground. A bird's-eye view verifies knowledge of some places and defies what you thought you knew about others; it also reveals the bigger picture and more secrets. But if I'd seen it first from the air, I wouldn't know diddly-squat about it—no significance of the earth, the trees, the feel of air currents, the odors, the smoothness or abrasion of slickrock, or the temperature of the water in potholes and rivers. Without ground knowledge, Fletch and I would be in another dimension, seeing only the configuration of synclines and anticlines, hollows and valleys, mountains and crevasses. How deep, how steep, how rough or smooth the walking miles, we couldn't know. Intimacy of the place would be denied us. Without the real wings of a bird, we were still part of the mechanized world up there, thinking ahead through the time machine of minutes, hours, days, and weeks. The automobile, the bicycle, the horse would put us closer, but nothing like our eyes, hands, and feet in contact with Mother Earth in her remote, almost unreachable pockets.

It was down there in the wild, uncluttered by humans, that I lived in the urgent present; every day a gift, each hour, all the minutes, down to the seconds. It was there, and only there, that the old saw "Patience is a virtue" had any meaning for me. Where I could sit through silence and watch a lizard communicate his signals, a beaver build his dam, a canyon wren fly a twig to its nest, an ouzel take an underwater bug to its mate, a pollywog sprout a leg or two, an ant chomp a leaf in half, a dry streambed slowly saturate with water from beneath and sweetly begin to flow. When I listened to the hum of sandstone, felt the light change my mood with its magic wand, tasted a wind that brought me knowledge of what was coming, and read clouds that told me why, I could smile at rain that impeded my progress and a sun that boiled my sweat, welcome shade that gave me rest, and talk to a moon that set me wondering.

That was patience in its truest form.

I thought of something John Graves had written in his book *Goodbye to a River*: that impatience is a city kind of emotion we probably need if we're going to hold our own in this society, but it goes poorly on a river. I agree that it not only goes poorly, but down there impatience can kill you!

We were following one of the larger drainages into the Colorado back up to its source in the high country when I elbowed Fletch and pointed. "Hey, that's the section of Cedar Canyon that Kevin and I haven't hiked yet. Doesn't look very long, does it?"

He answered over the noise, "We could check it out on the way to the river tomorrow. Maybe you and Kev could hike part of it if we start early enough. It doesn't look long, just narrow and deep."

"Narrow, all right. Looks like a hair in the butter from up here."

When we landed at the little mesa town that evening, we were met by the other two members of our river party, Kevin and Jason. It was decided to check out the "hair in the butter" for a possible half-day hike. We all knew the country. Jason was a professional river runner and guide; Fletcher, a photographer who'd done it from the sky, down, to the pollywogs, up. Those two would ferry supplies to the boats at Hite while Kevin and I hiked the narrows, then come back for us in the late afternoon at a designated side canyon about five miles from where we would enter, easy enough for the river takeoff next morning.

"But what if you don't get out in time for takeoff?" asked Fletch.

"Oh-hh," said Kevin, "we'll be out in time."

❧❧❧

KEVIN RIME WAS THE BIG SURPRISE you pulled off a back shelf in the toy shop, wound up, and found it could go anywhere: in and out, up and down, over, under, around, and between. He was built lean, compact, and not real tall—what you might call wiry—with muscles that didn't bulge beneath his smooth, tanned skin. His brown-eyed gaze was direct and inquisitive, yet the way he looked at you from beneath his brows with head tilted slightly down offered an appealing air of shyness. This was accentuated by a straight-line mouth tucked into a constant half smile, all framed by ears that fanned out to embrace the wind.

Born and reared in southeastern Utah's Mormon community, he had retained his own idea of what was bullshit and what was right, what the church decreed and what he knew was heretical to the land he loved. Long before most folks had a clue about the exotic backcountry that surrounded the small Mormon towns, before there were such things as national parks and recreation areas, Kevin had hiked more than a hundred canyons and blazed miles of jeep trails.

A man of few and uncomplicated words, he could slice the tail off a redundant discussion with one short, amusing phrase while looking straight at you with eyes that defied a negative response. Though he used words sparingly, Kevin could tell stories far into the night, tales that riveted you to the rock, his slow drawl and innate sense of the dramatic holding you suspended until he cut you loose. He had once talked me down off a near-vertical slickrock wall, his soft, confident voice telling me I wasn't in any danger, that I had all the time in the universe and all the smarts to move from left to right and down the crossbedding, one step at a time. "Don' look down here at me—makes ya dizzy. Look what's under yer feet, lookit them ridges."

Kevin had been my boatman down the San Juan and through Glen Canyon several times. Our first trip together was an early spring commercial run in very high water, where we'd made the mistake of drinking a river full of sheep shit that had percolated down from pastures of the Navajo Nation. That night I had a temperature of 102 degrees, so I put my bedroll with its head a few inches from a side stream of cool fresh water, placed my hands and wrists in it, and went to sleep. Next morning all that remained was a queasy stomach. Kevin barfed and shit half the night, feeling like both products as he staggered to the breakfast fire with a face the color of a green tree frog. I gave him three aspirin and rowed the boat for him until he could sit upright.

We were buddies.

Kev had a wife. Forever. Back then I had a husband, or a lover, depending on what year. I would tease Kev about his background, telling him he should have lived back in the days of orthodox polygamy, when he could fuck fifteen women with no guilt whatsoever—one at a time or all at once—since they'd be his wives.

When hiking together, alone, or with close friends, neither of us had a "thing" about clothes. If it was cold, we used them; if it was hot, we didn't. Mighty different from the other boatmen I knew, who wore not only long-sleeved shirts most of the time but long underwear as well. My one remark back in our beginnings kept things in perfect order: "Lay a hand on me and I'll nut you, Kev."

From then on, it was share the potholes; share the canyons; share the river and the magic; share the campfire, stories, beer, and booze; but most of all, share the fact that we are rare and goddam good friends. Forever.

※◈※

THE NEXT DAY, the first of September, was a day to die for. The country was washed clean. Pine needles glistened in the high country. The air was cool, brittle, and cleaner than wind, leaving just the scent of wildflowers in the low gullies where they grew profusely along the road. Down lower in juniper country, the air warmed, then turned hot against our faces when we leaned out the van's windows. Verdant groundlings laced their way across orange sand, and great totems of Wingate sandstone, with a green brush-cut on top, studded a dense blue sky. My eyes roved in a continuous cycle: earth to mesa, to mountaintop, to sky and back again, soaking up beauty, simplicity, perfection. And we were the only things in it, hardly seen. Not even a roll of dust trailed our vehicle as we drove unhurriedly over the damp, red earth.

There was even water in ditches beside the road, and when we drove down to one of the four crossings of the canyon we were to hike, the stream—usually a rare string of pothole beads—was chain-linked and moving right along. The flooding a few days before had tossed brush and driftwood haphazardly along the banks several feet above the moving water.

Just past a small airstrip, built for one of the still-active uranium mines, we stopped. Last year, in fifteen days, we had hiked seventy-five miles of this canyon from its headwaters to the place of our beginning at "the hair." The purpose was to complete the upper half now, the lower narrows sometime later, and ultimately, hike it, swim it, walk it—whatever—all the way to its confluence with the Colorado River.

We ate a lunch of fat sandwiches and discussed the trek. Both Kev and I had map-run the possible swimming, walking, and crawling five-or-so miles; knew that water, driftwood, and sand came out the far end because we'd been there; and concluded it would take about three hours.

Ah, the plans of best-laid men!

※豫※

AT TEN MINUTES PAST NOON, having equipped himself with his usual canyon gear—a coiled twenty-five-foot rope draped over one shoulder, a pocket knife, and six matches in a 44.40 western rifle shell with a .35 Colt stopper that he tucked into the watchpocket of his jeans—Kev was ready to go. I had a Rollei 2x2 camera on a strap, a waterproofed roll of extra film in my cutoffs pocket, a halter top, and a bandana—for what I don't remember. It was a given to pee beside the stream—no one but the two of us all the way to the big river—and the other, well, we'd done that already. The heat up top had become oppressive, and as we climbed down a short whisker into the narrows, the shade felt good. I could hardly wait to get to the bottom and wallow in the water. I thought about taking a drink, but when I saw the color, refrained.

⁂

THE FIRST QUARTER MILE was an easy amble: stream to ledge, to sandy bottom, through pools, to short pour-overs on beautiful slick-rock, and a gradual heightening, along with what felt like a hugging, of the fluted walls of Cedar Mesa sandstone. I'd spent a couple of months each year for the last four going in and out of canyons of every character imaginable—small, short, long, tight, rugged, dark, slimy, steep, dirty, dangerous, clean, wet, dry, fluted, boxed, boggy, deep. This one was a combination of all those, except *dry*.

"And dry I'll bet it never gets," I said to Kev. "I know it doesn't run all the time, but if it wasn't running medium-strong from the rains over the warmed rocks above, these pools would really be *cold*, yeah?"

"Might have ice floatin'" was his response.

Soon there came a drop we stopped to admire more than to negotiate. We'd have to swim it by slipping off a ledge several feet downstream, but just looking at the artistry of water-sculpted stone kept us lolling above the plunge. A tangle of driftwood had been lured into the sluiceway and trapped. I pulled out pieces of nature's artwork, shaped and polished and dressed in a finery that, in their youth, they never imagined; carvings with an expression of truth and dignity no gallery has ever witnessed. I couldn't take them with me, so I separated them from the others, placing them as high as it was possible to reach, knowing it wouldn't make any difference to their ultimate resting place—either the river, a higher bench, stranded like a bridge in a crevasse overhead, or buried in mud and sand.

I saw Kev going for the pocket in his jeans.

Out came the shell canister and one match. As a member of the Grand Canyon Driftwood Burners Society, who with one match can light a driftwood pile a few feet to a block long, he had within minutes, created a scene that no photograph could justify.

Our long, narrow cave ignited! Shadowplay upon the walls made the flutings, curves, and swirls in the lamellae dance in the blaze. As we moved along the ledge that placed us below the falls yet above where we had to swim, we looked back to see our driftwood plunge in flames, the whole surface of the water reflecting the inferno. The fire took over the narrows, shooting flares into the water and intermittently exploding the rock beneath, sounding like a subterranean cannon echoing through the underworld.

Fascinated, I clicked my shutter to the end of the roll and changed film.

"Better move on before we git bombed," Kevin declared.

Together we slid into the trench and swam almost a hundred feet before touching bottom. From there on, the camera, which I'd pulled through many a crevasse, became a hazard. The only way to keep it dry was to hold it on top of my head and dog-paddle the distance. This took more breath than swimming; thereafter, proper-sized pieces of drift became camera barges pushed from behind, thus eliminating the headdress and saving energy.

From where we torched the driftwood, we were never long out of water, from ankle to neck, except for brief minutes on small sandpits or short ledges that carried us above the stream. I couldn't fathom how a canyon, so many meandered miles from source to river, could be so narrow and so deep for such a long time—never opening up, averaging no more than twenty feet wide and in some places hardly twenty inches. Other canyons of my experience had wide spaces notched into their hairpin turns. Not this one. Its obstacle course ran through every conceivable formation akin to sandstone and whatever fell from the strata above, and unfortunately for us, was running more in a north-south direction than east-west, which would have given us a bit more sunlight.

Placidly, we waded through the next winding trough, sometimes touching both sides with arms outstretched, stopping now and then to look up at good-sized logs wedged between the fluted walls many feet over our heads.

"Whoo-e-e-e! Sure are a lot of bridges in here, Kev. I wouldn't even want to be a fish in the torrent that blasts through here when she floods!"

"Probably come out already filleted at the other end."

"Just like we would, huh?" I felt a fleeting shiver run down my spine, but just as quickly passed it off. We were full of gung-ho energy, ready to take on anything that came along. The big plus was the magic of the place: it made me feel like part of a dream, like being in another dimension, winding through a psychic illusion in a world never witnessed before or even imagined; like a mystery I wanted to solve but didn't know how to.

Kevin told me how he'd checked around trying to find if anyone knew of people who'd explored the Cedar Narrows before us. Wading along, he recalled that one or two uranium miners were rumored to have come through five or six years ago and that some guy had fallen in from the top and died. But he'd found no verifiable facts. Legend also had it that some poor kid, who wasn't the sharpest knife in the drawer, had wandered off from camp and disappeared—possibly in Cedar Narrows, possibly not. Nothing for sure. He could see why it wouldn't attract Sunday strollers. From the slant of light and his built-in timetable he estimated that we'd been in the canyon over two hours and hiked ... oh, maybe a mile.

"Ah-ha! What have we here?" Ahead of Kevin, I stopped.

I looked down at a twelve-foot waterfall, below which extended a throughway averaging two feet across that wiggled fifty feet or so before bending out of sight.

"Another swimmer" was Kev's flat observation.

"Maybe not," said the optimist, "Here, hold my camera. I'll take a look at what's around the bend." I inched down beside the fall, slid into the water, waded a ways, then swam 'til I was out of his sight. He must have heard excessive splashing over the sound of the waterfall and, after some grunts and snorts, my explosive "Holy shit!" before I came swimming back upstream five minutes later.

"Kev, that's the damnedest thing I've ever seen in my life! Around the bend, there's a cap of red, frothy foam rising four feet off the water around this first bend to the next one. I tried to find a way through—crawled around, slid down in the crevasse, trying to make a hole in the foam. But I got scared when it began to close in behind me. It wanted to go up my nose."

"Foam?"

"Yeah. There's a narrow ledge above the trough we can get onto, but I couldn't tell how far it goes, b'cause that foam is wall to wall."

Beside the waterfall I spotted a good-sized log and suggested we take it for a raft. It would serve to float the camera, his rope, and even us if we needed it. Luckily, we did not have to swim the whole way; we could stand part of the time, but when we came to the foam, Kevin whistled and said, "Wonder what's holdin' it back?" He then tried the same maneuver I had used, with the same result, and came paddling back.

Climbing up on the narrow ledge, we pondered the situation.

"Kev, let's use the rope. You hang on to it here, I'll take one end and swim down. If I holler or jerk on it, you pull me back. Quick!"

I played it out about halfway and was successful this time, disintegrating the spume by splashing it continuously ahead of me and making a kind of tunnel. I jerked on the rope and he pulled me back. The next move was to try the log. For balance, Kev took it under his right arm, I, my left; we put the rope and camera on top, held on to them, and managed to swim, wade, float, and break foam as we went. Again, it closed behind.

"Hey, this must be what it's like inside a sloe gin fizz."

"Ain't never been in one," he wheezed. "I ain't even thirsty."

"Me neither."

Because I'd taken note before we entered that foamy world, I knew that above us the fluted, magnificently colored walls rose and wove into patterns that artists of every kind have tried to capture for eons. But our eyes no longer searched out this beauty. Ours were magnetized to the water we floated, waded, and swam, appreciation lost in the challenge of finding a way through. Not many eyes would see this vault of water and stone, and though we had no thought of it then, several explorers would die here in years to come.

By the time we reached the obstacle holding back the foam, we could not determine how far we'd come, or how long it had taken us.

Raising my arm to splash the bubbles away, my hand hit something ahead of me. I released the log to stand on a ledge just underwater. With head poking above the foam, I brushed away the bubbles and felt around. Still holding the log, Kev came up to squat beside me.

A huge slice of rock had fallen from the wall to our right and lay flat as a slab of cheese across the channel with, we hoped, some clearance above the flow. How big was it? How far downstream did it go? What else lay beneath? I entered the trough again, gripped the bottom of the slab, and let myself float downstream full length. I could not feel the end of the rock with my tennies, but I could see a space of about twelve inches between the rock and the water.

I went back to the ledge, head spinning, thinking. The one thing I wasn't about to do was swim underwater for an undetermined distance, even if we had to go back the way we came. Like how? Anyway, the moment of decision was at hand: once through there, we knew we could not return against the current and the foam, *no matter what lay ahead.*

Readers may wonder why *I'm* the one pushing ahead on this explorer expedition, letting Kev, the real "earth mole," kinda follow in my wake. Kev is like that about his friends and the folks who love his country; he wants them to find out for themselves. It was long after this excursion that he told me what he was thinking that day. I must say his observations were right on. He told me I was like a steam engine, full of energy, and I was going to burn out if he didn't try to slow me down. He thought, after seeing the foam, that there was lots worse coming than what we'd already been through. He tried to ease me off by saying, "Let's do the rope trick again. You hold it this time, and I'll go."

"But what if the rock slants down to the water level?"

"Then pull me back if I yank on it."

I didn't think I could hold his weight, standing on the ledge, let alone pull him back up without falling off—it was too slick—so I persuaded him to let me try again.

He mumbled something like "So much for trying," as I took the rope and slid into the water, sloshing foam beneath the slab as I went. Immediately it closed in behind me and got darker. Ten feet … fifteen feet … water to my chin … head scraping the rock … near panic … I saw light through the foam and suddenly broke into a streak of sunlight, out in the open.

Wheezing, I crawled from the trough onto a slickrock mound, hugging it like a long-lost friend, my heart thumping like a seismic machine. Jesus, I made it! After a minute I rolled over, adrenaline still pumping, and called to Kevin to bring my camera, the log, and rope and come on through. "It's about fifteen feet—enough head-room all the way—and it's sunny over here!" Although my teeth were chattering.

In a few minutes, body and barge emerged from beneath the slab. He let the log go and crawled into the meager sliver of sunlight that was at that very moment creeping up the wall away from us.

"S-s-sunny, huh? Don't I wish. Still heading north. Won't get no more 'til the canyon turns, whenever that is." He gave a little shud-der and stood, jumped up and down, rubbed his arms and chest to get circulation going.

"What time you think it is, Kev?"

"After 4, I guess. Best move along."

I, too, stomped around and rubbed arms and legs, for the first time feeling the coldness in my body as we looked downstream at the next challenge—no, the next obstruction, rebuff, deterrent. Those long, sinuous trenches of indescribable shape and beauty had ceased to be a mere challenge. Now they were trouble. Figuring out a path through and around them had changed from excitement and glee to a campaign of wits and endurance underlain by an insidious tingle of fear. Fear of not finding, or fumbling, a way through before darkness overtook us; fear that led to fleeting thoughts of rescue and its improbability; and fear (mixed with embarrassment) at our lack of judgment about such a canyon. Strangely enough, fear of the one thing that could kill us didn't enter our minds: that our bodies might not be able to withstand the cold.

For several turns the bottom flattened out. The stream, running over sand and gravel, meandered from side to side, just ankle-deep. Occasional chunks of driftwood studded the floor. No one led. We moved ahead at a slightly faster pace than before, taking in height and narrowness, constantly searching the vaulted walls for niches leading to benches that could be walked or crawled along without pinching out before the next higher level could be reached.

There were none.

A drop in the upper rim let in more light and occasionally a streak of sunshine where we huddled in the warmth, soaking its fuel into our bodies. At one such place I removed my shoes to dump the gravel, rinse them out, and replace them; it was also the first time I voiced some trepidation.

"These half-assed cutoffs are freezing my buns, Kev. I'm taking them off—the titty hammock too."

"Me too. Legs feel like icicles. Don't reckon we'll run into many photographers."

"If we do, I hope they've got a boat—a real skinny one."

When the canyon actually *did* turn in a westerly direction, the sun had left the floor to paint what we could see of the upper rims a brilliant yellow-orange, and ... oh shit!—to light the surface of a long, serpentine incision that ran wall to wall with bloody water.

We just stood there staring at it, saying nothing, wondering what the hell now? Kevin turned back upstream.

"Where you going?"

"Got'n idea. Back in a minute," he said, hustling around the bend. He returned, dragging a log about six feet long and fairly straight. "I think we can bridge this across the water. Crawl across, walk, bridge again, crawl. Won't have to get so wet."

"Brilliant!" I shouted. "But shouldn't we test it first, see if it's only knee-deep?

"'Tisn't."

"How do you know?"

"Too wide," he stated, with that look that defied a negative response.

"Okay, buddy, let's give it a whirl."

And it did work—a little over half the way. On the third attempted bridge, my camera slid off my shoulder and hit the water with a splash. I still had hold of the strap and yanked it back instantly, but the leather case was not waterproof and water seeped in to cloud the lenses and wet the roll of film.

"Dammit! There go all my pictures of this wild place. Nobody'll ever believe we've been in here now."

"We won't neither, we don't get a move on."

Using the log, we dog-paddled out and stood shivering on the next gravel bar, rubbing each other's backs with our wadded-up clothes and stomping around, hoping to get circulation on the bubble once again. It was a slightly wider place than before. We both looked up, down, and around, hoping for some hint of a way out—on the left side, mostly. That's where the side canyon entered, where the road was, and likewise Jason and Fletcher.

Nothing. Nothing but woven stone that seemed to form a large prairieland tepee, its smoke hole out of sight, dark-skinned sides rippling as we walked along. The bridging maneuver had taken up possibly another hour of time—time spent half out of the water, to be sure, but time needed to get downstream to whatever the next obstacle might be.

I reckoned the Old Lady was being cruel now, her jaws an icy vice out there in the middle of a roiling red desert, unnatural, nasty, uncaring, *mean*. I stumbled and fell, bashing my camera against the stone, skinning an elbow and a knee; got up, hardly noticing, and fell again a few minutes later, this time on dry sand, again hardly noticing. Kevin's back, weaving and bobbing a few feet ahead of me, was blue, *really* blue. His arms hugged his chest; jeans were tied around his waist and knotted in front. To put them on would have made him twice as cold and twice as blue; the legs dangled cold and clammy beside his gonads, which about an hour ago had become his tonsils. My cutoffs and halter were strung up my arm and snuggled to my breasts for a warmth that didn't exist. "My canyons, my canyons," I whimpered, "why are you doing this to us?"

Within minutes our next obstruction appeared. Nothing like it before. Nothing similar afterward.

Seen from a hundred feet, it looked like the woven cloth that often covers the entrance to a large prairieland tepee, but *this* cover rose to where the fluted walls almost kissed overhead. Coming closer, we found it to be a stack of driftwood jammed into a narrow turn of the canyon and extending the entire width of the floor to twelve or fourteen feet overhead, where the walls pinched in. There was no way through or around it. We would have to crawl up and over the top, down the other side. How all that drift got this far through some of the narrow slits we'd negotiated, I couldn't imagine. Oh yes. The high-water mark of the flood could be seen sometimes fifty feet overhead. That's how.

Kev uncoiled the rope and tossed it over the top. To what avail, I wondered? It didn't hook on to anything, and when he pulled on it the whole thing ended up at his feet with a few pieces of drift. He re-coiled it, put it back over his shoulder, and began climbing up the center of the woodpile, testing a step here and there. Twice he slipped, bringing wood down with him, before he reached the top where he plunked down on a straight, milled board that instantly teeter-tottered and skied him swiftly down the other side.

For once I stood there numb and dumb, watching it all with my mouth shut.

Apparently he landed hard. "Yee-oww!" he yelled. Then only some shuffling and mumbling. Was he hurt? Was I s'posed to follow him? Uh-huh, guess so.

I came unfrozen and like a tranquilized duck, waddled, slipped, grappled, and grunted my way up the pile. At the top I screamed, batting away what I thought was a snake; then seeing Kev below with the other end of the rope still in hand, I got the picture and threw down the end that had hit me.

"You scared the shit out of me, Kev. We don't need that damn rope. Let's heave it!"

"Oh-h-h, sorry," he offered, recoiling it one more time. "Better not. Might need it to git us outta here." He reached for his behind and moaned, "I hit harder'n a boulder offa Lover's Leap."

That we were now deep in the maw of hypothermia was unnoticed by us. Our minds had slipped a cog; our bodies now responded to muddled thoughts with delayed, agitated movements, almost spastically. Kevin was probably the more concentrated of the two of us, but we both were dehydrated because we hadn't taken a drink since we entered the canyon hours ago. Even if we had known and been able to think it through, would it have altered our predicament?

Perhaps.

It seems unlikely now that neither of us desert dwellers had been schooled in the symptoms of hypothermia, that we didn't know the signs, the dangers, the word that appears in every guidebook, at every trailhead, even the topic of seminars. Perhaps we'd have stayed by the driftwood pile and lit it, both to get warm and to alert our friends who would see the smoke and know that something was amiss. Kevin still had five matches. Or we could have pulled some pieces from the pile and made a fire to warm ourselves enough so we could think straight; maybe even dry our clothes to use when we didn't have to swim.

But the one thought that hammered in our brains was *out ... out ... out!* And *out* meant downstream, downcanyon, whatever method, as fast as we could propel ourselves before darkness overtook us.

The runoff was no longer strong, sometimes barely a trickle. That's probably why it was so cold, especially to us in our exhausted condition. Kevin, slower now and limping a bit because he'd smacked his coccyx on the slide, still dragged a log over the shallow parts. A bit of luck, it turned out, because there were no more logs; all had stuck in the big pile back yonder. When we came to a very narrow trough, we straddled the log and used the walls to keep ourselves erect. This kept upper body parts out of water, but forced us to don jeans and cutoffs again to keep our genitalia intact. Anyway, it had come to the point that carrying them was more exhausting than wearing them, no matter how much their clamminess made us shiver.

We had ceased keeping count of time and distance, turns and pools, when we came to one of moderate length but wide and deep. With rope and camera on top, each of us held to the log, maneuvering with a one-arm dog-paddle. Halfway through, the rope fell off and disappeared. I went under twice with my camera when it fell from the log, but somehow managed to save it, and myself, from sinking.

When at last we crawled from the funnel, my legs refused to hold me up. I sat on the gravel bar looking at my bruised navy blue legs and Kev's equally blue torso where he leaned against the wall, and knew that if I had to take another swim, long or short, log or no log, I would drown. Meanwhile, the log floated back upstream and lodged in a bend out of sight, out of reach. Ahead, the canyon resembled the bellows of a giant accordion with a one-hundred-foot gash of dimly lit water in the bottom.

Shivering so I could hardly speak, I stuttered, "We should go back and l-l-light that big d-driftwood pile, Kev. Get warm."

"An' swim them trenches again?"

"Oooh, no. Why didn't we light it back then?"

"I forget."

At last my legs let me up and I came to stand beside him. "Turn 'round Kev. I'll hammer yer back, then you do me; see if I can get some blood back in ya."

He shook his head and turned to the wall. "S'all gone. Feel like a piece o' meat·been hangin' in the ice house."

I pounded on him for a few minutes until he returned the favor. Facing the wall and determined not to cry, I muttered, "Kev, I can't do it again—can't get in there—I'll drown."

"I won't exactly be floatin'. No more logs, neither."

"No more rope," I sighed.

We were in a relatively flat area twenty feet or so across, my head resting against my folded arms where I leaned into the wall, face down. I noticed we were standing in a scallop on a sandy hump. Looking up, I saw it had been washed down from a drainage above us, and a few feet above that I saw a shelf, which might lead to another, and yet another … but there were no footholds.

"Kev! Look! If I stand on your shoulders, maybe even on your *head*, I can reach that shelf and hopefully pull myself up. If I make it, you can take off your jeans and we can use them for a rope to haul you up."

He seemed dubious, but I guess he thought *anything* was worth a try. I sure did.

"I weigh about a hundred twenty pounds, Kev. You can take that on your shoulders, don't know about your head. If I get up far enough, you can prop my feet against the wall with your hands above your head."

"Uhhh, w-w-well, okay, let's do it. I *am* gettin' kinda hungry."

"What? You're priceless, Kevin!" I laughed (didn't know I could). "I'm too *cold* to be hungry. We have to get the hell outta here!"

When I lifted my foot to place it in his laced-together hands, my groin muscles were so painful I whimpered. Yet it's amazing what adrenaline will do, even worn-out adrenaline. I stepped from his hands to his shoulders, teetered to his head, then to a foot support, using every ounce of strength left in me. I pulled myself over the ledge and crumbled there, wheezing, crying, and laughing. "Kev, ol' buddy, I think we're outta here!"

"I ain't" came the simple statement from below.

"Throw me your jeans, ol' buddy, and you soon will be."

I don't remember all the minute details, only that he tossed up my camera and his jeans, I found a two-foot piece of driftwood wedged in a crevasse, and threw it down for him to stand on. With his sore behind it took two or three tries and the use of my feet dangling over the shelf before we were together on that narrow ledge, at least fifteen feet off the canyon floor, and leaning against a wall that retained more heat than those below, even though the sun had gone down over a half hour ago.

There were three or four more benches above us before the top of Cedar Canyon could be reached, any one of which could pinch out and rim us, making it impossible for us to do anything but stay where we were. But Cedar Mesa sandstone is far more forgiving than Navajo sandstone—something Kevin knew and I did not. I was convinced we'd have to stay on that tiny ledge all night. And another thing: we were on the right side of the canyon, not the left where the road, Jason, and Fletch awaited us.

"Kev, even if we get to the top how'll they find us? There's no road over here on this side."

"Yeah, there's an old trail to Horse Tanks. Jason knows it's there. Couple hours, we'll have a moon."

"Couple hours! Holy shit, by then I'll be an iceberg."

"Nah, there's wood up there. We build a big fire soon's we get to the rim. They'll see it an' git to us."

Feeling slightly encouraged and not wishing to mess around ledges in the dark, I inched behind him downstream, where he looked for a break in the wall above. Around a bend or two, sure enough it pinched off, dropping straight down to what we'd just come out of.

Before I could voice my despair, Kevin turned me around, saying, "Back to where we climbed out, and keep going. We'll find something. Might use my pants again."

About the same distance upstream, we hit a side drainage where we crawled around the corner on hands and knees to find it boxed in a few feet farther on, but there were boulders in the drainage and we were able to scramble to the next level.

That left two more benches to the rim.

Back and forth, in and out, over and under, around and between, each rise anywhere from fifteen to twenty or more feet, we finally topped out on the rounded sandstone cap. By then our clothes were nearly dry, but a cold, strong wind blew from the north across the hummocks and it was dark, the afterglow gone, the moon rising somewhere over Texas.

Kevin quickly gathered wood and lit a huge fire.

A quarter hour later, soaking up warmth from the fire, we saw lights from the van turn on, meander, thrash, and wiggle across uneven terrain, then stop, still a long way from us. The lights went to dim and within a few minutes, two flashlights wiggled and bobbed their way in and out of gullies until they came to within a few yards of us, on the *opposite* side of Cedar Canyon.

It was 9:00.

After two miles of moonlit walking in and out of six or seven more drainages; two more campfires to light the way for the van; many stops to drink from potholes still full of rainwater; acres of tired muscles and weary hearts; failure, then success, at finding a way, we connected, were loaded into the van, and were taken to the river camp for hot soup and crackers. When at last we crawled into our sleeping bags, it was after midnight.

❧

You'd think our trial in Cedar Canyon would have been a lesson to us. In many ways it was, but we had to take the second course—to be sure, to be sure. The following year, 1958, again September, in two days we did the whole show again, dividing it between the upper and lower halves, this time without the *running* water. Ahhh, but each long trench was full of scum and brush and slime. In place of smooth rock bottom and gravel bars there was *mud*. We found many caches of driftwood, but not nearly the abundance of last year's collection, certainly no huge stack obstructing the entire canyon.

The "foam pit," drawn down much lower and lacking its coiffure, continued on past the overhanging rock for more than a hundred feet. This meant one place had filled in with sand where another had emptied. It was full of reeking rot, like the business end of a skunk.

"I think there's a dead deer in here," said I.

"More like a dead cow," he answered. "Deer kin probably jump across up there."

This time I had a waterproof case for my camera, a plastic float for shorts, and a windbreaker. If we'd worn anything through those long trenches, we'd have been dragged under to become a permanent part of the miasma. Kevin's canteen was empty enough to have some buoyancy and use as a paddleboard in front of him; also for holding his jeans when he didn't wear them on his head.

The canyon itself was as weird and wondrous as we remembered it; as full of honeycombed depressions, vivid colors, lacerated stone, and high, inescapable walls; its woven patterns still indescribable. It was a canyon one might not wish to become intimate with, yet was worth far more appreciation than we had been able to give it in our condition last year. We saw, firsthand, how these sporadic streams altered from year to year, season to season, even minute to minute. This one was a good teacher for future challenging hikes in that stony country. Maybe it didn't cradle our love, but it definitely held our respect.

We stopped to nibble on candy bars in a pleasant sunny spot where multicolored walls dripped deep purple with desert varnish.

"Where'd we git out last year?" asked Kevin.

"Quite a way farther down," I answered. But looking around, we saw we were sitting right under it. It looked so different in the sunlight! We ogled it a long time, trying to figure out how we'd managed to get up such a high, uncompromising wall, or how we even recognized it as the only place that could have let us out. Then we

realized the sandy hump we'd stood on was now gone, washed away
in one more Cedar Canyon flood. The long, paralyzing pool that
I'd told Kevin I could not navigate without drowning was low
enough to bridge-walk the entire length. Once through, it would
have been less than a mile over gravel bottom most of the way to
our side canyon exit, with no pools to speak of.

Maybe. Only maybe. Perhaps the spring flood had brought down
a trillion tons of sand to cover the Great Mother's private parts. We
wouldn't know. What took us nine hours last year, we completed
easily in five—out the aforementioned canyon—to camp overnight
on the rim.

⁂

NEXT MORNING, we entered Cedar where we had climbed out. I
tried to picture this lower half as full of water as it was on our first
trip. There were pools, not nearly as many or as long—we swam four
or five—but it wouldn't have been much easier. Overall it was wider,
yet seemed to deepen even more. Walls soared higher, no way out on
either side. Much bigger drops and nothing but hanging crevasses
and notches way above the canyon floor, all draining from the right,
some whose headings I was certain we'd crossed the night of our exit
looking for the old trail to Horse Tanks, watching for the van.

When it turned in a south-north direction cutting back the sun, it
leveled out to an even sand-and-gravel floor, making easy walking,
barefooted.

At a bulge in the wall, Kevin stooped to pick up an inch-thick,
two-foot by ten-inch milled board, one end buried in the sand. It was
frayed, chinked, and beat up around the edges, but still all of a piece.

"Well, whadd'ya know?" He chewed on that for a bit, then turned
it over. His mouth dropped open. "Hey, this here board was in that
big woodpile we crawled over last year. It come loose from the top
when I slid down on it."

"Really, Kev? The one you hurt your butt on?"

"Yeah, lookit." There was writing on it, the routed-out letters
barely readable: PICNIC AREA.

"Y'know where this come from?"

I shook my head.

"From the national monument almost a hunnerd miles upstream. Come through Cedar Canyon, like we did."

I shot him a skeptical frown. "You sure it's the same board? Maybe it came from ..."

"Hell, yes! Same size, same kinda wood. An' there was writin' on it too, I remember. I was too busy with my sore butt to read it." He turned it over again and held it up. "See how beat-up it is? I felt jist like this sign *looks* when we climbed outta here last year!"

Since this was the longest sentence I'd ever heard Kevin speak, I wasn't about to disagree—and there was *that look*. I stared down at my bare toes wiggling in a tiny trickle.

"We were blessed, Kev. Could have been dead as that board. I still don't know how we made it out."

"Maybe 'cause we didn't give up," he grinned.

But I thought of the near impossibility—give up or not—of us finding the *one* spot that had probably saved our lives.

"No. I believe *if*, or *when*, or *why* the River Gods decide in your favor, it's pure luck."

Still grinning, Kevin replied, "Then let's be sure to thank 'em."

Sandstone Seduction

ON THIS NEW OCTOBER DAY, in the year of our River Gods, 1959, I have walked up a deep, shaded canyon through water, wet sand, and golden redbud leaves. My feet are cold in boots and socks, yet the sun, low in its arc across the southwestern sky, keeps smiling through a sweet-smelling autumn haze.

When I find it, the slickrock bowl is creamed in gentle warmth.

After the brilliant, blazing heat of summer, the ambiance of this place has shifted considerably. Then the bowl was like a sweaty exercise room; now, it's more like a balcony rimmed with light from *candelarias*.

Boots and socks—off with them! The second my bare feet touch stone, I become a thermometer. The mercury moves past my toes, up through my legs and body, to form a blush on my face—and what I see before me has already warmed my pulsing innards: this scooped-out place in an ancient dune of sand turned to rock has the look of a hammock, a cradle, a papyrus raft, or maybe Cleopatra's couch. Anyhow, it's a tempting space, a space that invites me to lie down, roll over, stretch out, and feel the texture of time-beneath-the-elements that has formed this perfect sanctuary.

Yes, I've been here before. The first time, not alone—the other times, always. It's not that easy to find. We first came upon it by accident, a *real* accident—stumbled on the ridge and literally slipped, rolled, and tumbled into this hollow to find ourselves unhurt, laughing, and completely alone. With no chance that anyone would be able to trace us, we stripped, slid into the pool at the lowest end of the bowl, came out dripping slick, and made heady love skin to skin with the stone—same color as our own. I could feel the rock sucking

151

Sandstone seduction

at my back where we entwined above the pool, feel it against my body like warm silk—silkier than his, if you want to know—as if I were the center figure in a ménage à trois. And I know it was the slickrock that made that coupling a more memorable one.

I'm warm enough now in this nude place to be the same, so I strip to my freckles and moles and walk down to the pothole, maybe to replay that fond memory as the water caresses me.

Aww ... it's empty ... rimmed with dead pollywogs that didn't make it to the hopping stage before the pool dried up and blew away.

Because of the shape of the pothole, I think it will be only one or two inches to bedrock. It is more, and I don't have a shovel, but when this sweet bowl is as full as it can be without running over its downhill lip, it's over my head. I was never able to touch bottom when it was full or even three-quarters full. Seep-seep-evaporate-seep-evaporate after the August–September rains have gone; I can read the weather pattern in the spacing of water rings above the bottom. They aren't uniform—some a foot, others three inches, some five to eight. There's a long cold winter speaking here, with ice on top, here in this quiet, dignified place.

❧

I WILL SAY FOR THOSE WHO have never seen, felt, walked on, or *heard* Navajo sandstone, that if you have a feeling for it, you can sense its birth, its formation. If you've lain upon a sand dune anywhere in any desert, you have felt not what it *looks* like, but a hard surface on what appears to be a pillow. A pillow it is not. You can move the top layer, soft as silk, and dig down. Silk falls over your hand and arm, the hardness gives way under you and you can burrow into the layer beneath, find it warm, make it fit your body. It will conform.

There is no silk beneath the Navajo. Fitting is up to you—you will conform. The flesh gives. If you find that place that fits your body, in whatever position you choose to sit, stand, or recline, you will know the same comfort that the live dune gave after you dug your place into it—the same warmth, the same softness, oh yes! And a new thing: a gift. When you return, it will still be there to fit you, and unlike the dune it will still be yours. Unless you get too fat, or skinny, or too long to fit; then go find yourself another place in the hundreds of miles of curvatures and mounds, dips and hollows, protrusions and extrusions, recliners and chairs, footstools and ladders, potties and peeholes, pillows and beds, and hammocks that don't swing.

Speaking of protrusions, on the way up here I passed her: "The Virgin," a shivering half figure of stone pressed into the mass; thigh, hip, and breast standing in bold relief. "Shivering" because of the striations that mark her body. She doesn't seem to know she's part of the man/womanhood of that whole mountain of rock, molded by the tears of Zeus, the breath of Thor, the lips of Venus. She trembles there, half done—no, not done at all until she's mated. That could be sometime within the next millennium, or maybe not. I always wish for her as I pass by, that she'll be made a whole being, sexually evolved, loved and caressed by those elements into a graceful being—all the shivering gone—with the assurance that she is one of the adored.

Yet forms that catch the eye are not what I'm trying to convey. There is more, much more, to learn about objects we deem inert simply because we don't know how to communicate with them. The years I was able to spend in Glen Canyon before its demise led to at least a partial understanding of those inert things, or let's say one to my satisfaction. You see, I don't want to know everything. A world without mysteries would be appalling to me. Though I try for answers, someone else's theory is not what I seek. I want to hear it from the rock. If I search long enough, feel the skin often enough, and listen intently, I will find the answers I need.

There are glad rocks, sad rocks, walls and ledges dark and brooding. In River tongue the name that whispers past calls them "Visssshh-nuu." To some this rock is cruel; to me only haunting, wise, and beautiful. All formations have personalities as convoluted and contradictory as our own, and we are either attracted or repelled by their presence. Yet how are we supposed to know about them without spending time in their company, studying them, being curious about them, trying to see through them to their inner life, wondering how they came to be the way they are? My soul was stolen long ago by Navajo slickrock. Its uncluttered intensity has the directness of an arrow piercing the heart cleanly, swiftly, fatally!—as if a mature and practiced lover had somehow found his way into the dunes. It is "come hither" stone, but not a tease. It declares itself eligible, then waits to see if a suitor is ready for love and marriage—a forever kind of relationship.

It has been observed by a few close friends and lovers over the years that when a man's relationship with me reached the point of commitment to steady dating, I would head for the hills; anything smelling of commitment to a lifetime partnership, I would vaporize.

Why was that?

Sure, I've been married, more than twice, but not for long. And those men don't enter my vision or flash across my memory screen as often as Glen Canyon and the gentle winding Colorado River that ran through it.

Why is that?

Is it possible to be attached to or love a place more than one does a human being? When you think about it, places are a large part of our psyche. We go to places we love—wildlands, rivers, deserts, seas, and mountains—go there when we're hurting from the treatment of other humans or the society we live in. We need those sanctuaries, those sacred places; they're medicine for whatever ails us.

Therefore, I must concede that when a place has altered my life, sent me in a direction other than the one I was striving for, and shown me possibilities I was unaware of, that place deserves more than one or two visits and a few photographs. It deserves my attention, my curiosity, my involvement, and finally my devotion.

The sandstones of Glen Canyon rest in the palm of my love.

Go! Hike the slickrock, swim the river, plunge the potholes, chimney the crevasses, twist with the canyon. Do it alone; that's where the finest discoveries are made. But before you go alone, here is a primer, not a preachment:

Learn the slickrock like boatmen learn waves and currents in rivers: respectfully and in various seasons. After which time you will realize there are places here that have the power to tempt, bewitch, and kill. I'm one of the lucky—bewitched, brought to the brink, then allowed to go on. It was an intense and frightening experience that infused all my senses. The many changing faces, moods, and textures of the rock need to be learned. Only then will you be aware of what the stone is telling you. The wise number for exploration is three. Two for reappraisal and engrossment. Alone for fulfillment.

MY WONDROUS SANDSTONE BOWL of flesh and warmth is high above the river and slanted enough to catch most of the sun's orbit until a couple of hours past noon. The air is still, not even a breeze; it hugs me gently—feels like I was in a warm pool just floating ... floating ... as if I could levitate from this spot slowly, sweetly, up to the rim. It's so quiet I can *hear* the sun conversing with the earth in the gentle way it has during the autumn months of the year. Nude beside my now-and-then pool, I raise my arms high to the sky and feel my whole resurrection take place in just these few minutes. Back to the earth, back to who I am and who I am not, back to my kin, the sandstone in my veins.

The dreck drains away. Peace overwhelms me.

Two ravens, their speech like dice rattling in a leather cup, sit above me on what looks like a sheaf of Navajo stone pages. Torrents have shredded and winnowed the sand into forms that resemble papers and books on an ill-kept desk.

"*Yakkety-auuuk. Ung-guck?*" (What the hell's that down there?)

"*Grak-oooie, ark-click.*" (Nonedible; just saw it move.)

"*Nn-guk.*" (Smells funny.)

"*Gurgle-argle-urk.*" (You got that right.)

The ravens pace and strut atop this casual creation, touch beaks and turn in circles, cock their heads, stare and shake more dice. Their lingo is so familiar, so much a part of this canyon, that I laugh and chat with them until they tire of translating and flap off in regal disgust, their curiosity sated.

My eyes trace a zigzag pattern of switchbacks under the cluttered desk where crossbedded ridges catch the sun's rays as it slips into the bowl. After countless visits to this spot, something new? I could probably enter and leave by this route never noticed before now. Our eyes are poor things in this world of arrested swirls if all it takes is an inch of sunlight to point the way. Think how long it would take for anyone to discover the thousands of possible trails threading over and through this trackless sea of humps and hollows.

The last time here was a glazed, windy day. I came planning to get away from the blast in this protected place. Sweat dribbled down onto the stone where I stood on the rim. I took off my clothes to make my own evaporative cooling system, and hurried down toward the pool. In an instant I was a human emery board. The sand that didn't stick to me swirled and bit, stung and blasted my bare bod until I sought the refuge of the water, only to find it covered with a gauze of pink sand so dense it looked to be the dry bottom of the pool. I touched the surface, waded in, and lay back hardly covered, to find myself bedded down with swarms of wiggling pollywogs! They tickled me everywhere. I giggled and flopped about so much I'm sure I squashed a bunch of them.

Living with the slickrock, I've made some startling discoveries; even better, mysteries never dreamed and never solved. And to my astonishment I found it a very sensual place, not just visually, but engaging *all* the senses. I never thought I was crazy to have such an attachment to simple rock and stone—it seemed a natural evolvement. There have been times when the river, the canyon, or the sandstone has spoken to me, rather than me speaking to it, or asking questions. Those times are as vivid today as they were then.

⁂

FALL. The most perfect time of year. The side canyon pulled me through every kind of sandstone magic—pools to swim, ledges to crawl, open spaces with sandy bottoms and redbud trees, fluted narrows, banks drenched in maidenhair fern, monkey flowers, and penstemon—to where there really could be no more surprises. I leaned against a water-cut rift no wider than my living room to take the scene in through every pore, and to bless the gods that let me find this Eden.

I was about to turn back when I heard a sound I'd never heard before. Someone, something running across the slickrock in soft leather soles. Instinctively I felt a promise of something wild, beautiful, personal, something I was supposed to see. Like a beckoning, the sound urged me on upcanyon.

I climbed a sluiceway, to top out at the bottom of many small cataracts where water played soft musical notes beneath an overhang. Everything was in faerie light, refracted down through the curvaceous sandstone walls rising two hundred feet on either side. To my right, bordering the stream, the stone resembled the open fan of a pleated skirt. Above that lay a ridge of chipped ice, then long sweeps of Navajo tapestry, topped with a lacy border of honeycomb depressions dribbling colors from maroon to pink-gold down fifty feet of wall. Some of the depressions were large enough to crawl into, others no bigger than your head. Homes, of course, for owls and canyon wrens and those spunky little lizards who constantly hug these walls to make sure they don't go away.

My God! The place was out of this world. Alice never knew what a wonderland was.

I lay down on the cataract ledges, rolled over them, and hugged them, drank the pure water, stood, and pulled the mosses over my breasts and let them drape down my body, literally *dressing* myself in nature; all the while feeling as if this was a perfectly natural ritual I had always performed.

The patter of running feet came again.

At the same moment a streak of sunlight shot into the canyon, startling me. It beamed on part of the honeycombs, and in the center of the beam, in a comb no bigger than the circle of my arms, sat a perfect jug with two handles, decorated in a pattern I could not discern, but clearly decorated — black on buff.

A prickling within raised goosebumps on my skin.

I strained to see it, to make out its actual size in the maze of hollows and holes, and scanned the wall for any possible way — above, below, or from the side — that anyone could have found a route to place it there. There was none. Two, maybe three minutes, and the streak disappeared as quickly as it came, the pot could no longer be seen, and the running feet died away.

⁂

BECAUSE I'M CURIOUS about Nature and why she does what she does, I keep looking, feeling, and asking questions. When I explained how I felt about sandstone to friends, I discovered that the sensual aspect wasn't unique, so I started asking others about their experiences with my favorite stone. Taking note that women often had erotic responses to its smooth curvaceousness, I became curious whether men experienced similar reactions to anything that wasn't pure flesh and blood, and wondered if they thought there was more to feeling sandstone than merely touching it. I made certain they understood I was *not* talking about jerking off in the wilderness. From that questionnaire I received a quote from an intellect of note:

> *I think it was after jerking off in the wilderness that I decided to become a geologist. At times it seems as though the gift of seed to the rocks has returned stony children. … The rocks have been more responsive than some people I know. Erotic response? Not usually,*

and not hardly ever. Sensual, stimulating, intriguing, vaguely
attractive—but not something you could palpate. Feelings and
emotions and spirit are not, in themselves, erotica. And what do you
mean by erotic? ... there are so many emotions that can be evoked by
rock that aren't erotic, but could be confused with erotic or spiritual.

What I meant by "erotic" is something written by a woman
whose sensuality exploded in ways she'd never dreamed. If you
look and listen to the rock at all, it will tell you to rid yourself of the
cumbersome stuff you wear—entreat you to join in the fun and freedom of its lumpy-bumpy world—and learn something about yourself. Hiking those narrows, climbing the crevasses, bounding across
the cap atop the hot, clean, sun-drenched stone with the teasing
wind or rain upon one's body; lying on the sand, in the pools, standing beneath the mosses, is the only way to be one with that world.
This woman was wooed and won by the elements: the rivers, the
pools, and that curvaceous stone.

I felt the tensions leave my body each time I swam the pool, like the
creek was cleansing me of all the stuff I dragged around with me.
Then I climbed out onto a large pyramidal rock. ... I found amazing
shapes in this rock, which just fit my body. This one was shaped like
two buttocks with a saddle in between, and my butt fit in there
perfectly. ... I had to arch my back over the rock, which opened my
chest and heart to the sun. ... Well, it was so damn sensuous, my
whole body, heart and soul, couldn't help but respond. The sun came
down and opened me up and it was like making love to the earth.
I had an orgasm that was so gentle, yet so explosive, its completeness
melted me into the heart of the rock in the middle of this water
world—the creek rushing by me and the river taking the creek.
I was in the earth, part of her and the sun. ... I felt like I had been
taken, in a very nice way, and claimed by the river, canyons and
pool that own my soul.

I found some who could define the sensual only when *looking* at
certain formations, but would put aside their *second* thought as "too
far out" to use the sense of touch, maybe lie down, or stretch out
bare, feel, and let the stone feel their skin, their body, and ahhh ... let

it curl up in their minds. Even in winter the canyons of The Glen demanded your bare skin. I questioned yet another geologist whose intimacy with rock leaped and bounded past the scientific, through the visual, into the visceral.

> *I have licked sandstone so many times, just gotten on hands and knees and passed my lips right over the surface, either the smooth on narrow canyon walls, or the sandy-rough up on top. And Navajo Sandstone … that rock has gotten inside of me … whales and thighs and water and moons. MY GOD, ITS SHAPES!! SHOULD WE EVEN BE ALLOWED TO SEE SUCH THINGS? I started using the word sensual all over the place.*
>
> *You must have found in bringing up the erotic nature of stone with people, some number of them drifting away into remembered orgasm. Is this what "ergonomically designed" means? That it seems constructed to fit your flesh, a hundred miles of rock begging for your hand. I want to go sprawl naked even in January with the low warm sun—as long as the air doesn't move—and kiss the nape of the earth's neck. For those who don't understand what you're talking about, they will probably be satisfied with a pile of porno magazines and a poorly lit room. It's better that way. Not enough room for them out there.*

When I suggested to someone that reveling in that nude world was like taking a bath in awareness, they asked, "Of yourself?"

"Oh, no," I said. "Awareness of the earth, the elements, that blue roof up there, the old stone dune with its birthmarks, that fitting hollow, the sound that sometimes comes from the stone when I put my ear to it." Would that person understand if I said there were places I had lain on my back in a cupped palm of fleshy stone, my arms and legs outstretched, and *felt* the earth turn, pressing me against it, embracing me in my chosen spot? Probably not. But I have a southwestern-sandstone-river-rowing sister who would not merely understand but give it words I could never hope to find.

> *For me sandstone is filled with secret veins that only the flesh can find. Press the stone and feel its flex. Its beauty shapes perception with a harrowing embrace. The sun rises east of my hip bones. Color*

strikes like blows. The light ratchets up its blaze and flashes through
each nerve, a net of flame, a field of exquisite friction. I am seized
by something that can never be wrestled down, a feeling not unlike
sorrow and ecstasy compounded. Then comes the sweet drift of
longing, and I must hang on to the earth's curve for dear life,
breathe the comfort of stone during my ride. Skin of slickrock,
skin of woman, there is no difference.

And skin of man, there is no difference. The luscious sandstones
of Glen Canyon began their beckoning call to me after my first year
in those sequestered erogenous zones—those deep sinuous paths between Mother Earth's labia, so private, so impermissible I'd back
away. "*Should we even be allowed to see such things?*" And those
proud erections pushing through fleshy stone. Some were tall as
buildings, others like little boy peepees; some in neutral, others limp
and comical, dangling over a scarp, all cockiness gone.

All of us know a few who just can't, or won't, see the kinky
humor in rock formations and who are shocked by them. They will
turn a rosy hue, or look away from Nature's undressed forms poking above earth's crust in shapes raw and shameless in their effrontery—afraid someone like me will make an indecorous comment,
which of course I couldn't help but do. Yet to some it could appear
as a painting, one-dimensional, nice to look at, but who'd want to
come here? Still others would see ... what? Just sandstone? An obstruction? Something to be climbed? A place to hide? As when fifteen people witness a car accident, no one will see what the others
saw. Nor do I always see the same thing.

I've been up here in a bruising rainstorm, looking for the quickest way down to the boat, the cave, the overhang; watched the rock
retch, heave, and scream into the arms of a loving river; seen it
teeter and resettle, quiet as you please—not a whisper of its deadly
dive to oblivion with just a single person's weight on it; been here
when lightning struck a few feet from me, just bare me alone on
this bald rock, knowing I wasn't the only object sticking up and
vulnerable. But Nature's not selective. Would she pick me, the
flesh? Hopefully, no—she'd choose Buster, the big stony phallus
over there.

As I step on the crossbedding that has so often saved my life, it crosses my mind that it would be unbearable to me, and to the stone, if it called to everyone. Certainly I'm aware that my *place* and time here are a gift, the gift of being allowed an insight to the ways and moods of something seemingly inert.

Ah, no. This sandstone is anything but inert!

With smiles and snickers I remember my dear *amigo*, the late Fred Rodell, who was forever enthralled by the erotic shapes in Nature, gleefully pointing them out to blue noses and red faces. Fred whacked away at pretentiousness with brilliant, ribald humor. When I met him in the sixties, he was still a tenured professor at Yale Law School. He would come to Aspen for the summers, hang out wherever I was singing, and lay on me some of the funniest, filthiest limericks ever conceived. He had a passion for clever smut, and just as much passion for the West, its wild rivers, its bare shapes and spaces. He knew my love for Glen Canyon and mourned its loss with me at the Aspen Inn, late at night, over scotch on the rocks. One night he pushed a paper across the table to me, and smirking said, "Did you know sandstone attracts animals as well as people?"

> *Now the sexual life of a camel*
> *Is stranger than anyone thinks,*
> *And includes in its passionate orbit*
> *Abnormal assaults on the Sphinx.*
> *But the Sphinx's posterior region*
> *Is clogged with the sands of the Nile,*
> *Which accounts for the hump on the camel,*
> *And the Sphinx's inscrutable smile.*

❦

I THINK ABOUT FRED on this October day of returning to my sun-warmed sanctuary with its sometime pool, and know what he'd see from my perch a thousand feet above the river. I've climbed five hundred feet higher than the hidden bowl and am looking down on miles of humpy sandstone. All those fleshy bodies lolling against each other; legs thrown over chests, arms reaching between legs, tits, and bottoms pointing to the sky; all locked in a raucous orgy, rolling and tumbling their way to the river. That's what he'd see.

When I called it "come hither" stone, I didn't mean just sensually. There is a kind of gesticulation in the rock, in the almost invisible trails through and around it, a code that I learn to read, in the forms that surround me, like spoor. They suggest a path leading to something far more profound than the touch of skin on stone.

Here above these rhythmic, rolling dunes I find overhangs, caves, and alcoves cradling a warm sun; tonight they will suspend a fickle moon. These sequesters disdain the rain and lull the rampant wind to whispers. They are secret spaces where in centuries past others have stayed. I know, because they left a trace.

It lies toward the rear of this shallow depression, mostly covered by hard-packed, windblown sand. Glancing at it several times without really looking, taking it for a piece of firewood I may or may not use—I sit near the lips of the shelter, looking out, knees pulled beneath my chin, arms locked around them, The Glen's arms locked around me. Here, now, at our favorite time of day—when we love each other most and tell our deepest secrets beneath a lowering sun—I listen. The wayward wind speaks in many tongues, coming from all directions. Before taking its final plunge downcanyon for the night, it sucks up a huge mouthful of sand and blasts it into my shelter, driving me on hands and knees to the back, where I can barely sit upright.

As the sun teeters on the edge of the Kaiparowits, its last rays blossoming in my hollow, I pull the piece of firewood from beneath the sand.

To see and touch an artifact left in its place, *untouched*, for a thousand years is to dissolve time and space and make a connection. This is some sort of tool carved from split juniper—or possibly ironwood, certainly hard and heavy enough to be ironwood—about twenty inches long, and thin; the handle about an inch thick, the rest of the instrument about half that. It is twisted slightly and curved at the end, possibly where it once joined the main trunk as a branch, and part of this curve is broken off, leaving a jagged edge. The whole piece is covered with whittle marks from a stone tool; the color is maroon, with a thin stripe of cream through the middle, from handle to curved tip.

"What did you use this for?" I hear myself saying aloud.

I crawl, then walk, out of the alcove, hefting it in my hand, swinging it back and forth. "Is this a war club?" I ask again. "You could have split somebody's head open with this!" I check the broken end, which doesn't seem so jagged now, merely worn down as if it had been dragged through dirt and sand for a long time.

"No," I correct myself, "not sharp enough. I know what you used it for. You dug furrows with it for planting, and sometimes for smacking the deathblow to fish or snakes or rabbits out of the snare. That's it, isn't it?"

More profound than the touch of skin on stone. More profound are thought waves on thought waves, through the ether of beginnings, to bridge the thousand-year-old gap between us.

"This is the way you traveled, from bar to planting bar, and from canyon to canyon, rather than down along the river through dense undergrowth and mud, right? That's why it's up here. And you slept in this alcove too sometimes, didn't you?—caught in a storm, or on a hot day wanting out of the sun. Probably had your woman with you. Yes. This place feels like the two of you together. Thanks for leaving your tool."

Thank you for the connection.

The SCUD

IT WAS THE YEAR I didn't have a boat, didn't have a boatman, didn't have a passenger, didn't have nuthin'—felt like I didn't even have a friend—but I had a river, by God, and I was going to get to it and run it, even if I had to do it on an air mattress. The river *was* my friend.

Odd how things fall into place when you push the "dammit-I'll-do-it" button. Two weeks later I found a friend who loaned me a "craft" he had run through Glen Canyon the autumn before; two twelve-foot inflatable baloneys, the kind I swore I'd never set foot in. Well, it was that or nothing: a wooden deck that fitted over both, holding them together; a support at the rear—I think it was the rear—for a used nine-horsepower outboard motor I bought for $35, with a packet of shear-pins thrown in. Next, I did a crash run of my address book and turned up two green kids who expressed a frenzied desire to run Glen Canyon with me. (Given another year or so, it would be deep-sixed by an ugly plug known as Glen Canyon Dam.) They would share expenses and help with chores. I knew that even if I couldn't have my good boatman or his boat this time, I could have the necessary equipment for the trip, like kitchen boxes, Dutch oven, grill, buckets, tarps, ropes, etc.

We met in Blanding at Frank's house (the boatman I couldn't have), who then trucked us some eighty miles down the muddy road with all our gear, to Farley Canyon, where Woody met us in his jeep and trailer below a six-foot washout in the road. It took all of us nearly an hour of slip-slide-away to ferry the gear from Frank's outfit to Woody's, whereupon Frank departed with hardly more than a disturbing smile and a perfunctory hug for me, his old river-running friend, and took off like a skunked pussycat for the San Juan trip he was late getting to.

While the flatbed slithered around behind, Woody whimpered and whined all the way down Farley about the goddam storm and the few sprinkles it was still dropping, saying we probably wouldn't get to the river at all after what it had done to the road, how the flood had yanked out two young cottonwood trees by his trailer house that he'd jacked up five times in less than a week because the creek kept snitching pieces of its foundation, and what the hell was I doing going down Glen this time of year?

"Well, gee, Woody, I always go down this time of year; and what's happened to your sense of humor? I think you need a beer."

"Sure do. The supply truck couldn't even get this far a couple days ago."

I gladly gave him one, knowing it would only make him babble more, and in a way I could sympathize. After all the summer Glen Canyoneers left remote Hiteland and glided back to packed City-land, Woody didn't have many people to ferry across the river, talk to, or run after, so he ran off at the mouth instead. I put my greenies, Donna and Dale, up front to catch the flood of words and moved as far back in the jeep as possible so I could try to understand why I felt so lost and lonely.

Pretty soon it dawned on me.

I, Miss Smart-ass, would now be the one responsible for getting us to Kane Creek ten days later in a weird craft I'd never seen before, with a used motor I hadn't tested, two people who had never run a river, and a "guide" who'd never solo guided! My confidence began to flag when I realized why Frank had had little to say on the ride from Blanding. He too was worried, knowing how determined I am to do what I set out to do, and most likely was reluctant to let me find out for myself the hazards of being "boss guide." Or maybe he thought it was high time I *did* know. Anyhow, when we reached the river, I knew why he may have had second thoughts.

Ol' Colly Raddy was running 30,000 cubic feet per second!

The storm had abated, but Ol' Colly Raddy had not. I'd never seen him so high—in September. Standing there watching the swirling, humping, bank-eating, Moenkopi-red flood tide yank at tree roots and bite chunks out of gravel bars was unnerving enough—adding the sound it made and feeling earth's answer beneath my feet, buzzed my solar plexus and lifted the hair on my arms. I could almost believe I was in Grand Canyon instead of my peaceful Glen.

Woody took us about a mile upriver from the ferry to Slim's cabin, where Slim and his Moki-hunting visitor, Leo, helped us unload for the second time that day. We heaved it all onto the wet ground about thirty feet from the bank, me wondering if the river would come up and eat it in the night, half hoping it would so I could relax and enjoy myself. Both men had offered to help us pump the muthas up, help us pack, lash down, and get underway tomorrow. I'm sure it looked like I not only needed help, but also a large portion of luck and twenty River Angels to lead the way. I'd known Slim for several years now, knew he had beaucoup river miles under his belt and could tell at a glance that my eager friends didn't know diddly-squat what was, or could be, in store for them. And he'd seen what I hadn't: that between the two of them they could barely lift a Dutch oven. The main component for river trips, muscle, would not be onboard. Slim offered: rather than build a fire and slurp around in the damp, why not bring dinner up to cook in his kitchen? He and Leo added more and we had a whopping meal. The rain stopped its intermittent spitting and the weather turned normal and beautiful the way it always does that time of year. We took showers under Slim's outdoor tank and stayed up until almost midnight trading river stories. Laying our sleeping bags on the bar in front of Slim's cabin, we watched big hairy stars pop out of the black. Counting them, I felt tension and misgivings ease into the chortling river as I drifted away just before Orion rose in the east.

By sunrise the river had dropped six inches and was still sinking. Nonetheless it sounded like thick, whipped chocolate—really hell on outboard motors, but mine was supposedly river trained. I hadn't planned to use it anyway except in a tight, for making up time, or to go back upstream to see something we'd missed. We'd always run the Gentle Glen on oars, but as I watched the Colorado percolate, figured I might need to fire the bugger up.

After gallons of strong coffee and the huge breakfast Slim cooked for us, we were ready to inflate the rafts. Starting with a big hand pump that usually does the job, we discovered that these army surplus things were built with twenty-four compartments that had to be inflated independently. *Mama mia.* I didn't just look that gift horse in the mouth; I jumped halfway down its throat!

Slim had a thing called a Tote Goat he used between his cabin and the store up Farley Canyon. He showed me how to start and shift it, then suggested that while they were using elbow grease, I could run up and get his sparkplug pump on loan to Woody. After slamming the thing into a few bushes and almost dunking it in the outhouse, I managed to steer it to that destination and return with the pump. It blew the sausages up right smart, and by the time Woody arrived to tell us how it should all be done, Slim and Leo had put the entire contraption together. By early afternoon the SCUD (as I have named it) was waterborne, deck lashed firmly down, motor tested and actually sounding good. Heaving a sigh of relief and gratitude, I thanked my luck for Slim and Leo. There's no way we could have gotten that goofy rig together without them. But by that time it was too late to start loading and leave, adding a worry that hadn't fazed me in the past: would I be on time to meet Frank at Kane Creek ten days later if I lost a day? Slim gently suggested that with the river this fast, I could easily make up the time.

Then I found my hand in the cookie jar.

If we didn't leave until the next day, they would go with us in Slim's aluminum canoe at least as far as the Rincon. After they got us underway, they'd pack up and mosey on down, stopping here and there for Leo to do a little Moki-in' and find us wherever we were camped. It would be impossible to miss the SCUD. More cookies! He'd bring his small Clinton motor in case the one I had didn't perform as it should. I didn't know jack-shit about outboards, but Slim had spent half his life bitching and tinkering with his main mode of transportation; after eyeballing mine, he probably thought it couldn't hurt to slip another ace in the deck.

We enjoyed a whole afternoon of fun and games. Went up past North Wash, the Dirty Devil, and Sheep Canyon to Dark Canyon,

Birth of the SCUD

almost eighteen miles. The river was high enough to make those riffles glassy instead of rocky—except for Dark. We didn't even try for that, though Slim had once made it above with a lighter boat, a bigger motor, and less driftwood. We hiked to a cave and ruin high above Rock Canyon, then lit a huge driftwood pile the flood had left on the beach below it. As the sun dropped behind the Red Benches, we took pictures of its reflection in the deep purple light of Narrow Canyon, then headed homeward, stopping at Slim's fishing lines to pull in two large catfish for dinner. At the cabin we found the river holding steady.

After the great afternoon we'd spent exploring, I managed to wash my quakies and qualms away under Slim's shower, wonderfully

Katie and the SCUD

warm from a whole day's sun on the tank. His whole setting was a
riverman's paradise. And that shower! Total efficiency — all any
human could need or want. The five-hundred-gallon tank standing
on a wooden scaffold thirty feet from the house was sheltered from
the wind by a sandstone cliff. Water piped from a nearby spring trick-
led into the top; at the bottom a nozzle with a lawn sprinkler attached
made up the shower. A section cut from a Jeep tire and nailed to the
scaffold served as a soap dish, and underfoot, liberated from an old
motorboat, lay a deckboard. *And that river:* within earshot, eyeshot,
and gutshot to keep you on your toes, not to mention the carmine
cliffs behind it. With all that majesty, I let the breeze dry me, then hit
the sack and went to dreamland counting unhatched chickens.

Journal Entry: September 13, 1961, Camp, Mile 136.5, Warm Springs Creek

WE DEPART SLIMSVILLE before 10:00 on 28,000 cubic feet per second, motor whirring away just to see if it works; then I cut it and let the river take us along. I get my first warning/surprise/alert about four miles downstream at the bend of Dorothy riffle. Big boulders line the curve, drawing the SCUD toward them like a magnet. When I damn near dislocate my shoulder pulling back to miss them, I get the wink that this scow is nothing like the sleek, well-balanced, *maneuverable* boats I've always rowed, nor is this river exactly like the one I'm used to running in the fall. Farther on, the "wink" becomes a bop on the head at Four Mile Canyon, where we nearly upset against a huge rock that heretofore was several yards offshore.

I wise up and opt for the motor.

We aren't stopping for many hikes or riverside ruins because of the day-late start, and I'd probably miss the landings anyway, being disoriented by high water. Beautiful Monte Christo Island, where we used to love to camp, has almost vanished! At Tickaboo Creek, I land on big gravel and rocks; beach gone. But the creek is running clear, and I aim for its potholes like a river otter to its den; rinse off river silt, and float free of clothes in the cool, smooth bowls formed in bedrock. Need to teach the greenies how to run a raw river in the raw. Not to worry, I know how to pick my friends.

We are a hot and dirty crew when we reach camp tonight. I look eagerly for signs of Slim and Leo, but they don't show. I'm so tired I can hardly move, but I get dinner and do dishes with little help from Donna and none at all from Dale—he seems to be sick or something. I dunno. The damned motor quit two miles above camp. Haven't the faintest idea why; I'm full of apprehension and dread; we can't *row* this SCUD all the way down the river, can't even get it to the bank without fifty pulls from fifty feet away, and without the motor we won't get in *anywhere*. Dear God, I hope Slim and Leo haven't changed their minds about coming to meet us! My bath upstream tonight in Cleopatra's Sandstone Bowl is the only thing that saves my sanity and my dreams from a horror show!

**Journal Entry: September 14, Camp, Mile 125,
Island Below Moki Canyon**

WHEN THE RISING SUN hits Tapestry Wall and my sleeping bag,
my spirit wants to rise along with it to a sparkling blue sky. Not this
morning; I'm too tired to care. River has dropped another six to
eight inches, but is staying mighty muddy. Coffee revives me somewhat until I go down the slickrock shelf to the SCUD. All twenty-
four of its darling little compartments have lost half their air. If it
had been fully loaded, it would have *sunk during the night!*

River Gods, are you pissed at me? Did I do something to offend
you on this, my fifteenth, Glen trip? *No ma'am. The thing didn't
sink, did it? We didn't carry it away, so blow it up again.*

And we do—load up and shove off about noon, on oars—the
motor still out of service. Dale is even sicker today with heatstroke.
I lay him down on the deck, hat over his face, cover him with a wet
towel, and pour water over him. Downstream we stop at Olympia
Bar, an old placer mine where the Bennett Wheel once turned to run
the machinery. I somehow navigate the swift river and pull into the
dent of a wash below. We plunk Dale in the river beside the beached
SCUD and I take Donna up on the ridge to marvel at what's left of
the old placer mine. Fifteen minutes later, we hear Dale yelling.

Great gods! has he been washed downstream?

No-o-o. He's been disturbed by loud popping noises. The
SCUD's twenty-four compartments have reinflated in the heat and
are popping their seams! We quickly unroll their little penises, let
out some hot stuff, and tuck them back in their respective shorts—
all twenty-four. Mother of God, is this going to happen every day?!

There are two or three small canyons I want to stop and explore,
but fail. Being used to a beaching maneuver that starts less than a
hundred yards upstream, I pass the place before I can get from
midriver to the bank, let alone from the far side.

I need to clue you in about this hunk of blubber. It is almost as
wide as it is long, with two sorta rounded noses, a short V between
them—the better to catch driftwood—and looks like two hippos
trying to fornicate while floating. Do hippos float? Well, these do,
sort of. They certainly move like hippos—slowly, reluctantly, maybe

not at all, except with the current. My oars feel like toothpicks in bubble gum. Maybe if I put the two greenies on one, me on the other, we might—I say *might*—get from one side of the river to the other within a mile's distance. [I don't realize how aptly I've named this beast—rhymes with mud, doesn't it?—or find out *why* this is so until we dock at the very end of our trip.]

All day I have been looking hopefully upstream, listening intently for the whirr of an outboard motor, ambivalent about keeping up the pace or slowing down to wait for Slim and Leo to catch up. But tiredness and negative thoughts (that I keep to myself) insist on getting the upper hand.

Woops! Hansen Creek *rapid?*—that was never here before. It slams us into the vertical wall and nearly buries us. One nose goes up, the other under, as the kitchen box crashes against the rampart, knocking off the lid, which I grab just before it floats away.

I seem to be having trouble chewing what I've bitten off, but rather than admit it, I start feeling sorry for myself. Then I get my knickers in a knot at Frank for letting me go it on my own. In this worked-up, teeth-grinding stage I manage to pull onto a beach, tie up, sit my greenies down beneath a willow, feed salt pills to Dale and give them a lecture: instructions about helping at mealtime, loading and unloading, getting fresh water, drinking it, tying up, getting wood, building fires, staying cool (which I ain't right now); simple things I'd think anyone would know, that ends with "My name isn't Samson. I can't do this alone. I need *help!*"

"We know, we know," says Dale. "We've been watching and wondering how to help you, but you've been so angry with the boat, so ... so ..."

"Bitchy," I offer in sudden recognition of my pitiful self.

"Yeah," Donna smiles, "you could say that, and worried too. But now that you've told us what to do ..."

"I'm sorry, kids. You're right, I am a bit worried. But I hope you'll remember my bark is worse than my bite."

Dale laughs. "We know that or we wouldn't be here. Hey! I feel better already, and you know something? I've tinkered with two-stroke motors before. When we camp, I'll see if I can find the problem."

I feel better too, now that my worry burden is being shared, now that I know I've got a potential grease monkey onboard.

A plan to camp at Moki Canyon goes k-plotz when we find the entrance deep in brush and loaded with ants. What in hell do these critters do when the river comes up to flood their commune? Do they dig for China? Seal the hatches? Sprint for dry ground? I know what they do when the river goes down. They call in the troops and regroup—they're everywhere. They *dig* the mouth of Moki. Means we're outta here and won't get to hike it in the morning; no way could I get the hippos back upstream without an eddy half the size of this river.

Quarter mile below, I find an island poking several feet above river level, its upstream beach flat, clean, and untracked; driftwood neatly stacked on higher ground just waiting for our fire. We are partially unloaded when I'm *sure* I hear that sound I've been imagining all day. Looking up, I see a flash of the late afternoon sun against the aluminum canoe at the mouth of Moki Canyon. We drop everything and run like wild things up the beach, waving towels and screaming, jumping up and down to attract their attention, even though I know they can't hear us over their motor. It looks like they're moving back upstream and taking my hopes of a joyful night along with them, when Slim cuts the motor, they hear us, and head down. We prance around, shouting and laughing, having a regular whoopee dance. Anyone would think we'd been marooned for months awaiting rescue.

As they pull up their outboard and paddle onto the beach, I hear Leo say, "Hey, they ain't got nuthin' on." And it's truly the first time I realize I don't. Dale has only an open shirt to cover his redness; Donna, a mere sash hanging from her hips. Well, I figure it's too late to make something of it, so I grab their bow rope and we help them unload. No one seems uncomfortable about us. Later, when we're getting dinner and it cools off, we go put something on.

I've never in my life been happier to see two people. We have fried chicken, biscuits, asparagus, plus a drink of Old Overshoes, conversation, cookies, and coffee that Slim pronounces "Larapin!" I have my ritual bath in the river and am peacefully bedded down with the others for a night of sweet dreams when, through the stillness I love so deeply on this river, come the idiot man-made tones of rock-and-roll.

I leap from my bedroll, hollering, "Who in hell brought a *radio?*"

It's Leo, who turns it off pronto. The poor man probably wonders why he's getting his head bitten off; after all, he's seen my guitar and knows I *play* music. Feeling sheepish after my outburst, I go over to his sack and try to explain.

"I just can't cope with *mu-zak* in this quiet, near holy place, Leo. The work I do has me listening to all kinds of plunking, day and night, like it or not, so when I come to The Glen I don't want to hear anymore."

"Oh, sure 'nuff," agrees this gentle, laid-back Mokiman, as he stuffs the offender into his duffel. "No need for it at all."

"Believe it or not, this is the first time I've heard a radio in all my years on the river. Guess that's why my outburst was so rude. You'll have to forgive me."

"We be fine," he smiles. I can tell: his teeth shine in the sliver of a moon that's beginning to show. I return to my bed, watch a few clouds scud into the south, breath a sigh of relief with these two great guys here, and go to sleep. Soundly.

[For the record: Leo became one of the most magnificent canyon buddies anyone could ask for. In later years, after the reservoir drowned all of Glen's canyons, we hiked over twenty others that hadn't received such a sorry fate, some of them more than once. Long hikes they were—ten, fifteen days—drainages into the San Juan and Colorado Rivers. When we hit the canyons, he'd plunk all of his paper-white, bare skin beneath waterfalls in Grand Gulch, in Slickhorn, White, Long, Gravel, Dark, Bowdie, and Gypsum Canyons, to name a few, for a "fine soakin'." Perhaps we released something in him that night below Moki. His eyes were like 10×25 binocs—could pick out a half-covered arrowhead or a potsherd from a hundred feet away—that's the reason we named him Moki Sam. Leo had a little Paper Piper (built it himself) that he sometimes flew from his Kansas farm on the Old Missou to the Colorado

Plateau. Or, if he didn't feel like flying, he'd drive his *quiet* BMW motorcycle all that way to join us. I never heard the radio again.]

Journal Entry: September 15, Camp, Mile 108, Gretchen Bar

SMELL OF COFFEE wakes me. I'm handed a big mug of the steaming elixir and told that breakfast chores are not my business today. Someone's moved the SCUD to deeper water—my job certainly, but I'm mighty glad they've done it, river goin' down. Means I have to seriously watch where I dock for the night. Must be around twenty thou; stick we put in last night is clear out of water.

I have a moment now to reflect and make discoveries of my young crew. Donna is a passive nature lover. Sights, sounds, visions leave their impression, but beyond that, she forces herself into competition with nature without letting these impressions sink in to give her a more poignant meaning. She loves the canyon and expresses love for it, yet as much as she climbs, skis, hikes, and enjoys other outdoor pursuits, her participation seems more driven than desired. Bits and pieces strike her, giving pause; fitting the pieces together escapes her. Donna could never look as though she'd lived an outdoor life. Her body—Rubenesque, with small waist, large hips and thighs— though not clumsy, is too heavy to be lithe. What strength she has lies below the waist.

Dale is also appreciative of the beauty around him. He absorbs it mentally; will have an appreciation of Glen Canyon and its imprint on his memory far longer than Donna. I watch his eyes as they move up the walls and into the side canyons, over the water, and along the banks of the river; watch his concentration as he puts the meaning of it together. There's also a longing in that gaze for something more physical than he can afford. Dale might remind you of a bookish kid you knew in school—slight, non-athletic, delicate of bone that supports little muscle—and though he'd like very much to embrace his surroundings more physically, hasn't the strength for it. Fascinated he is, but tires too easily to cope with nature and the wild.

After a fat breakfast of Slim's biscuits and gravy, we bolt the Clinton on the SCUD and depart with five headless nails the guys have fashioned to serve as shear-pins. My free packet's been fed to drift-wood already; can't turn this tub quickly enough to miss it. Three miles down, the motor quits. Dale gets it going and it poops again—starter won't pull. Holy fuck-bombs! Am I some kind of jinx? Slim and Leo to the rescue once more, when we stop at Bullfrog for fresh water. First time in my river career I can't take my traditional swim through the only tossed-up water in Glen Canyon that resembles a rapid and not a *riffle* this year. God knows what would happen to blubber and bodies if I did.

Lost Eden Canyon. The name churns my gut. The whole Glen will be a Lost Eden in a couple more years. This three-forked canyon has history untold, both ancient and modern. People I know have been married here; two ravens have raised families here; around the first bend beneath a fifty-foot alcove partially surrounded by cattails and maidenhair fern lies a deep emerald pool that stops most passage; those few who know the way around and above this beau-tiful obstacle might find a perfectly formed dolphin shaped by water's hands lying in the sandstone, flipper curved and mouth agape. Once I chimneyed halfway up the pool's inflow, feeling as though I was clasped between Mother Nature's thighs—a woman in a womb. To the Anasazi the middle fork was home, where now little green turtles play; canyon wrens, lizards, and singing toads per-form; a huge sand dune leaps a cliff wall of the south fork to whis-per, moan, and dance its way across Iron Top Mesa or the Water Pocket Fold. And up on the cap where large wind- and water-shaped iguanas stare across the mesa, the sandstone hums, or drones like faraway bagpipes. All the history, all the mystery, all the magic soon to disappear.

Dale is so infernally slow that Slim, Leo, and I decide to explore the south fork where we don't have to wait every few yards for my greenies to catch up; anyhow, I'm sure they can use a day without my comments or suggestions, as well as space to appreciate it in their own way. But it's late afternoon when they come out of Eden Lost and we must scoot nine miles to camp on Gretchen Bar. The canoeists go ahead to set up camp while I and my faithful crew wrestle *Twenty-fourtubes* over the Kayenta shelves at Lake Canyon and away from sandbars. I have them up front on the snoots now, with long sticks shoving aside drift to save shear-pins and keep from dinging a prop. No use. At dusk a pin goes. While replacing it, the other nails slide into the river. Norwest clouds move in with a forty-mile upstream wind—it begins to rain.

Forget it. You don't want to know any more about this day—or night.

Journal Entry: September 18, Camp, Mile 76.5, Hidden Passage Bar

Two nights have passed with intermittent flashes of wind and rain from a storm farther up north, but the days have been sunny for wonderful hikes with good friends and plenty of help with our temperamental motors. They've been fixed as best can be with parts of old mining machinery from Gretchen Bar, bacon grease instead of lubricating oil for packing the gearbox, and a new batch of cutoff nails to shear; and *Twentyfourtubes* have quit puffing and unpuffing, probably because of cooler weather. But I didn't sleep too well last night. Here at Rincon is as far as Slim and Leo go—from now on I'm on my own with little help. I hope we have *some* fun, that I don't get too weary and the tub doesn't drive me barmy before the end. Right now I'd like to stab every section with a dagger and dump it—a log raft would be ten times better!

River's on the rise again, probably back to thirty thousand; storm up north must be a good one, just hope it stays put—up north. Here there is only light cloud cover. I don't know why we've named my motor Annabel; she'll be doing the pushing this morning. They pack us up, bid good luck, shove the SCUD into the maw, and wave us out of sight. My eyes spill tears as we disappear around the bend.

Just below the Rincon is the longest straight stretch in Glen Canyon—almost four miles. Walls of maroon Wingate sandstone corridor the river with sharp-edged slabs that stand vertically, one against the other, all draped in a metallic blue patina. Mean-looking stuff, hard to hike around when it chunks off. On the right bank is a series of canyons, hanging with mouths agape, fifty to seventy feet above the water. These random slices (through what looks to be solid iron) have always left me wanting to find a way into them, knowing full well they must hide secrets unfathomable. Today being no different, I do the usual: move way left so I can see farther into those tempting mouths. Standing on the deck, steering Annabel with my foot, I look up at each temptation as we pass. In one I see the tops of trees; in another, bowls and dropoffs; smooth rounded domes of Navajo sandstone appear high on the rim behind a third.

"*Look!*" screams Donna, pointing downstream. "*Holy moly!*" croaks an awestruck Dale.

I jerk around to see, from the mouth of a hanging canyon one hundred feet ahead of us, an eruption of red mud, sand, rocks, and limbs that shoots halfway across the river. Trying frantically to steer into brush on the left bank and stop, I holler at the kids: be ready to jump out, hold and tie to *anything*. But of course the SCUD doesn't want to do that and we keep going with the flow, still somewhat left of center. Now fifty feet from this raging fire hose and feeling the squall it is making, I goose Annabel to pass the maelstrom as quickly as possible. She coughs ... sputters ... dies ...

At that moment a tree trunk six to eight inches in diameter and as long as our raft bursts from the watery volcano, spins through the air, and dives into the river toward us. Emerging at considerable speed, it crosses in front of our bow where we sit, helpless, frozen in shock; then rolls over, noses into the current, and bobbles on downstream. When I can breathe again, I realize if the motor *had* kept going, the log would have bored, dead center, right through *Twentyfourtubes*!

With everybody on the oars we actually manage to get to the bank and tie up. Mesmerized, we spend half an hour watching the raging fountain gradually disappear. It drops a lot more talus on the slope below when it's in high flood carrying debris; next, it moves back off the river onto the slope where it dwindles to an almost clear stream, eating a small channel in what it built up in a rage. By the time we leave, there's a mere trickle over the lip and down the bib. None of the other canyons have shown a trickle; just this raging torrent erupting from a single declivity.

From under the tarp comes old faithful (?) Clinton. A couple of miles and it strips a pin without our hearing, seeing, smelling, or feeling anything to make it happen, and after replacement refuses to start. Annabel again.

And so it goes the whole day. We play (un)musical motors, first one, then the other. Dale takes over half the deck with greasy rags and tools, where he tinkers, adjusts, screws, unscrews, and replaces, the poor guy looking like a real grease monkey with gunk smeared all over his hands, arms, and face. When driftwood takes a blade off Annabel's only prop, rendering her useless for the duration, we don't dump her in the river; we can use her nuts and bolts.

I do manage to pull into Hole-in-the-Rock so we can wash our hair and bods in a sweet clear stream and take a rest from all the ruckus, but there are no canyon hikes today. Both the Escalante and the San Juan are running right smartly, though I can see on the banks that the river had dropped about half a foot.

Late, late afternoon, five miles above camp, Clinton's high-speed jet breaks off. My God, what next?! Without a motor for the rest of this run, I'm way past my rump in rubble. If only this hulk would obey the oars, our trip would be a piece of cake—well, maybe a biscuit. We pull, we push, we strain, we swear, and somehow (with luck) we make camp 'long about dusk on Hidden Passage Bar.

I want my mama!

Journal Entry: September 19, Camp, Mile 70.5, Twilight Bar

OKAY, MR. RIVER, I get it. You figure it's time I learned some lessons; that all is not posies and perfume; that Frank had good reason for not wanting to camp and cook after dark; that you would come up and go down whenever you bloody well felt like it; that danger to humans lurks around every bend of your deceptively innocent beauty; that the *slightest* inattention, let alone bravado, will have us swimming; that we'd better have more survival tricks than you have countersurvival ones; that rowing once in a while is nothing like rowing *all day*; that you can, and will, unsecure many tie-ups; that mud is not just to take a bath in; that being a guide, and therefore responsible, is unlike being the happy passenger who only goes to collect firewood. And that when you're feeling free, wild, and mean, it's best to wait out your tantrum for safer passage. If we don't *have* that much time, tough shit, not your fault. But we are hiking today, by damn. I didn't come here just to fight with you.

I have a vivid memory of this son-of-a-bitch scow swinging on the end of its bow rope this morning—no place to tie the stern. We try to load it, shortening the rope every few minutes as the river rises (again!) nearly a foot between breakfast and shoving off.

Camp will be just six miles downstream tonight and the hike will be up above Music Temple, just across this sheet of flowing water. Dale will stay with the transport and spend time working on the Clinton, our last hope for any sort of maneuverability, because getting into my favorite tight-mouthed little canyons on oars will be impossible.

Donna's and my mood change is palpable when we hit the slickrock. She's a good climber, yet neither of us is expert enough for what we attempt. Our elation over separation from the hulk and the river has made us less cautious; on one ascent we come very close to losing it—and ourselves. So-o-o, watchit, sassy-ass! River Gods may not always let you off the hook. At least I've kept an ace—descent by another route—and we have a glorious day in a tree-filled, stream-fed canyon amid sensuous mounds of petrified dunes and potholes, a place few have seen aside from those who made this paradise home a thousand years ago.

Down to SCUD reality, we find that Dale's tinkering on the motor has brought positive results. That's the *good* news. While he was tinkering, however, Rome was burning. Mr. River has decided to suck off another eight inches, leaving the muck-o SCUD-o *embedded*! After trying for an hour to budge Jumbo with no success, we remove everything—even the fucking deck—and still it *will not budge*. We take buckets and throw water around the edges to loosen it; then—with both ladies (?) pulling and Dale at the front end, pushing with all his little might—at last we grunt and foulmouth it into deeper water; at which point we hear *squeak-squall-SPLAT*-"help" from the bow, where Dale loses footing and the nose flops on top of him, swatting him into the goo up to his neck.

I simply cannot handle this!

Laughing hysterically, or crying, I'm not sure, I slide into the gookcumpucky beside him, trying to ask if he's hurt. How thoughtful, how considerate of me. Right now I don't care if he's dead!

No, he's not. Donna and I drag him out from under the toilet seat; we all wash off, put the pregnant pig back together, and as the sun zinks zlowly in ze West, we zigzag zix miles to camp on lovely Twilight Bar.

Fergiddit, Mama, you can't help.

Journal Entry: September 21, Kane Creek, Mile 40.4, the End

SINCE THE NIGHT'S CAMP on beautiful Twilight Bar, things have gone much the same as every day, save that Mr. Clinton has performed his duty without complaint except for shearing his pin now and then. With the river upsy-downsy every day and night, often the blubber rafts (remember there are two of the muthas decked together) will collect a whole campfire of driftwood between their snoots, funneling it right into the motor's whirlygig, no matter how much shoving away my passengers do.

Naturally, they want to walk up to Rainbow Bridge, so when we get about two miles upstream, I do my best to make a landing at the trailhead on Forbidding Bar. My friend Earl happens to be coming upstream from Kane Creek in the *Tsai-Na-ni-ah-go Atin* (Art Green's Rainbow Bridge tourist boat, which sports two 75 hp motors at the rear; the name is Navajo for "Place Where the Bridge Crosses Over"). I hail to him to come and help us in. As he comes alongside, he throws us his stern rope. Dale, up between the bows, grabs it, but before he can tie on or I can get the Clinton into a helpful push ahead, Earl moves forward, and *pop!*—like a champagne cork—Dale hits the drink. He forgot to let go. Luckily he doesn't go under the SCUD, and once again I don't know whether to laugh or cry, so I laugh—we all do. As he floats by in his life jacket, we snag him, fish him out, and try again, but we might as well be treading water; can't even get out of the main current. After nearly pulling our deck off and before the rope breaks, Earl gives up, asking what the hell we're packing to make us so damned heavy. We still don't have a clue.

Aside from an upstream wind later that afternoon so strong it holds the SCUD immobile in the water, the rise of another foot of chocolate 'n' chips river the next day, banging into several walls at side canyon mouths trying to get in, and shearing the *last* pin in Slim's valiant little Clinton five miles above takeout, there are no more disasters to turn this run into a tragedy. Pitting my luck and our combined strength—what's left of it—against the river's chicanery, we slam the SCUD's noses up onto the slickrock at Kane Creek, leap out, and tie up before it can back its tail into the eddy, hauling us all with it. I'm grateful nobody's here to see this ungraceful landing. After all, I am a performer, have a reputation of sorts, and like to give a good show.

As we begin to unload, my dear river pard Frank arrives to help de-rig. He's so happy to see us alive he doesn't even ask how we fared. I tell him soon enough. When all is unlashed and removed, I'm thinking: if these excuses for something that floats hadn't been loaned to me by a friend, I'd gladly take a knife and plunge it into each blubbery balloon. But in lieu of such rashness, we patiently unwrap and let blow each one of its twenty-four little peckers. Then Frank attempts to haul the first one farther up on the slickrock so we can roll it up and wrestle it into his truck.

The *thang* will not budge.

He emits a low whistle, rolls the nose to one side, looks underneath, whistles again, and stares at me in amazement. "Ye gods, girl. It's a wonder you're here at all!"

Perplexed, we help him lift and fold back the nose enough to gawk beneath and see *the entire bottom packed solid with four to six inches of river silt*—probably more at the rear—adding more than five hundred pounds to our load! This poor thing was formerly an ocean-going life raft with a false bottom for buoyancy, letting in seawater through twelve holes the size of saucers. Needless to say, it worked in reverse on a great muddy river during flood stage. No wonder I couldn't dodge anything, and all those walls *hit me*; no wonder our little outboards were trashed; no wonder Earl couldn't budge us with *two* 75 hp motors. It would have taken a derrick to move Jumbo-the-Elephant!

"We can't get these in the truck, Frank. No way."

"No."

"Can't leave them here."

"Nope." He walks around, rubbing his chin and kicking them.

I know what he's thinking—so am I. "But ... ah ... mm, what'll Buck say when we ...?"

"I'll explain it to him," offers Frank. "I'm sure he'll understand."

So what do we do? All four of us heave, shove, push, grunt, swear (me), and wiggle them off the sandstone—*into the river*. With sadistic glee I watch them snorkel into the current, bob a few yards, then *drown!* Without us in them. Then and only then do I rehearse my conversation to come.

"Hi, Buck. Sorry about the SCU—uh, the rafts. Nothing else we could do, really. Even if they nearly killed us, I'd like to offer to pay you for them."

"Ah, you don't have to do that. Frank explained what happened. It's okay. They didn't cost a whole lot."

"Well, I still wanna pay you. Like to honor my debts."

"No, really."

"Yup. I'm gonna send you some money. I figure they're worth—uhh, lemme see—two cents apiece. I'm sending it right away. 'Bye."

The Ride

IT WAS THE HOTTEST DAY of the year when I decided to do it.

Sure as hell, it wasn't anything planned in advance. Intuition works best in a case like this. I remember dreaming up something similar a year or so back and threatening that I would do it someday, but the notion didn't even get out of bed with me that morning. I was still deep into the sorrow of loss.

He was such a wonderful friend, such a joyful man, full of life and living it, of love and giving it. He could torch you with his sense of humor, fire your laughter until you peed your pants to put it out. An artist, a sensualist, and, I suspect, a creative lover as well. Gentle. A listener. A man who treated women the way he handled his sculptures—molding, caressing, teasing them into creatures of beauty and supple grace until they glowed with a life they didn't know they possessed. I watched that happen with more than one of his many women friends—women he'd never made love to, women he saw every day in his shop, in the shop next door, all around town, really. Everyone knew him. It's a small town, fewer than five hundred of us.

Then, about three years after his move from the Big Rotten Apple to this little burg that he so loved, tiptoeing quietly toward another peak in his creative talent—not with money in mind this time, only love—and with all the freedom to do whatever he chose whenever he wanted and with whomever, his generous heart betrayed him. Harvey up and died.

And the heat moved in.

We held a memorial for him in the park. A big one. Everybody came and brought food, drink, and things to say and remember about him. Our town is still one that lets its folks express their grief

185

in their own way, lay it out, and mix it up so it doesn't hurt so much. No preachers. Just all of us talking about him, telling stories of our time with him, things he said, things he did, what he meant to us. Harvey's spirit was right there that day, moving among us, telling us to get on with it, laughing at us, caressing us. And we all knew it. For me it was really tough because I had to sing his favorite song. I ain't no Judy Garland, I can't sob and sing at the same time, and I was holding tight to a big aching bubble as I tried to get the words out. Then I felt Harvey pat me on the bum, right in the middle, right in the hardest part—hardest part of the song, not my bum—and through my tears I almost ended up laughing, which is no better than crying when you're trying to sing.

Then the heat bore down.

THE FIRST YEAR HE WAS HERE, he was my next-door neighbor. I won't forget the day he first walked down the street in front of my gate with a couple of his friends. I was out watering the nematodes that like to make my carrots into funny little men with penises and hair all over them, when he stopped laughing at whatever his friends had said, turned his flax-blue, slightly bulging eyes on me, and supposed: "Ooooh! You must be the lovin' lady, the lady I'm going to live next door to?" ("Lovin'" as opposed to "lovely," I noted right away, and he knew that I noted, which is what blew me away.)

Harvey had class!

I am a lovin' lady, though I try hard to disguise it, which is why a lotta people don't call me a lady. I could care less. (I've always maintained to those who believe in such messy physics moonshine that being a Scorpio, right there on the cusp of Libra, the balance of the scales keeps me from being a total bitch.) Gimme a break. Harvey did.

He sure enough rented the house next door. Every morning from his back deck when I came out with my cup of coffee, he'd wing his sweet morning greeting across my yard, "How-dee-doo, MizKittyLu. You feeling fine today?" He never started working until after 9:00 because his electric sanders and shapers and drills would make too much noise. (A caring man among his other talents—like he loved music:

jazz, folk, Cuban, but he played it benignly, not at two thousand deci-
bels like some twits in our built-like-a-Greek-auditorium town do.)

By the time I returned from my morning ride, I'd find him nearly
smothered in clouds of alabaster and marble dust, tooling away at
some beautiful sculpture he was creating. He'd ask me to come over
and check it out, see if it looked all right. Wow! He sure didn't need
my two bits; his pieces were always elegant. Never mind that it was
a medium he'd never worked in before. His imagination was limitless, his gift divine.

Then he bought a broken-down little house up the mountain a
ways with an outbuilding he could make into a studio, and began its
renovation like a doting father building a dollhouse for his beloved
daughter. I don't think a nail or a board went into that place without
his kiss or his blessing on it—that it be happy there, happy like he
was, and "thank you very much for being such a beautiful piece of
wood and for coming from such a fine tree in such a lovely forest."

"But where, Harvey?"

"I don't know, but it's a fine tree. Just look at that lovely, graceful, and oooh … sensuous grain!"

Key word. Harvey was indeed a sensualist.

He had an open Jeep, a little runt of a thing it seemed for a guy as
big-boned and tall as he was. Drove it with his girlfriend through
rain or shine, snow or hail, through forest and desert. In summertime, all over the back roads, windshield down, canvas off, toodling
up and down the mountains in his hirsute and shorts, his ponytail
straight out in the slipstream. In winter it was khakis, jacket, and
headband, maybe with the top up, maybe not. Rarely did I see the
side-curtains except on the floor of his studio.

About a week before he flipped his coin for the other side, I
stopped by his shop with some friends to show them the lovely
things he made. I often did that, especially after he'd grown a new
wig-bubble and made something that nobody even dreamed about.
It was ladders this time. Crazy ladders, like some that might have
come from a ceremonial kiva back a thousand years ago, except that
they were so beautifully and imaginatively carved, they'd have to
have been used only by shamans for special initiation purposes:

twining snakes and lizards slithering up the rails and whole Pueblo villages on the rungs that you stepped between as you went up from desert floor to mountains near the top. They were transcendental.

His blue bulbs seemed to be dancing to extra-potent jazz that day. He pulled me into a corner and whispered, "Just got back from the Apple, baby, and I dropped a shitload of problems back there that I won't ever have to deal with anymore. I'm never going back. Wow, do I feel great!"

I was so happy for him, knowing how he hated going to New York for anything, except to show his rarefied Arizona girlfriend something she never need worry about missing.

⁂

AFTER THE MEMORIAL, the heat became grotesque.

Nothing short of our Main Street knee-deep in rattlesnakes will keep the damn tourists out of here, but the weather that week was proving to be a deterrent of the same magnitude. Shopkeepers were kvetching and moaning "no business." Never mind that most of them came here as artists or flower children to enjoy life, grow a little pot on the back deck, and just incidentally make enough to pay the bills—before they opted for a Chamber of Commerce, after which violation, as Ed Abbey said, you can kiss your town good-bye. Friends were snapping at each other like looney birds in a tank of toxins and the humidity was a wet down comforter under a 110-degree heating pad. Even at 8:00 in the morning, pulling on my Lycra shorts and top was a sticky chore.

That's when I decided to do it.

⁂

I RIDE MY BICYCLE up the mountain about three miles from the house five days a week, before the traffic becomes repulsive, if possible. I've been doing it for almost thirty years, so people are used to it and pay me no mind. (Had the first mountain bike in town—1980 I think, when I was sixty years old—and took all the outlying cowpaths with the same sort of joy and devil-may-care as Harvey did with his Jeep fifteen years later.)

That morning was no different with regard to the joie de vivre. I always love the ride because of the canyon, once I get above town. The rocks are so beautifully cruel; deep maroon, red, and orange and pale sheeny green in ragged pinnacles and spires, spit from the pit of the earth into great ridges and crevasses that time can't seem to smooth over. The smell of juniper and mountain earth is heady under early morning sun before cars and motorcycles take over the highway with their noxious fumes, and there's a sometime-creek rippling below the winding road where canyon wrens sing their sweet song down the scale. All this adds up to perfection, or as close as you can get to it—on a paved road.

It's my meditation time, too, that ride. I sort out everything for the day, the week, sometimes the month. It's where I learn the lyrics to new songs—up, on up, to a rhythm of the pedals' turning—where I find inspiration for a story, a show, a letter, or a melody. And the reward! All downhill at twenty-five to thirty miles per hour, cooling the sweat, blowing through my helmet, down my back and neck, even through my shoes. Ya-hooooo!

So ... 8:00. I got on my Trek and pedaled up through town. Didn't stop at the P.O. for my mail, it wasn't in yet; besides which, I was looking very hard for special little nooks and hidey-holes that could assist me on the way back down. My heart was beating a bit faster than usual, the adrenaline of anticipation already started.

I must not have been paying close attention to everything like I usually do, because the beep from behind startled me. After thirty years I can hear cars coming both ways before they get anywhere near me—it's an acoustic mountain—I can identify locals from tourists and tune in the driving "mood of the day." There is one, you know—fast or slow, frantic or relaxed—it infects the whole road like a virus. That day it was relaxed, nobody on the road but me. The beeper wasn't a local—locals don't beep—so I looked in my bike mirror and saw ...

Harvey's Jeep!

I'd been thinking about him so hard, my sadness turning to giggles as I rode, picturing what a hoot he would get out of this caper, that for a second I just accepted it. When I remembered he was gone,

I nearly fell off my bike. But it wasn't his Jeep, just some slow-driving, far more than ordinarily polite dude trying not to run over me. I got to my rock under the tree, ducked in, sat down, and poured half the water bottle over my head. Cooling down, I rested there in the shade for about fifteen minutes. Even so, my heartbeat was much faster then usual.

So ... 9:15. I had chosen my spot on the way up.

As I zoomed down the mountain and through the upper residential section to the turnoff that goes to the open pit, I was so exhilarated, so hyperventilated, that the wind made me shiver. No one in front of me—good. No one behind—even better. Very few cars on Main Street (the only level spot in town), and I didn't see anyone walking the street.

I darted in behind Robby's antique oar truck, yanked off my Lycra, everything but helmet-socks-shoes, mounted the Trek buck-ass, and pedaled furiously through the center of town, past the P.O., past the shops, the bars, Town Hall, police office ... Oh-oh! Never had I seen our town marshal (as he liked to be called) out in front of the cop shop, but there he was, in a blur, talking with someone beside him. He looked up, automatically began a wave ...

"Hel-l-o-oh, (double take) Ka-t-i-e-eeee?!"

I was gone!

Faster then, working the brakes, no more level ground. As I passed Harvey's empty shop, I looked up and cried out "Harvey, this is for you, Harvey. Bye-bye!"

The last half mile to my front gate, I was laughing so hard I could hardly steer and hoping to hell no one would pull out in front of me, when up came Wally, one of our town crew, in the frontloader. You got this? These are no-passing, two-lane roads, barely, and behind him was a whole string of tourists, ten or more cars long, chugging along at three miles an hour.

Hoo-eee! What an opportunity!

"Olé!" I yelled, as I sailed by. "Welcome to _____!" (You can't have the name, you won't like it here.)

In my mirror I saw arms flapping out windows, and a couple got out and stared downhill, not at all sure of what they'd just seen.

My uproarious laughter had turned to streaming tears and coughing by the time I hooked a U-ey in front of my gate, hauled in, decked the bike, and headed for the shower, where I sat down under the spray and howled.

Still wired and laughing, my tummy sore from it, I dressed, got in the car, and drove uptown. I knocked on the police chief's door, walked in, and said, "You wanna arrest me, Ray?"

He just looked at me, shook his head, and sucked in the corners of his mouth to keep from laughing. "I thought about that," he said, "but what exactly would I do?"

"Yeah, that could pose a problem," I answered, picturing him chasing me down with the cop car, getting out, yanking me off the bike, steering me onto the seat, nude-o, and driving me up to the office.

"Phones are ringing like crazy" (so was his). "You certainly gave the town something to talk about."

"That was the object of the exercise, Ray. Everybody's so damn glum they need something to distract them; besides, hardly anybody saw me. There weren't more than three or four people on the street."

"Enough. I took a census and asked them, 'Well, is anyone deeply offended?' Only the retarded son of one of our emporium owners raised his hand and said, 'I am,' so I told him to go chase you down the hill and tell you so."

His phone was still ringing. Ray ignored it. "You going to make this an annual event?" he queried.

"Absolutely not. I like to quit when I'm ahead. Meanwhile, I'm going to enjoy what all the hardnoses have to say—the old farts who need their blood stirred up. As for my friends, they'll just laugh their butts off."

There was, as expected, quite a reaction: notes, phone calls, and letters—only one anonymous, which wasn't really bad. The next day, tacked up on the post office bulletin board, appeared an ode to me and my stunt, and folks were smiling again.

The town had lightened up and I had purged the heavy loss of our dear Harvey.

Before the weekend, it rained and cooled the town down right smart. I ran into friend Mod-Bob at the P.O. and stopped to chat.

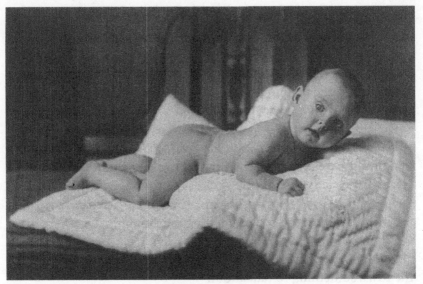

Young Katie

Underplaying it, he eyed me sideways from beneath his brows and sneaky-like, whispered, "I saw ya."

"Oh, yeah? I didn't see you. Where were you?"

"Sittin' on the bench ... in front ... out there ... by the Nellie Bly. Hollered, but you weren't lookin'."

"Nope," I laughed, "I was in kind of a hurry."

"Uhhh ... ya think anybody got any photos?"

"Gawd, I sure hope not!"

"Yeah ... uhh ... right." Then he looked at me straight on, eyes dancing, his face nearly fractured by his smile, and said, "B'cause I thought you had your backpack on backwards."

The nerve of that boy!

The Cottonwood Leaf

IT WAS HOTTER'N A FRESH FUCKED FOX in a forest fire! Which is hot, you must agree, even if you're not a fox. Adding to the heat was a mega-bunch of flares licking up forests all over California, Wyoming, and the Four Corner states.

In a bunch of big Bolognese—garbage scows, we used to call them—we rafted down a river in one of those corners, trying to keep cool. Maybe if we'd been in Alaska it would have worked, but the sand burned our feet if we dared take off our Tevas; the mud, which ordinarily I adore, was slippery with green algae goo; the river was as slow (but not nearly as muddy) as a campaign speech; there were *way* too many people; it was July; and I was on a *commercial outfitter's trip!*

All of the above, I swore thirty-five years ago, I'd have nothing to do with. So why am I bitchin'? Because bitchin' is my thing. I'm happier that way, really bitchin' at myself for doing something I know better than to do. I know better than to go hiking in the Grand Canyon in August (down the Eminence Break), know better than to hike the slickrock in snow or mid-July (in the Dirty Devil drainage), know better than to camp on a clean, inviting island with a river on the rise (in the Once & Future Glen Canyon), know better because I've done all those dorky things, and won't do them again, right?

Wrong.

I have an excuse. Well, a half-assed one. There are few things I love as much as a river. Let's just say my dear friend, Scott, is one of them. I love and admire him so much that I'll do whatever he asks of me. It's a half-assed excuse because at least a week before the trip, he gave me an out, said he didn't want me to go if I didn't feel up to it. Furthermore, I knew it was a reunion with his extended family, and extended families talk to one another—constantly, if they haven't seen each other for a long spell. He didn't ask, but I knew he wanted me to bring my guitar and sing about the river for them. I'm sure his purpose was to show them the grandeur of our canyons and great southwestern rivers, to put them in tune with the land he loved and give them an understanding of why he chose to live here. Maybe it was necessary for Scott to prove something. Hell, I dunno. I just thank the River Gods I don't have an extended family, unless you call my son Ron extended.

Then, to add insult to injury, the commercial outfitter put another ten souls on the same voyage.

Holy shit! As if they couldn't have taken them on *another* run. If that's what commercial river running is all about, it sucks. Scott hadn't expected that at all. He was sure he had a full load for the outfitters: eighteen including me and my paramour, more than a damn 'nuff to haul down a river! Add ten other folks from Chicago, New York, and points elsewhere, and you have (including five boatmen) thirty-three humans. A Georgie White Special.

Whether or not I needed verification for all the reasons I've quit running rivers since the mid-eighties, when I knew for sure my good times had ended, I got them all on this run. Fair enough. I know how blessed I've been. The last time I ran this stretch of spectacular scenery, I was alone in my Sportyak (boat—rigid, with *oars*, not paddles), rowing my way through rapids long gone at this present stage of water; hooting and screaming and laughing in the rain; trembling at the height of the waves, the rocks, the current; and pulling like hell away from the undercuts to keep from drowning. Fifteen of us in our own boats. Nobody had to worry about a spot to flop, lie down, sit up, cool off, piss, or shit in the woods.

Now, a decade and a half later, I'm feeling sorry enough for myself, swelling up like a poisoned pig in the heat, but twice as sorry for the boatmen. They work their butts off. After rowing most of the day on slow water against the inevitable upstream wind—not a single complaint, mind you—they pretend they aren't pooped, whistle and sing, and serve up fine meals. Thirty-three mouths is a lot to feed three times a day, especially on a river where everything has to be loaded and unloaded, located and distributed, set up, cooked, and served. Yet, if and when I pulled out the guitar to sing around no campfire they were there to listen—everyone else, except Scott and two or three others, was long gone, asleep or disinterested. You got that? *No* campfire. A river trip without a campfire is like a forest with no trees. Even when campfires went from real (free driftwood everywhere) to pseudo (bring your own and stick it on a garbage can lid), they still lit up the night. Bond fires, they are—pulling us toward each other and the light.

So the day went: eat, sit, yak-yak-yak, jump in the river, sit, eat, yak-yak-yak, jump in the river, sit, eat, yak-yak-yak, go to bed. The outfitters supplied five rubber duckies to play in, so we traded them off, ran some of the fluffy water, and stayed wet awhile. Then back in the scows, dry off quickly, jump in the river, sit, eat, etc. R&R no longer stands for "rest and relaxation"; it stands for "rules and regulations." How not to "feel" a river is rule number one: Live in a harness all day long. On the rafts, in the duckies, swimming, fast water, slow water, no water, you gotta wear a goddam life jacket. Try swimming in one. Once upon a time we wore the things when common sense told us to. For swimmers, feeling the river's moods and currents, its eddies, tug and flow, is the real joy of being there. Wearing a life jacket is like making love with a condom, and "freedom" is a word no longer synonymous with rivers. I need a tattoo or a permanent river tag attached that reads: "If I drown on this river because I refuse to wear a life jacket, it's *my fault*. Any asshole who tries to interfere, or thinks he will be sued for my freedom of expression (to die or not to die), *will be shot*."

I had a good bunch of time to think while moving about the world's most ungainly waterhorse trying to shut out the people noise, hear the river-song, and find a comfortable place to sit, lie, stand—there isn't one—and I wondered what entices people to go on river trips these days, since they're nothing like they used to be—neither the people nor the rivers. I knew why this trip had materialized, but what about millions of others? The greatest inducement has to come from hype: Chambers of Commerce, magazines, TV, road advertising, the Net. We now have my old friend Ed Abbey's Industrial Tourism on full boil.

But hype has nothing to do with the river itself.

I looked around. There weren't ten people, outside the boatmen, who knew any more about the river they were being carried on than they did about who laid the asphalt on the highway. Didn't know where it came from, where it was going, what fed it, what lived off it; what other uses it had besides floating us; whether it was drained, diverted, or dammed, and if so, by whom. Nor had they bothered to find out. They just went on a trip like they'd go to the beach, to a resort, for a train ride, or to Las Vegas. Any of our boatmen could fill them in; it's part of a tour guide's job, and furthermore, boat guides are damn good storytellers. But I know from my river friends that most of the passengers on the commercial floating condos in Grand Canyon go because "it's the thing to do." They can hunch a shoulder and say, "Been there, done that." Well, they haven't *been there* and won't be until they spend about three months in the canyon. They haven't *done* anything but a roller coaster ride until they find out how quickly the canyon can bring them to their knees and with any luck at all teach them who they really are, even if they don't want to know.

The reason this indifference irritates me so is because I have a very different feeling about rivers. All of them. Everywhere. To me a river is a sacred thing; not because I was born in the West where rivers and other waters are scarce, but because I know how hard it is for rivers to get where they're supposed to go, to overcome the massive meddling by man from their very source, through the long or short journey, to the sea. A free-flowing river is a life-giving, lifesaving artery; a dammed and diverted one is sick and doomed to die, as will everything in and around it.

During the halcyon years, when I was able to run rivers whenever and with whomever I chose (no more than three or four souls), they were places of solitude where the only sounds outside our own were those of Nature's network—pure and intoxicating. Water music, bird music, animal music, wave and wind music. The human voice was always hesitant, on hold, waiting for sounds that were phenomenal and thrilling because we didn't hear them often. Sadly, most folks don't hear them at all for they have never learned the fine art of listening.

Not too long ago, I joined a wilderness travel group to hike the Cordilleras in Chile. If ever there was a place dominated by spirits—a sense of them with every step, every breath one takes—it is there. Mountains! Crags! Ramparts! Granite, rutted from the bottom of the ocean, now sits on the highest peaks dipped in snow. The bare spine of a continent. Rock from the bowels of the earth somehow cleaved up like knives to slice open the sky. Every step on the trails is more than a foot above the other; you take a lot of breaths when you hike the Cordilleras. The very air is awesome in its purity, and I would think it easier to listen to what comes in on that air, foreign to our own dwelling place, than to blow out a sentence about a fucking baseball score just heard on the wristwatch of some twit up ahead. I'd about managed to grasp some of the intangibles that surrounded me, only to be batted from the sphere by a baseball score. (I hate baseball!) I wanted those mighty crags to suck me in and keep me there long enough to feel something about them, and listen to what the Mountain Gods had to say.

It was the same song, second chorus, on this river trip. There weren't thirty seconds from the time the first person rose in the morning until they were all bedded down at night that someone, somewhere, wasn't talking-screaming-hooting-laughing-howling-crying-yipping-squawking-yammering. Four kids could lay claim to at least a quarter of the noise, but the adult contributions were dominated by a single male's midwestern twang that resembled the whine of high-speed tires on wet pavement. It was omnipresent—always in the background, foreground, or echoing off the canyon walls—would vary in pitch, like going up or down hill, but if it stopped for a few seconds I'd looked around to see if there'd been an accident.

The owner of this constant was not stupid. He was a man in his early forties, strong, with handsome features and physique. He moved with an athlete's assurance and grace, was highly competitive in sports ... and conversation. He would argue one relative down, then another, or agree with a third; he'd cajole his daughter, snare his brother, toggle his cousin, tease his sister, and baffle an unwary stranger, going from one to the other in rapid succession with a repartee that hit dead center. The man abhorred a silent second. How could he find that much to say? How could he talk through his nose like that without buzzing it off? Was he in love with the sound of his voice? Was he compulsive? Did he need psychiatric help? It got to be kind of funny. "*Habra haste por los codas!*" they say in Mexico (Even talks with his elbows!). He was truly amusing a lot of the time, and his relatives laughed and sparred with him, seeming to know all about his affliction.

It's midway through the trip and we're at lunch. Nice sandy beach. Hot, as usual, but there's shade under big cottonwood trees. We've shed our harnesses for this brief time on land and are waiting for the boat lads 'n' lasses to prepare lunch. I'm lying under a sweet green canopy, doing the cowboy thing with a cottonwood leaf, and listening to the cicada competition—"our team's louder than your team"—as the choruses pass from tree to tree.

Who ambles up but our man.

At first I don't realize he's talking—his voice has the same timbre and frequency as the cicadas. Then, after several buzzing sentences, I hear, "Do you want to ride with me in the ducky this afternoon?"

Amused by the blend of voice and insect, I answer without thinking, "Sure, Jay. Gonna be a hot afternoon. I'll enjoy getting soaked." Then I think, Egad! That buzzing's going to be in my ear all afternoon!

At that moment I flash on the cottonwood leaf and the genius of an idea forms in my heat-addled brain. I take the stem from my mouth and show it to him, saying, "Bet you can't do this, Jay. It's an old cowboy trick—they do it to pass the time while riding herd, sitting on a corral fence, or just relaxing in their bedrolls watching a sunset."

He studies it, turns it over in his hand. "Stem's tied in a knot," he says. "So what?"

I hand him a fresh leaf. "See if you can do it."

He gives me a skeptical glance. "Just tie it in a knot?"

Doing the cowboy thing with a cottonwood leaf

"With your *tongue*. No hands. No help. No cheating."

When he stops about ten minutes later to eat lunch, he still hasn't tied it, but the only buzzing I've heard since he began the task is from the trees.

A little snooze in the shade. And through my reverie ... kids splashing and squealing down by the boats, a Frisbee game on the beach, cooler and food container lids slamming shut as the boats are loaded ... and somewhere in the background, sure enough, Jay's voice dominating a conversation.

"All aboard!"

While I'm putting my harness back on, I ask Jay if he's mastered the trick yet.

"Almost had it," he says. "Not as easy as it looks."

"Here, try again," I say, and hand him another one.

His captivating smile is big and broad as he takes the leaf, twirls the stem between thumb and forefinger, and asks me, "Is this a subtle way of telling me to shut up?"

"No, Jay, not subtle at all. I'm *sure* you can do it."

He sticks it in the strap of his life jacket. We get into the ducky, and for the next two hours, through riffles, stuck on sandbars, reading water, or easily gliding along, I can barely get a word out of him. Aside from spontaneous yelps and "Whoopee!" in the fast water, he answers in monosyllables if I ask him a question, or lets a conversation die after just a few words, as if his chattering string is broken.

After a while, I begin to feel guilty. I'm about to turn around and say, "You can talk now, Jay," when I remember something his very smart and lovely eight-year-old daughter revealed to me in a discussion about adult behavior.

"Don't you think grown-ups are gross sometimes?" I asked her.

In a small and very innocent voice she answered, "I guess ... some. But mostly they just talk too much."

So. To myself says I: *If it's broke, don't fix it!* And for the rest of the river journey, even the cicadas seem to quiet down.

Frozen Ro-tundra

THERE ARE SOME, I suppose, who don't mind having their derrières exposed to the arctic winds of the frozen North. Those who live there, maybe—they've grown used to it. But being a desert dweller, I'd rather cuddle up to a catclaw bush than have my poopdeck exposed to elements that freeze the stuff as it drops.

This is not the kind of adventure Joey and I envisioned when we decided, one early August, to run the Noatak River in Alaska's Gates of the Arctic National Park, three hundred miles north of the Arctic Circle. Friends had run it before us, shown us photos of a whoop-dee-do wild and beautiful river abundant with fish; its banks decorated with a few grizzlies, arctic fox, elk, moose, and caribou; its acclivities with Dall sheep and bald eagles, to name but a few unusual sights for desert dwellers.

I should have paid more attention.

"Beginnings are a bore," says my friend Bruce Berger. Only now and then, beginnings send a message, usually unclear at the time, but if we had light-year vision we'd be able to see that red flag waving before a torn-out bridge. When a trip begins with the lilting flow of a gentle cataract, we can only hope it will increase in tempo—whatever little blips and stutters clog the serene—and tumble into more and more serendipitous delights as the days pass. But when it begins like a snake trying to swallow a hairbrush, shouldn't we heed the message? Alas, we rarely do—our gears already shifted into *go!*

We were an hour and a half early for the flight from Phoenix to Fairbanks—better early than late—settled into seats, happy and smiling, ready for takeoff. Wrong seats. Moved to correct seats, other side—couldn't see Mts. Hood, St. Helens, and Rainier as I'd planned, but oh my God, I could see the clear-cuts. Mile after hundred miles of chessboards on the snow-covered mountains; cuts so steep that avalanches are prevalent, the tops of mountains completely bare; nowhere a whole range or even part of one left untouched. To my great relief the ground clouded over past Vancouver, blotting out the chess players' wreckage.

Arrive Fairbanks.

Baggage cart machine takes our money, keeps the cart. Phone motel, get a *busy*—no coins return. Second try, no answer—eats more quarters. Third try, got 'em! Motel sends car for us. Settle into room. Wrong room. Wait half an hour for clerk to decide which room and then drag our gear from 114 to 107.

It is nearly 5 in the afternoon and we are jet-lagged for a snooze before dinner. No way. Planes rev, zoom, land, take off. Kids yell. Parrots screech. Wait a minute. What are parrots doing in the Arctic? My observation deck was kinda fogged over from the flight when we checked in. Then I remember there were seed hulls all over the floor by the registration desk and some things with feathers pooping in cages. Ah-ha, they were his! How very thoughtful of an innkeeper to own wake-up birds. After an hour of toss and turn, we give up and ask for the courtesy car to take us to dinner. Here we sit outside on the deck to enjoy a couple of drinks, serenaded by the melodious snarl of Jet Skis racing up and down the Chena River.

If our instincts were sharper than our mental derailment of them, we would stop, look, listen, reset the goal and our mental picture of the trip we're about to make, backpedal, flip a coin, pick something else. God knows there is plenty to see, do, hear, discover, and become enchanted with in Alaska, a land we know relatively little of. (I was here once before, but didn't have the opportunity to shave as much as a whisker off its fascinating face. And, as I was to discover, neither have half of those who live in Alaska's cities, where they stay, just as we do in ours down yonder.) I even have friends we don't bother to look up, who would point us toward a dozen treks even better than the one we've set out for. But the red flag simply quits waving on the torn-out bridge to new adventure.

After our deafening dinner, we go back to the motel and actually sleep from 11 P.M. — in spite of the racket from heaven and earth — until we get "the bird" at 7 A.M. next morning.

⚜

OUR QUARTERS LOOK as if a bomb has struck. Clothes are strewn, flung, draped, balled up, or hanging from every protrusion in the room—a few from splinters in the rough wood—as we try to separate our gear for the river from what we will leave here for the remainder of our trip. (Little do I know that what we leave will find its way to a hidden place in the unknown. We won't even remember where we stashed it.)

Should we take this extra waterproof tarp? The outfitter is supposed to have that kind of thing. Hunch: take it. What about the heavy liner for my sleeping bag? It's 80 degrees out there! We're going wa-y-y north of Fairbanks. Take it. Do we buy those knee-high rubber boots we couldn't get at home for the glacial prices we see here in the store? Absolutely!

For this Noatak run I have enlisted a friend who has rowed rivers from South America to the Arctic. He, in turn, is leasing services and supplies from a company here in Alaska that has outfitted every kind of trek from arctic sledge to glacier skiing. There will be only one other couple joining us—experienced river runners who have spent many of their days canoeing the Boundary Waters on the U.S.-Canadian border. We'll be five souls, have three boats, and plenty of time to go at our own pace.

One P.M. We're to fly from Fairbanks to Bettles, about three hundred miles as ravens go, where we will lodge for the night, then bush-fly to the Noatak River tomorrow. F-f-frontier F-f-flight S-s-service. Very casual, these folks. We wait an hour for the plane. Our pilot doesn't like it—magnetos not doing their job, or whatever. Return from runway to hangar and take another plane. This gives us a moment's pause, but once in the air the view becomes so magical that the "moment" is left at the airport, forgotten.

Ahead are cumulus piled on cumulus, with cirrostratus bisecting their billows; a bolt of low sunlight flaming the southern end where some wisps have broken away to float down and join the land. On the ground are tangled, multilayered brush and trees of the absolute wild; a silver river winding through like a skein of witch's hair, braided, knotted, let loose to flow over a shoulder, down a back, over a rump. A slight shudder passes through me, looking down on that dark green pelt of wild earth. It puts me in mind of a friend who left the frantic forty-eight in the late seventies to come here and build herself a home.

How in Christ's name did she do it?

For starters, she strapped eighty pounds on her back, carried a 12-gauge shotgun that wasn't exactly light, and walked, waded, stomped, and slithered some ten swampy miles from the nearest village through the kind of impenetrable stuff I see below me, to find the site for her house, mark off and stake it, return, and file for ownership. Sort of like a mining claim, not a homestead. She knew where she wanted to be, but she needed the foot trail—actually a moose, wolf, deer, and bear trail—for the many times she would be hoofing it in winter when the grizzlies were snoozing. She chose a spot a quarter mile uphill from a river that would serve to transport material for building the house in the summer. Came winter, she hauled everything in on a little red sled behind snowshoes or skis. Joanna is one tough lady. As for the gun, she told me she never had to use it on a bear she didn't mean to kill (for food) for the fourteen years she lived there before moving back to semi-civilization. Once only, when she wasn't there, a black bear broke into her house and entertained himself to the max.

From Fairbanks to Bettles takes about an hour and a half in this little four-passenger job; winging northwest; crossing and recrossing the Tanana and Yukon Rivers, the Tatalina and Chatanika, plus a hundred streams, creeks, and flushes that vein the landscape wherever you see them through the tangle. Bettles is a collection of gas and oil tanks, heavy trucks, husky kennels, cabins, trading post, and airstrip beside the Koyukuk River. Jim, our guide/boatman/cook/gopher/friend, has come to meet us. When we unload our gear, my film can is not in the pile! I swear I saw it go aboard. Before the pilot takes off for his turnaround to Fairbanks, Jim goes through the plane with a packer's practiced eye and finds it stuck behind a port-a-potty. So glad my can lid is down tight.

After we're assigned our cabin, have a snack, check out the trading post, read the sign—BETTLES—Population 8—Lowest Temperature –70°—Highest +92°, take some photos, walk along the river for an hour or so, check out the moose racks on the grounds, talk to the huskies, take some more photos, eat a leisurely dinner, and enjoy a bottle of wine and some river talk with the boatmen, I glance up to check on the big clock in the sky—only to find it at much the same angle as when we got here. Hmmm. I hate watches when I'm going to be outside with the real elements, so I ditch it deep in my luggage for the duration.

Hesitantly I ask, "Jim, uh, what is the time here?"

"Eeee-leven Peee-emm," he says, eyebrows dancing as he smirks. "I didn't say anything because that's how you learn about daylight saving itself all the time up here. When I first came, I didn't go to bed for two days 'cause the sun never went down."

One of the other boatmen cracks, "Makes it easier to see the bears. They can't creep up on ya in the dark 'cause there ain't no dark."

❧

NEXT MORNING, Mark, our bush pilot, tells us: if we agree, he will fly Joey and me to the put-in first with our gear, food, water, tents, and wait there for the arrival of Jim and the other couple who have not yet shown. (Seems someone forgot to change their reservations to F-f-frontier F-f-flight S-s-service.)

Still blindsided by beauty and the imminence of a spectacular wilderness river trip, I don't ask what happens if we don't agree, and after nodding our assent, he hands each of us a can of Bear Repellent. Damn me if it doesn't say that on the can. Click. In my talks with Doug Peacock, I seem to remember, either this shit doesn't work or if it does, it has a reverse action. Then I figure, what the hell? I'd rather be eaten by a bear than chewed up in a traffic accident. Mark assures us we'll only be there two or three hours before Jim and the other couple join us.

At this point I look up to see clouds rolling over the Brooks Range where we're headed. Clouds of incredible variety: vicious, smoky, tumbled, and streaked with sun; the whole range cut down to size by their immensity. In retrospect, I understand what happens to the human mind in places as grand and glorious as this. Our instinct and intuition, along with our common sense, go dormant beside all the grandeur and newness, allowing us to see, without asking what it all might mean.

Here the sun is brightly shining.

As we turn toward the airstrip, Mark shakes his head. "No, no. This way. Plane's out on the river."

"In the river!"

"*On* the river. We're using a floatplane. You know, pontoons instead of wheels. We land on water." He gives me the "stupid tourist" look and I return a sheepish smile; it's the same look I've given to others at least a million times.

We leave at noon.

The flight is surprisingly smooth in a wee four-seater stuffed with barrels, much gear, and us. Mark dodges most of the cloudy stuff, following a braided river up a valley heading west-northwest. We wing over glacial lakes and backwaters, crossing and recrossing the snaking Continental Divide—wouldn't have had a clue if he hadn't told me; I thought all of Alaska was west of the Divide. Dumb tourist. The plane seems to skid as we round a jagged rock uplift by a horseshoe bend in a river that is swallowing its banks. We sneak between this clouded mountain and that vibrant green, sunlit one, sometimes coming so close I can see hair rise on the backs of Dall sheep. Yet, Mark's skill, his knowledge of this range and a photographic memory of peak-dodging through it, allow us to relax and enjoy the flight.

In less than an hour, we're down alongside the right bank of the Noatak River, skiing on a little tarn, in these parts often called a slough. The earth is tundra now; nothing but knee- to waist-high scrub, mostly matted ground cover and some grasses around the edges of the tarn where we've landed. Up a three-foot bank to higher ground and maybe a hundred yards from the plane is a drop-off into the Noatak. In the distance, on this level span, I see one upside-down canoe, patched here and there with duct tape.

The frozen tundra as seen from the air

"Where are the boats?" I ask. "Surely, that's not ..."

"No, it isn't. I'll bring one on the next trip with Jim and his passengers and another one with the final load." Seeing my questioning frown, he continues, "We strap them to the pontoons. Do it all the time—works really well."

I don't understand why they aren't already here, but since there's no time to waste asking more tourist questions, we unload the plane and in less than fifteen minutes Mark has taxied, skied across the tarn, and is on his way to Bettles, to return, so he said, around 4:00.

As soon as the plane is out of eye- and earshot, it begins to rain.

Joey and I wander over the tundra seeking the best place to put our tent, and find a spot for the kitchen. We can't do a whole lot in the strong wind, intermittent heavy to light rain, nasty low-hanging clouds, teasing blue sky, and occasional sun. Having been told at one of our briefings to walk only on existing trails, animal or otherwise, we try to comply; tundra being a delicate, easily destroyed surface that will not regenerate for years, similar to the sandy/silty microbiotic soil of the Colorado Plateau.

Out of the wind and rain

Two tents get put up and we manage to carry, roll, or drag most of the equipment to the highest spot around. Between spates of heavy rain, we wander over to the bank of the Noatak, looking down ten or twelve feet into its swirls and burbles, wishing we were out of this and on our way downstream where the sun is making a grand display against the northwest end of the Brooks Range. Turning around to retrace my way back to our tent, I halt in midstep and start laughing. Circling one branch of a head-high shrub is the familiar green, upraised fist of an Earth First! sticker: *No compromise in defense of Mother Earth*. Wonder if anyone we know put it there? Anyhow, it gives me the first smile of the forever afternoon.

Back in the tent, we wait … and read … and wait. I can't tell if the sun is going down, around, or under in this depressing weather. All I know is that it never gets really dark. Like the boatman said, easier to see the bears. We don't. Just as I'm about to have real doubts about life in the frozen North, about 6:30—yes, I've taken to my watch again, it's the only way I can even tell what day it is—Mark finally arrives with Jim and the other couple, but no canoe, because of too much gear.

Sincere rain greets their arrival.

After hurried introductions, we help unload so Mark can return for the last load of food, more Coleman fuel, Ann's vegetarian stash, camp gear, canoes and paddles—none here yet—and more water. Water, water everywhere, which only animals can drink. Ann and Eric, well-seasoned outdoors folks in their sixties, watch the takeoff and disappearance of the plane with a lingering apprehension that prompts me to ask if their trip from Bettles was okay.

A mite disgruntled over the screwed-up reservations, to say nothing of the bracing weather, Eric tells us he saw very little between cloud dodging and mountain hopping. Ann agrees that she felt some interesting updrafts and downdrafts, but it rained a good part of the way.

"Yeah, same thing here, it looks like," observes Jim. "Let's get the kitchen set up and the other tents."

The men rig a cook tarp off of Jim's tent onto the longest twigs found anywhere on the tundra so Jim can light the cookstove out of the wind and rain. Meanwhile, I rifle through the gear for a waterproof ground cloth to spread under our tent because it leaks. Is this outfitter really together? When the last load gets here this afternoon? evening? morning? tomorrow? it'll be light enough to fly the whole night—all I want is to get gone, down that river—if they don't forget the paddles. Having kayaked, paddleboated, and rowed, but never canoed, I still can't wait to split this sponge.

It is almost 10 P.M. when we eat. Maybe the sun went behind the mountain, maybe behind a denser cloud, maybe I'm in Russia. To me this looks like a five-day rain, one that's here to stay.

It is. And so are we.

✦✦✦✦✦

I NEVER DO FIND OUT if I can assist paddling a canoe with Joey, Jim, Eric, or Ann. It continues to rain the whole night and most of the next day. We lie in the tent and read, sit under the kitchen tarp, drink coffee or tea, tell stories, and wait for the plane. The wind is relentless, and perhaps two or three times in twelve hours, a tease of sun appears. The plane does not.

We move the tents to higher? drier? ground.

Temperatures continue to go down, the river to come up. It was something like ten feet down the bank when we first viewed it. By the end of day two, it's more like two feet below our feet. Gradually, then with increasing velocity, the Noatak chokes on itself; with nowhere to go but into and out of the tarn, it surrounds us completely. We can no longer get to the mainland. We're on an island that is approximately 900 feet wide by 1,200 feet long, with one duct-taped canoe that we've pronounced un-sea-water-ice-or-snow-worthy and *no paddles*. In a pinch, which seems more than likely, we can use the canoe for meager shelter.

We watch what we use and go easy on the drinking water. Who's thirsty? Just open your mouth. But seriously, there's not enough Coleman fuel to boil what we drink. Ann's special food is a dicey problem; it isn't here yet. I'm a bit less tense than I would be if it weren't for Jim, an expert for knowing how to keep it together, what to ration and what not. With all his experience he's the best person to have a-tundra. We talk a lot about having positive thoughts: Mark will return as soon as he can get through—this weather can only last a few days—there's food enough for a week if we're careful—we can collect rainwater for drinking—everything will turn out all right and we'll be downriver soon. Bless all the gods for these knee-high rubber boots. But after a two-and-a-half day wait, it's hard not to think what *could* have happened if Mark hadn't been able to get here with Jim, more food, water, and gear. It would be just Joey and me alone on this sopping, shrinking island.

We see two planes but they never come near us. Hmmm. (1) They've forgotten we're here. (2) Each pilot thinks the other has come for us. (3) One crashed. (4) Impossible to get here (wrong— another plane went and came back from Lake Matcharak). Jim says that doesn't always mean they can land here. So they don't. We have all been in tricky situations before this, and found that panic takes energy needed for survival. Luckily we're not on some guided tour with a group of novices. By now, a number of them would be well on their way to severe nervous disorder.

Music helps. I sing after dinner, breakfast, lunch, whatever it is, though without my guitar, or great sandstone walls to reflect the voice, the sound gets soaked up in rain and squishy tundra. But it's better than talking, and lyrics take us to another world of hope and dreams, give us something else to ponder, invent, laugh, or wonder about.

If you've never spent 24, 48, 72, 96, 120 hours of daylight in a rising pond on a lily pad, in a wild, unfamiliar place, hoping you won't be left there to rot, you may not understand to what extremes the mind can wander. When you can't read another word, can't move from your tent, don't have a deck of cards, have exhausted all topics pro and con, can't sleep anymore, and are trying desperately to keep your gray matter on positive thought; slowly, like rising dough, wild and nonsensical to utterly ludicrous visions will enter to save your sanity. My wig bubbles were energized when I had to leave our shelter to perform the simple task of dropping scat, and found it to be a big problem. There are no porta-potties out here, no places to hide. This island is flatter than an old maid's chest. Yet, to sneak over the edge into a river drainage that is now about a foot from taking you with it, or to slog into the tarn that is now part of that river, is not an option. Certainly we shouldn't defecate on the precious tundra, since we can't even walk on it unless we follow a trail. So-o-o, lying here in our tent, I begin to have fantasies—even time to psychoanalyze them—and conclude that this particular fantasy is based on envy.

I have always wanted to witness a man piss an arc from some high place, as they are wont to do, and have it freeze. Would it hurt? Anyway, it would be colorful (if we had sun). Even under cloudy skies, it would be more colorful than a squat-dribble-type freeze with no lights to play on the rainbow, so to speak. However, there is no fantasy when it comes to the poopdeck. Here we have pure realism. Oh my! To let down thy drawers in falling sleet and a brisk wind at zero temperature is an experience few can appreciate. One must not let this stuff go into the river, though I don't know why. "Hares do it, mares do it, even copulating bears do it. Let's do it." Never mind. We must do it on that "delicate" tundra, and unless we yank up a hunk of endangered moss to cover our scat tracks, there's no place to hide it on this sopping tundra sponge. A few inches beneath, the earth is frozen solid. We're in permafrost country.

And we pace—pace—pace, up, down, and across our island each time we get out of the tent, when it isn't raining. We'll grow mold if we just lie here and read. Anyhow, we've come perilously close to our last game of musical books. So we slosh around in our rubber boots, which have begun to feel more like rafts, at first trying to keep to existing rills, but after three or more days we give up. What a poor substitute sloshing is for rowing and learning about this fine, now very fat and fast, river and how it carves its way from here. We keep an eye out for bears over on the mainland. They can swim over here even if we can't swim over there, and though we have no way to hang our food, Jim knows how to keep it contained and what to do with any scraps that might attract them. Again we move the tents, squashing low shrubs, in the hope we can elevate them above the swamp.

One evening—I think it is the fourth day—we are treated to a live Wildlife Adventure program.

After dinner it stops drizzling and we all walk down to where our tarn flows back into the Noatak to see if the floodwaters have dropped at all.

Two ducks are floating on the slow-moving water fairly close to the opposite shore, quacking serenely. Then Joey's eagle eye picks up movement on the bank. After a moment we see two arctic foxes hiding in the grasses, creeping low, stalking the swimming ducks. For a few moments, Mr. and Ms. Fox butt down side by side, out of sight of the swimmers, just watching. Then—and you can almost hear this conversation—she says to him: "Plan A, dear. I'll walk along here where they can see me while you circle around in front of them." He glances at the ducks, licks his chops, sneaks through the brush and away. Acting as a decoy, she pussyfoots along the bank while the two ducks, certain of their advantage in the water at least ten feet from shore, wiggle their sassy asses, and keeping a duck eye on her, move ahead slightly faster. The bank bends toward us, but they don't seem to notice. Intent they are, watching Ms. Fox, when *crash!* off the four-foot bank right in front of them sails Mr. Fox with mouth wide open. He hits the water inches from the lead duck, who does what?

Ducks, what else?

Mr. Fox disappears underwater for a few seconds, but has forgotten his snorkel and has to surface almost immediately. Ahh, no dinner tonight, at least not that one. The ducks have flown. So much for teamwork.

We stand on the bank, holding our sides laughing. The only real entertainment we've had for ninety-six hours. Our laughter continues far into whatever-time-it-is as we recount fox tactics, analyze strategies, wander into all sorts of animal behavior, and discuss the nature show from every angle, scientific to anthropomorphic. Heavy on the anthro side, an old folksong pings into my memory, one I learned from a Burl Ives recording back in the late forties. Others remember it too, and so we hum and sing parts of it into the wee small hours that finally drop us into dreamland.

> *Fox went out on a chilly night*
> *Prayed for the moon to give him light*
> *For he'd many a mile to go that night*
> *Before he'd reach the town-o, town-o, town-o*
> *He'd many a mile to go that night*
> *Before he'd reach the town-o*

WHEN I CRAWL FROM THE TENT on the fifth day to take my morning's morning, sometime about 10, my throat is sore, my nose snotty, and what I know will sabotage this adventure is in full bloom. A bronchial infection. Added to this, I see the surrounding hills topped with snow.

About the same time, everyone else is witness to the whiteness. We gather beneath the cook tent, stomping around and drinking coffee. It's not the same as other mornings. For one thing it isn't raining. And something besides atmosphere fills the foggy air. It's our attitude. We aren't taking this anymore. We have got to get the hell off this sinking lily pad *now*, *today*. All brains on deck.

Jim: "Let's go have a look at that canoe. If we stuff rags in the holes, it might give us a few trips to the mainland with some necessary items."
Eric: "No paddles."
Ann: "If the canoe will float us, even taking turns, we can't row with our hands in that icy water, they'll freeze off."
Joey: "We can make a paddle out of something: piece of plastic on a couple of sticks ..."
Me: "I saw a native paddle in Bettles. They take a branch, little over an inch thick, split the end up about a foot, bind it with thong or string to keep it from splitting further, and at the bottom of the split, lace a five-inch twig to keep it spread open. Next, they put three or four consecutively shorter twigs up to the wedge, then weave leafy saplings in and out of the twigs until they have a nearly solid surface."
Eric: "I think it would take a whole day to make one of those, even if we could find the fixings."
Ann: "Joey's idea about a piece of plastic would take care of the woven twigs."
Jim: "The canoe. Let's go look at it."

We turn it over and decide that it might actually float—with a bit of stuffing here and there—slide it across the precious tundra into a foot of water, and push down to see if the bottom, at least, is leakproof. So far, so good. It's about two hundred feet to the mainland, some of it bordered by grasses rising above the water, so we don't actually know if, or where, we might bottom out before getting to the bank.

We go back to the kitchen to mull this over while we eat a very light breakfast of bagels and cream cheese, orange juice, moldy toast and jam, and a little more coffee, because we're near the end of our drinking water and the Coleman fuel is almost gone. Mugs in hand, Jim and Joey search for pieces of plastic that might serve for rowing parts.

Then we hear it.

Between two low mountains capped with a layer of mist, a plane appears. With no formalities of circling—the pilot already knows the direction of the wind or reads it from ripples on the water—the plane drops, beelines for the tarn, and skis in, looking heavier on one side where a canoe rides. I spot this instantly. One canoe, with paddles, not two.

It taxis to our lily pad.

There is a special urgency this time because the plane is over half filled with emergency rations for other drop-offs and pickups Mark has to make. This means only one of us can return with him. Ann and Eric have elected to tough it out, wait for the second canoe, and make the run. I'm the logical returnee with my hacking bronchitis, gear, and lighter weight; but I hope to hell Mark will be able to pick up Joey and get back to Bettles before more bad weather sets in. Fifteen minutes later, we're gone.

Halfway there, we see smoke rising from thick brush on the steep side of a mountain. Moving closer, we spot four people in obvious distress, gesticulating wildly, waving a yellow tarp. Mark circles, sights their position, wiggles the wings, and flies on. (I learn later that they burned one of their sleeping bags to attract attention.)

Midway to Bettles, Mark lands on a lake where more folks are stranded. He leaves some cargo, picks up one person who barely fits, and tells the others he'll be back in two or three hours—or someone else will. Since I've "been there, heard that" already, I can only pray I'll see Joey sometime before midnight ... tonight.

Elsewhere, during the five days and nights we were awash, Mother Nature has really done a number on the land. With the kind of weather that fosters the saying "There are no old bush pilots in Alaska," the Koyukuk has flooded Bettles and taken several cars, plus other trash, along with it. Close to the middle of the river, what I thought was a runaway barge turns out to be a huge oil truck half submerged in the flow. It just squats there at the mercy of a pissed-off river that is slowly burying it.

While I wait apprehensively for Joey, I go to the office of the company that supplied Jim's equipment. There I learn the aim, the rationale, the excuse—whatever you want to call it—for the two canoes that were *not* at the put-in for our trip.

"The Park Service won't let us take the canoes and leave them out there before a trip because it damages the tundra, the ground cover."

"Excuse me? A couple of overturned canoes are going to damage the ground cover?"

I can't believe what I'm hearing. Then I recall the dozens of similar national park and monument, recreation, and Forest Service rules and regulations in my own state, and groan over the actual harm they cause because some deferential superintendent hasn't the balls (or boobs) to move against what is obviously stupid, if not dangerous.

"What in hell do they think five pairs of boots do to that precious tundra in almost a week, walking all over to keep from freezing, to say nothing of the poops, the tarps, the tents, the …?"

"I know," she interrupts. "We've argued that point for over a year, and this isn't the first time we've lost money on the tours." The woman motions with her thumb. "Park's office is over there if you want to express your opinion."

I rave at the guy for an hour and hope his ears are still burning. I also hope that his boss, and the boss above that one, and the next find themselves up some creek in the frozen tundra, far above the Arctic Circle, without a paddle!

Mark arrives with Joey about 10:30 and we toast each other with a warm and potent bedtime beverage.

The clouds move in. Again.

Split Bar

ARGUMENTS ARE FEEBLE this morning after last night's discussion when I told both my companions I wanted them to go on without me. Even as we slid into our bags, agreeing to "sleep on it," I knew, as they did, it was a done deal.

For years—since my exploration of Glen Canyon with close friends—I have yearned to encounter myself *absolutely alone* in the wild. So why haven't I? Maybe the old hiker's mantra has put me off—three for safety, two for caution, one for the foolhardy—even though other canyoneers have urged me to go it alone or I'll never experience a bonded relationship with the land rather than with people.

My friends are ambivalent, both concerned and relieved. I'm in a state of joyous apprehension. Already I've planned to hook an exploratory U-ey during this next week, find other trails and a different way out. If anything goes wrong, if I break an ankle—did that many years ago and it was a bitch; swimming, crawling, swinging on vines, and yelling for help—here I can yell my head off if I fall in a crevasse, get rimmed, or drown in the river, and nobody will know until I don't come out next week. My head tells me, when you set out on such an excursion, adventure, or enlightened journey, you had better accept that it's okay if you die there; a really nice place to die, or it's time to die. Or maybe like Everett Ruess, you're experiencing so much beauty that it's killing you, and you *will* die, dammit, because it can't get better than this!

So here goes Miss Foolhardy!

Preparations for the split—repacking our packs, dividing food-stuffs—have our adrenaline at the bubble. "You'll need this. Take more jam. We don't want the tube of peanut butter. Kool-Aid? I'll take the grape if you guys don't want it. Here's another dinner." I wonder about being able to use the time that is mine alone with no other human interference or conversation, no plan or motivation concerning anything besides myself. J. hands me his paperback, saying, "It's for reading in caves." We laugh a lot, give each other hugs, I heist my thirty-five-pound pack and turn downstream. "Goodbye, have fun." "You too." "Be careful." "I will."

Where the canyon bends, I turn to wave, leaving them beside the river on what we've just named Split Bar.

⚘

THE FIRST THING I NOTICE is, I'm sore from yesterday's overexertion that sleep didn't soothe, and so conscious of being on my entire own, careful not to fall and wet my pack, that for the first time ever I find a staff, a damned hiking stick to use each time I cross a river that's only ankle-deep in most places. Next, I freak myself out remembering last night's bit of bladder irregularity, thinking, I could have a serious infection with no way to treat it. Six, seven days from rescue!

Bullshit. I feel fine and healthy.

The sore muscles begin to iron out, alternating in a fight with charley horses that want to take over and make me lame. This pack is really heavy. I don't remember it pulling back on my shoulders this way. Tighten the hip belt. I notice our foot and boot prints along the banks, but I don't seem to be following them consciously. Should I? Absolutely not. I'll make my own crossings.

Discovery! Coming upstream, crossings differ from those going downstream. I'm down, looking up, I can't see that the river knows more than I do. Now I cut him off at the pass. The sun is full into the canyon and starting to get hot. Why am I wearing all these clothes? On the odd possibility that another soul will enter here? Tough titty! My bare buns will have to be *their* problem. I was here first. My right foot hurts. Oh, I remember, I stabbed it last night on a root hidden in the sand on Split Bar. Is it bleeding? I stop, remove my tennie, and can't even *find* the place that's supposed to hurt. I try for a pee, but can't get anything save a squirt. Something's really squirrelly with my bladder.

Katie hiking solo

Will you stop this crap? You're okay!

Damn! I missed a short side canyon I have marked on the map because I'm so busy worrying about myself. Oh-oh, haven't paid much attention to a river that's been rising (about mid-calf now) since I started walking this morning. Instantly, "Name the Horrors" syndrome takes over: flash flood! boxed canyon! lightning strike! drowned pack! Is this panicky situation going to keep up indefinitely? To feel, listen, soak up the canyon's beauty, and puzzle over its mysteries is the reason I wanted to do this alone. Is my whole solo going to be like this? Surely not. I know the rules. I've hiked thousands of miles in canyons over the years. Years.

Oh, my God, I've gotten older. How could this have happened to me?

The Glen and I embraced twenty years ago, and since then I seem to have slowed down. Well, yes. Now I have more sympathy for my erstwhile companions as I drag-assed behind, feeling weary and sorry for myself. A flush of sadness rushes over me when I think back on the times when each canyon devoured me, pulling me ahead of the others to clamber over obstacles that would reveal whatever the next bend held in secret; everyone else having to wait while I *assaulted* the canyons.

Shoe on other foot.

So … okay … I'm older, but not *that* old. Only fifty-four. As I walk the shore and cross with caution, I suddenly realize how much fun I'm having. I start laughing, then burst into song, listening for an echo that doesn't answer. Finding the river higher taxes my streamside climbing, but I cut through the brush and hug the walls with no effort at all. With that, I hit my stride, start looking at something besides every footfall, start smelling and hearing the canyon's sounds, bringing all the senses together, *en pointe*.

There it is! The song that tingles my spine, pulls me into the rock, takes my hand, and leads me to canyon intimacy. Like the music of a gentle cataract, a series of light waterfalls, a float through sweet-smelling air, comes a freefall of notes from the throat of the happiest, most magical bird in the world. The canyon wren. Its little *pfftt* at the end of the song, which most people miss, often tickles me more than those joyous tumbling notes—like landing on a soft feather pillow at the end of a graceful glissade.

It is early afternoon, water to my knees; the river stones are enjoying a pinball game with my ankles, seeing how many hits they can make in one crossing. Slipping becomes a reality, even if falling down has not yet happened. I am thinking seriously of camping in the alcove we used on the way in, even though it's early. A river on the rise can mean several things, even if there are no clouds in the sky. There's a town many miles above here that uses water like a hydraulic mine; when it quits, the river takes back its own. Since the color hasn't changed much—isn't flood color—I don't think it will rise even halfway up the ten-foot rock ledge to my hollow. At any rate, I'll know in a couple of hours and will move if I have to.

Arriving at the alcove, I go through the mind-changing bit—stay or go—because water has covered my knees this last crossing. Dumping my pack on the level slickrock bench in front of the alcove, I go to check all my surroundings. There's an elephant drinking from the river on the right bank opposite my camp cave—what a neat rock formation—extraordinary company! I set three gauge sticks in the banks; get water to settle and put the purifying pills in; swim and purr in the tiny eddy; sit on the ledge writing notes; study the map I'm thinking of burning but don't have the guts to yet; worry again about the bladder thing; listen to the river burp and give me a tone to judge its rise and fall; talk to a friendly bird; and slowly sink into the sandstone, my friend for all these years.

A drop of rain!

Not a cloud when I snoozed off. How long ago? Sun, a touch above the rocky rim—must be five-ish. (I had a dumb timepiece that tells a piece of time at a time, but I threw it in the river when I caught myself looking at it too often before lunch. Why in hell would I want it here?) Trees are conversing with some gusts of wind, and whatever moisture blew in has come from downstream, not up. Still don't see a cloud. Did a bird whiz on me? A monarch butterfly just wafted by. My elephant friend is feeding off a sandbar in place of where he was drinking a few hours ago; the sticks are high and dry. The river has dropped four inches. I'm staying here.

I make my firepit in the sand, off to the side of my burrow; gather wood, mostly drift—of which there's plenty; pour myself a rum-ade; and sit, feet dangling over the ledge, facing a deep turquoise sky above a five-hundred-foot wall of rusty Navajo. "*Salud, Elephante!* Keep drinking up that river. Make my *mañana* easier." Birds are saying goodnight, toads are rendezvousing, the river croons and whispers, dragonflies couple, and bats careen in the twilight. The cottonwoods give a standing ovation for this extraordinary musical theater.

This *is* unlike other hikes. I can't recall a similar experience of oneness, loneness, almost like abandonment. Even stranded once, far out in the desert with a broken-down car, I knew they would be back for me in a few hours. To say that we are herd animals is to understate. We've lost the joyful art of observation and we misunderstand the healing power of solitude. We calculate too damn much. This lofty brain of ours is going to be our undoing if we don't get back some of our instincts, our intuitive good sense, our wildness.

When I was but a pup, reaching for my teens, my mother would ask me to "go into a trance" when she had to make a tough decision about money or certain moves we should or should not make. She thought I had a sixth sense, a kind of gift that could lead us in the right direction. It was during the Depression, and we had to be very careful how we managed things or we didn't eat. I would lie down, breathe deeply, concentrate—even if I didn't truly know what that was—and rather than weigh one decision against another, wait until the ether parted and handed me a preference. That's the only way I can describe it now, but it seemed to work for our little family. I don't know if she always accepted my conclusions, but I think she did most of them. I've lost that gift from lack of practice, lack of attention, lack of trust. I'm going to work on it while I'm here. If I fall in a hole, I'll know I've lost it altogether.

Not just blunted instinct and lack of intuition make us unfit for the wild. We've coddled ourselves to the point that our skin is so thin it burns under a couple of hours of sunshine and bleeds with a scratch. We've pillowed our beds to feel like marshmallows, not like the boards we ought to sleep on, and armored ourselves against all sensitivity to outside elements. Good sense tells me the cave dwellers hereabouts didn't need half the clothing we need to stay warm, and that they didn't worry much about wearing cover-ups when they were hot. It also tells me there weren't many potbellies lolling about, folded up in their fat, rolling from the cookpot to the grave.

Attention!

What did I just hear? Oh, shit! Someone's coming up the canyon. Surely not. It's almost dark. *Splash-plunk-swish-plunk-plunk.* Go away, go away, I don't want you here! I move to the downstream corner of my shelter and peer around its pillared edge. In last light, I see two sleek heads in the water below me. They look up, startled, flip, slap the water, *pop! pop!*, and dive. Bubbles top the river's flow to the far bank. Beaver.

I go for my wimpy human aid, the flashlight, find matches, and light a fire, determined not to use the flash again. I will adjust my eyesight to the light that is—whatever it is—and *live* here without an overload of twentieth century inventions. What about the pack, the mattress, the sleeping bag, the food, the clothes, the rum ...? Never mind. I'll do the best I can. And don't tell me the Old Ones didn't have woven slings to put over their shoulders, or around their waists, to carry all sorts of things from this camp to that, over the sandstone, on the trails, and across the rivers.

Well, I'm not here to prove that I can live-exist-thrive without modern backpacker aids. I'm here to find out how to use my antenna in a different way for other reasons, to learn if they sharpen up or dull down when away from ugliness, noise, pollution, conversation, and consideration for others. (If we are caring humans, the latter will take up at least half our time in thought, plan, or action.) I expect to hone the principal senses I may need to save my ass out here—an ass that's been saved, so far, by praxis in my social world. And those senses that sharpen here: I want to see how long, or even *if*, they stay sharp when I butt them up against "civilization" on my return.

Somehow, through the lens of intimacy, a bigger picture emerges.

No one has to tell me why my uninteresting, dehydrated dinner tonight tasted like a banquet feast. With every bite I tasted musky, earth-river seasoning. It floated on the gentle downstream breeze and I sniffed it up like one does the aroma of a French chef's rare steak. Only this was *primo*. Wild earth smells tune the taste buds far better than dried, bottled, or canned flavorings.

Time for bed.

I make one in a sandy depression on my slickrock balcony, ten feet or more above the river. Pockets of sand have blown here, or been swirled in on high water, and are layered in strata, like the mother-stone. There's an alcove in the wall behind me I can crawl into if it rains. The firmament has sneezed out a billion-trillion droplets of light, so incandescent I can read by them if I choose. The toads are tuning up; a great horned has whoo-whooed me; the river's in a slow samba over some rocks below my balcony, and the moon will rise after I'm asleep.

I dream a canyon wren sonata.

❧

THE WIND WAKES ME AT DAWN.

I begin to bitch and grump about it immediately, since its sandy brush has invaded my bedroll, causing me to scratch my itches and blink sand-filled tears from my eyes. This place is supposed to be heaven. What's all the ruckus about?

Well, you little twit, your cool, wake-up bath is down there, inviting you to wade in and enjoy its soothing swirls against your itchy-bitchy skin. What are you waiting for?

I sit, swim, paddle, and lie in the river until Father Sun bites into the canyon rim, then go make coffee. My balcony faces the western walls where I sit, sipping, to watch a painting-in-progress. Colors shift, fade, change, and glow from black, midnight blue, and streaks of rust to indigo, buff, peach, salmon, and rose red; in the lower right corner the painter splashes, for contrast, a bowed, feathery head of wild green hair that trails into the river.

Decide not to leave this camp for another one tonight. I want to know if this same painting demonstration takes place tomorrow—missed certain flourishes of the brush while cooking and watching other places on the canvas and want to learn more about the technique of the artist. Maybe he'll present a slightly different brushwork, something even better. Anyhow, the demonstration is free.

The map. One more day and I swear it will start my fire. On it I read, about a half mile downstream, a side canyon, barely a blip, that says hike me! I eat cereal, make lunch, pack the daypack. Don't forget water purifying pills (never needed in Glen); take moleskin and Band-Aids; leave the damn sunglasses. Accessories. It's my age, giving me the boot again. *Qué lástima!*

Already it's heating up. Sweat pours as I thread through river, quicksand, willow banks, cottonwood compost, and mud—*without* the infernal staff I must use when carrying the big pack in high water—up sandbanks, slickrock benches, and crumbling Kayenta, to an exclamation mark in the three-hundred-foot wall. What makes the exclamation is a huge chock-rock that has toppled from some high instability and looks tightly jammed into the bottom of the crevasse. Above it, the sides open for fifty feet or so, then come together again in a curvaceous embrace. The fit below, however, is of poor quality and I discover I can wedge my small being between the chock and the wall, walk and crawl twenty feet, skirt the fallen rock, and leave the world as we know it.

Oooh ... dark in here ... and cooool ... and musky-earthy-smelling ... and damp ... and so still ... not even the river chortling from outside. My feet don't move on the sand and pebble floor. I slip the daypack forward and lean my bare body against the cool, smooth wall powdered with peachy sand, hear my breathing, and feel the thud of my heart against the stone. What time zone have I slipped into? Beyond the fact that it isn't the one I left outside, I forget about it. I'll go where this one takes me. Already I know I won't need my shoes or anything in my pack, and the sounds of their removal may be the first alien waves off these walls in many moons. No footprints, animal or human, no birdsong or whistling of the wind. I take the peach-colored sand that sticks to my backside like a shawl, and walk.

After a few bends the floor gives way to water-sculpted bedrock, but there is no water here. The floor climbs quickly, the walls lean in, a pattern that in similar crevasses means an abrupt ending. But reason need not enter here, the journey is preordained, the canyon will not end. I climb over boulders and cross beneath dry pour-overs, look up at impossible passages, smile, and find my way around and through; energy and certainty from another lifetime propelling me through space.

Around a bend and up what looks to be a difficult twist, I see more light than before: an opening up of the canyon and the heart-shaped leaves of a redbud tree backed by a varnished, sunlit wall of Navajo sandstone. The tree stops me in my tracks, my favorite of them all. Beauty in here has not escaped my senses; it's just that I know I'm to await my destination before I let it engulf me. The twist is difficult, water-worn, and smooth. I make my toes and fingers into suction cups, topping a twenty-five-foot rise I know I could not climb any other time but on this space walk.

I'm on a wide ledge, looking into a bowl where another vein enters the heart of this body of stone. The redbud seems to have sprung from the ledge near a tiny seep in the wall behind it. The slow, rhythmic sound of dripping water echoing against the surrounding stone ramparts greets me. Hypnotic and musical. A secret sound, teasingly private and alluring.

Desert water, like precious metal, appears in isolated pockets, potholes, streams. I come upon it with the excitement of discovery, as if I've uncovered the mother lode. Actually, I have. Even if I don't need to drink, I have to touch it. Something deep inside, some primal instinct I can't explain. Or I may want it for cooling off, for the sweet, sensuous *feel* of it. But if none of these, I must just *look* at it for the beauty — for the colors flowing on its surface, or lying immobile on its glass — for the wonder of its being where it doesn't seem to belong.

Desert water. The lifesaver, when it loves. The killer, when it rages.

I don't mistake the sound. It *is* water dripping, but where is it coming from and what is it falling into? The bowl is dry, woven stone. I move a bit farther along the ledge, lie down, and look over. Twenty feet below, nestled in stony swirls, a small, moss-rimmed pool materializes, its surface painted in blue and orange ripples. Three, maybe four drops of water, from somewhere out of sight, play a song on its surface. Each note falls with an echo behind it, composing a melody I half recognize from long ago.

Feeling exceptionally blessed with this day and this place, I pull back, rest my head on my arm, and fall asleep.

The odor wakes me. Not strong, but unmistakable. I would know it anywhere. Cat!

I feel the hair rising along my back and shoulders—ancient warning signals like those of our four-legged friends. The musical score I was so enthralled by has vanished in the percussion of an animal's lap-lap-lapping from the water. Even if I move to look over the edge—which I both do and don't want to do—I will see only part of the pool below. Will I see the cat? Worse, will it see *me*? The natural canyon air is rising from it to me, so maybe …

My heart is playing drums loud enough to be heard for miles around, but slowly I move forward and peer over the edge.

Its head is down to the water, busily drinking, making ripples, letting me savor the splendor of its mottled coat, its big tufted ears and curled-up, thinly striped, white-tipped stubby tail.

Bobcat. Cousin to the lynx. Not supposed to be on afternoon walkabout. My-y-y, what big feet you have! And such audacious mutton chops!

He stops drinking, walks into the water, and sits down, smiling I'm sure, cooling his balls. I've decided it's a he—too large, wrong coloration, for a female. Then he bats the water with one paw, spreads it out, and licks it clean, almost covering his whole face. Next paw—but no. In that moment he sees something he's not sure of: the reflection of my head on the less ruffled water. He noses the water, turns his head sideways, and looks up.

Can't help myself. "Hi, pussycat!" I say.

He leaps straight up, turns a zippo in midair, and is gone before the spray falls back into the pool.

⁂

AT LAST I'VE GOT THE RHYTHM of the river figured out. It comes up mid- to late morning, goes down again in late afternoon.

Stoked by the adrenaline of my pussycat encounter, feeling brave and snotty going back to camp, upstream against the flow without the staff and just the daypack, I slip and fall midstream, skin my bare butt, and bruise my knee. Where did all my rapt observation go? What happened to my senses *en pointe*? So it's okay to dream lying down, or sitting up with a drink, but not okay walking around? No-no. I remember. Matter of time. It takes a few days to "get in step with the stone," to be in tune with sensations unique to your surroundings. Like the feel of river current, and the telling sounds that signal shallow, deep, solid, loose, quick, free, or let's drown her, pack and all. In tune with light and shadow that leads or deters you, and odors that tingle your sniffer. After a few days, the senses fine-tune to the environment, and constantly thinking about them is no longer a must.

I start my fire with the map tonight and am so proud of myself that I shiver. I smell cat in the night. All in my dreams, of course, of course.

⚜

MORNING. Fleecy clouds puffing up in the sky. While watching the sun's painting demonstration on the great west wall—far different from yesterday's—I see prints around the elephant's trunk and go have a closer look. *Whoosh!* Not pussycat, not bobcat. Big cat! How nice, they are still around. They don't want to eat me or my lousy dried food, certainly not my peanut butter. Curious they are, like us; wondering what that strange smell is amid the water-leaves-rock-sand purity of their home place. I'm certain that I smell as queer to them as they smell wild and exciting to me. Logical as all this human chatter sounds, my head nerves tingle just looking at the size of those paw prints.

I pack up and walk the walk again.

Did I leave something behind? This pack feels ultralight today. Nah … it's the lightness of euphoria. When I come out of the river I'm as natant as when floating on it—do not feel gravity or my own weight, let alone my pack with camping gear and sneakers. (If I climb *heavy* out of the water it's because I have something weighty on my mind, not my back.) Bare feet take the earth in a caress, toeing its skin of silken sand and soft cool mud, its pebbly bones and sandstone curves, now and then dancing in a crotch of fallen leaves, feeling the blessed earth. How impossible for us to make such intimate contact, smashed into shoes most of our walking lives.

There's an arch up this next side canyon that I want to see, glimpsed while coming off the cap a few days ago. At least, I *think* it's this canyon. So what if it's not? I will have the great good pleasure of seeing something I've never seen before and may never see again, except in my mind's eye, forever. Through your words, Mr. Thoreau: "We cannot see anything until we are possessed with it, and then we can hardly see anything else." Or mine: Once you make a beautiful place an extension of yourself, the vividness it adds to your whole life is immeasurable.

I almost forget to dump my pack at the mouth of the side canyon. In fact, I'm several yards up its winding course before I realize I'm still carrying what I don't need. When I take it off I almost levitate. And only now do I notice the shoulder straps coated with sand. Humph, a few days ago I would have expected great drops of blood to be dripping off my breasts from the abrasions. I tuck my camera in a fanny pack and pull on my sneakers. I don't think why, just a thing I should do in this particular place.

It is far wider than my last foray, and though the sun is shining brilliantly outside, in here everything is deep blue and lavender, intimidating the Navajo peach, orange, and flesh colors. The fallen rock is more slab-shaped than sweetly rounded, more angular and rough where it has broken off and tumbled to the bottom; too recent (perhaps five hundred years) to have been beaten by whopping flash floods, then caressed by the small stream that presently flows clean and musical, fingering the jumbled bottom.

The light changes abruptly and I look up to find myself standing almost under the arch I've been seeking—no idea it was so close. Climbing a few feet higher, I find that great fallen rocks have formed a step-across over a deep blue pool beneath the stone rainbow. A sinuous flume leads water into the upper end where it dances through bubbles. I extricate my camera and walk up the first huge rock slab, intending to leap to the next one—about four feet across and almost level with it. I'm ten feet from the leap when I stop dead. Something's amiss. Two more tentative steps and I know immediately. The big rock moves ... slowly ... downward! I spin around, almost dropping the camera, dig in with the shoes, and race back to the point of beginning.

Like a secret panel closing slowly, the big slab returns to bedrock, a secret undetectable once more.

Hmmmm. Intuition working. Or did I learn from experience what I've never forgotten?

⁂

THREE OF US WERE HIKING the cap rim above Music Temple in Glen Canyon, just below the confluence of the San Juan River where the walls reach their highest straight fall to the river—a bit over 1,200 feet. We wanted a photo of the confluence with the rim in the foreground where, in a fault line, half hanging in space, a jimson weed—Datura inoxia—was in full flower. While the other two plotted their shot, about eight feet from the edge, I stood back adjusting my Rollei to take a photo of them taking a photo, and was about to snap the shutter, when they seemed to move out of frame. Both men were busy staring into their cameras and didn't notice they were rocking toward a 1,200 foot drop. I screamed, "Back up! Get off! The rock is moving!" They saw and felt it at the same time, but panic overtook the one closest to the edge, who fell on his stomach after two steps and froze, as the rock teetered toward oblivion. The other one and I managed to stand on the rising edge—by then having risen six inches from its base. Hoping it wouldn't crumble, we talked our friend out of his freeze, to his feet, and the run to safety. The rock settled back. The three of us together could not budge it or even find a fingerhold where it snuggled back into the stony dune that gave it birth. The devil's weed tossed serenely in the breeze, on the lip between life and death.

⁂

WHEN I FILL MY BOTTLE above the dancing bubbles and drop in the purifying pills, I notice algae bearding the sluiceway and clinging to some of the rocks underwater. This has always been a warning to me of abused or polluted waters, but I'm so enthralled by the beauty beneath the arch that I let the thought slide by me and spend the next half hour in the glory of the pool's color and stimulating chill, its sensuous roving fingers on my body and the incandescent play of trick-light and shadow on its surface. Swimming beneath the teetering rock, I look up to find it would have stopped its tilt on another boulder somewhat lower down and out of sight from above. So ... remembering our panic, the one in Glen Canyon might not have keeled over after all. I know there are many more seesaws waiting for the unwary trekker in this fractured land. Over the years I've stepped on hundreds of *small* ones, but these two are limousine size. We know that landmasses shift and pivot over the centuries. Erosion and death happen in a continuous flow—no mini-second between—to all parts, people, and places on this round earth, so we must call upon instinct and what's left of our primitive genes to help us pick our way safely between the centuries.

I've called the business of mastering slickrock hiking "getting in step with the stone": paying attention to balance and pressure, reading and navigating the land like a boatman does rivers. However, the art of finding ancient paths and destinations in this country asks much more of us.

Out on the big slickrock slopes and benches, our eyes learn to see routes that, when we *try* to look for them, simply aren't there. If we scan the whole terrain for the quickest, easiest, or perhaps the only route to wherever we're attempting to go, and *our* route is similar to the Old Ones', we will see paths rise up off the stone, without the painted yellow yeti feet to show us the way. Some of those paths are uncanny, so filled they are with the flesh and bone of those who came before us. How do we know they are paths? Ancient byways? Destinations? There are signs. Stone flakes (chippings), a shard of pottery, a wooden tool, something washed into a crevasse that doesn't belong way up there on the naked arms, legs, and shoulders of the sandstone canyons. There may be incisions, or drawings on the rock—dim, clever, hidden, but there if you are looking. Our eyes learn to scan, our feet to measure stride, our arms to stretch, our hands to hold for a swing around this or that boulder.

Craig Childs, author of *The Soul of Nowhere*, has the eye:

> *What is revealed is an interior landscape that will never be divulged*
> *by a map or photograph. It defines a person's vision, how one will*
> *move or pause ... something not so much seen as sensed. It is*
> *something transitory, a moment when the tone of light and the shape*
> *of the horizon, perhaps the sudden sound of an animal or wind, meet*
> *at one place, revealing the indwelling landscape.*

Indwelling is the word. Learn the indwelling and you will find
the way.

⚜

TUMMY RUMBLES. Nothing in the fanny pack to eat. I drink some
of my pilled water, stick my feet back into tennies, hike down to my
pack, find the tube of peanut butter, squeeze a glob or two into my
mouth, and drink more water to wash it down.

Late afternoon.

I stare at a twenty-foot bulging wall with bangs of desert varnish
hanging over its brow—one dark, winking eye shedding teardrops
down its cheek—and know right off that I can't tote a thirty-five-
pound pack up those Moki steps, no matter how tempting they may
be. But I must. *This* is the way out. I plunk my bare butt down on
the wet sand and look around.

The day is storybook heaven. Bees hum everywhere; wasps putty
up their multi-hogans; toads honk, *re-deep*, and trill; monarch
butterflies mirror their brazen colors across the water; and hardly a
minute goes by without a song bursting from the throat of a wee
canyon wren. Yet all is not kosher. I've a queasy feeling in my stomach and I needn't tell you what I left back there under a big rock a
while ago.

I retreat half a mile to the main river canyon.

By nightfall, I'm really sick. I drink some tea and heat some soup.
Nothing stays down, and I feel feverish. I'm rarely ill, so I don't
even take aspirin with me on hiking trips. Maybe I will next time. Is
this part of getting older? No, just dumber. Things have changed

and I haven't taken that into the equation. What was then (in Glen) is not now. More people, more usage, more everything but wild solitude and nature's purity. This canyon has been walked, stalked, and invaded all summer long and I only waited half an hour—the bottle says wait an hour—for the purifying pills to clean what ten years ago was cleaner than any pill could make it. We once filled our canteens at the mouth of this river.

I wet a T-shirt, lay it on my forehead, and try to get some rest, but I'm in and out of the bag all night long, worried about how I'll get up those Mokis without having to backtrack ten miles or more. And it's the wrong side for my car at that. Sometime during my restless, tangled sleep, I hit on a plan, and just before dawn, I fall into deep, relaxed unconsciousness, without insulting my sleeping bag.

❦

WASPS WAKE ME. They've found the peanut butter. I dropped the tube last night and the lid fell off. Do they think it's mud? "Hey, guys, I wish you all the best. You can have it. Planned to chuck it anyhow, so I can get up those Moki tear-steps." I feel weak and empty, but otherwise okay. Temperature gone. After cereal with powdered cream and water (*two* pills and eight hours this time), some Kool-Aid and an apple, I think I might live. Burying the peanut butter and other stuff I won't need for the next three days, I trudge back up the side canyon to the impasse.

These steps have been rechipped and are far better than the old notched log that served as a getting-out place many moons ago. I have lightened my pack by about five pounds. The nylon cord I have just might be long enough for me to get my raggedy ass up the steps to where I can belly down and hang over—without doing a header on the slickrock below—and haul the Blue Beast up beside me. I fill my fanny pack as full as possible with the heaviest things, stand my pack up against the wall, tie the nylon to the frame, slip the other end under the fanny pack belt, and climb up.

Damn! One step from the top, the cord falls to the ground.

Leaving the small pack, I go back down. First I think about getting a strong stick to make the nylon longer, but realizing it won't

be flexible enough, I find my jeans, tie the cord between the legs and
open zipper, pin the cuffs around my hips (yes, I *do* carry safety
pins, big ones), and climb up again. The extra two and a half feet
allow me to barely sit on the ledge, haul cautiously till I reach the
cord, and slowly pull the Beast up to join me.

All this takes most of the morning. Since I have nearly seven miles
to do today, I hoist old Blue and hit my stride. For some reason not
clear to me, I put on clothes for the first time in three days. This
makes me feel obscene and encumbered, and after one canyon turn
I stop to take them off again.

Time to amble and observe has pulled me into wayward thoughts
of comparison, avoided up to now, with the challenge of being alone
and alert. This small tributary of arches and caves, seeps and potholes
is beautiful, but I can't go crazy here like I did in Glen. In spite of
being alone, this whole show is less electrifying, less profound. Was
sharing that electrification with each other part of the hype—bal-
looning its essence, its mystery—is that the reason I find this a radi-
cally reduced version? Nah. There hasn't been a Little Arch, a Dove,
a Grotto, Driftwood, Twilight, or Cathedral among them. I'm thinking "soiled dove" for this place. Most of what can happen to me here
is predictable. Mystery has been submerged beneath the rising tide of
population. It's no longer virgin territory, nor was it even then, when
the Glen was truly pristine, when we had the unparalleled good fortune to embrace its secret places ... years before the rape.

Have I passed the stage of "joyous apprehension"?

⚜

AT FIRST I THINK it's the drone from a bee or wasp hive. Looking
around, I don't find any. I start humming and singing as well as talking to myself, but the high-pitched hum invades everything—birdsong, shouting, woodpeckers, cottonwood leaves clapping, and
nose-blowing. I look up to see if I've crossed beneath an electric
cable, knowing damn well there isn't one for miles.

Hmmm. I walk on, climb here and there, crawl through narrows,
become enticed by a seep dripping into another green algae pool,
and still the noise is there. I hear the stream's trickle, but why the

hell is it *humming*? By midafternoon I'm truly bugged, but afraid to discover what must be happening—that the sound is coming from within, not without. At last I put my hands over my ears to make sure.

Within.

I've read many a tale of prospectors, hermits, adventurers lost at sea and on land who, after several days, months, whatever, develop a ringing in their ears—don't remember reading about how long it persisted. I try banging my palm against the side of my head to knock it out; try submerging my head under a small waterfall, filling my ears with water; try wrapping a bandana around my ears and stuffing them with toilet paper. *Zzz-z-z-ing!* My brain is a tuning fork on high E-flat.

How in Buddha's balls am I going to sleep tonight?

After I make camp, have my drink, and cook my meal, I try to read the cave book by firelight, even though I'm not in a cave. I know I won't be wallowing in sleep tonight with this new tuning fork on my shoulders. Finally, too weary to fight it any longer, I lie down and watch the stars trying to outshine each other.

Must have slept, because I'm awakened by loud crunching and rustling noises. Fire's gone out—dark as doom. Aiming my flash, I see that two very industrious mice have chewed their way through my pack and are consuming nuts and raisins like Romans at a three-day bacchanal. The sound is deafening, my head aches from it, and yet I'm six feet or more away. I toss a stone at them and they scoot. Then I press my hands to aching head and ears.

The hum is gone.

Have I just passed through some threshold of sound as we know it? A cortege of ants is catering crumbs from my evening meal to a banquet at the queen's palace, and I swear I can *hear* them trotting the trail. I get up to take a pee (as ladies do) and the sound is not that of a cow pissing on a flat rock, but of ocean waves crashing on a rocky shore. Now I'm sure I won't sleep, so I build up the fire, which pops, cracks, and farts like an infernal machine; sit, patch the mouse hole in my backpack; and wonder how long this *ultra* sound will continue. Faraway coyotes lament the loss of a hare. I *feel* their distance, though the sound is more penetrating than ever before. Stars tell me midnight is nigh, so once again I lie down and try for sleep. My last remembrance: the sound of palace troops tramping the ant trail nearby.

⚜

THUNDER!

The ground shakes with it, but when I pop my head out of the sleeping bag, the morning sun blinds me and I duck back in — ground still softly booming. When it stops, I ease out and look up to the rim to check for weather and clouds; the walls are only around three hundred feet high in this part of the canyon. Looking down at me are three horses, shaggy manes blowing in the wind. Two, then three more, join them. Eight wild horses.

I wave and holler, "Hi, guys!"

Like a chorus line they peel off. First a head disappears, replaced by a tail, as one at a time they turn and go thundering across the dusty mesa. So much for the first show of the day. The second one, a couple of hours later, is a bit more exciting.

Something about the luxury of time is unsettling to those who deal with the workaday world—even to me, who doesn't have to keep to a rigid schedule and has had this kind of time before, knowing bloody well what to do with it. Am I getting antsy to be doing something more inspiring, more challenging, than walking this very narrow, utterly beautiful canyon? It's the *last* thing I would expect.

As I walk and ponder this unusual sensation, still looking intently at everything, smelling all the familiar smells, hearing (now reverted to what I'd call normal) birds, bees, water trickles, wind whistles, and frogs, I watch with amusement as a snaky strip of water makes its way slowly, then rapidly, over dry stone and damp. It snakes beneath ledges where it puddles for a few minutes in hollows, then continues doggedly on, like the tongue of a thirsty animal, its outer edges are wreathed in foam.

Foam. Holy shit!

My head snaps skyward so fast I hear my neck crack. Not a cloud anywhere. *Doesn't have to be, stupid, you know that. Looked intently huh? But failed to observe what you should have, like a way out of these possibly flooding narrows now!* Fear makes a geyser of my adrenaline, a geyser that momentarily floods the brain and sends adrenaline to those parts of the body that need it for survival—my feet and legs.

Subconsciously I must have been keeping my eye on the cliffs that entrench me, because I *do* recall a place about a quarter mile back where the walls dropped to low rounded knobs that I thought would be interesting to climb, merely for another perspective on my surroundings. When I spin around to run back, I see the tongue has passed me but is not in as big a hurry as I am to get where it's going. I rush past and hear a booming noise that I take for the flood train coming down only to discover it's my pulse hammering on my eardrums.

A couple of hundred feet downcanyon, I begin to slow. The fear geyser has given out. My legs sting from panicky exertion and my breath comes in dry wheezes. Don't hear anything yet, but know I soon will. Water is on the way. It could flash or rise slowly, depending on the gradient, the hollows and diversions, the magnitude of rain—wherever it is. One thing is certain: I should be farther out of reach when it finds me than I am at the moment.

My thinker starts ticking again, and from past experience I know there's nothing more fascinating than watching nature on a rampage. No matter how fearful, the spectacle never fails to pull me in. I don't want to be flushed from this canyon. I came here to enter stone; to take, steal, or borrow whatever I need from it; to be a part of its grandness, its great strength and endurance; to gain insight and take pleasure in all its forms. If I want to watch and share whatever might be taken away or given by this flash of water, I can't let myself be flipped out by fear. I need to ride it and guide it like a boat through rapids. Follow the bubble trail ... down.

A couple of quick turns of the canyon and I find a bench I can climb up to with my pack. The channel, at least fifty feet wide here, will take huge flooding before it reaches me, a dozen or more feet above the bedrock. Certainly I'm in a state of alarm, but to me *real* fear is intellectual—of being left in limbo, maimed beyond recovery, paralyzed, with no control over my wounded life—not fear driven by adrenaline. I've no *fear* about the end of my existence on this planet. But I don't want it to hurt.

I sit down on my pack and wait.

Ten or more minutes pass before the snaky little tongue comes licking around the corner at a slightly faster pace than what drove me to this perch in such a frenzy. No booming noises, no roaring splashes. It hardly says, *whisssh*, wiggling over the slickrock bottom.

"Well," I say, disgusted. "You sure ain't nuthin' to get excited about. I thought I was going to watch you throw a tantrum. At the rate you're going, you'll dry up before you go another mile!"

Minutes and hours in this country mean nothing, except when one is under duress, so I don't know how long it takes my licky friend to fill a nice-sized pothole before ambling on its way, before the silt settles out; before I decide a bath in something deeper than a pie pan will be ideal. I fish around in my pack for soap and even a wash rag before moving down to this nice new pool, taking off my tennies and slipping in, *ooohing* about the luxury of it all: the sky is blue, the sun at apex, the birds ... none.

A noise like a B-24 bomber assails my solitude, rumbles, then sounds as if it has crashed somewhere upcanyon. In my languor, wits do not collect themselves in rational order, or even toward panic, until ... the ground beneath me shakes, ripples dance on the water, and twenty lions roar all together! Like a comet, I'm out of the pool, stuffing my foot into one tennie, when, around the bend and into the opposite wall, a three-foot jumble of red gunk, branches, trees, mud, sand, rocks, foam, cowshit (and cows, for all I know) crashes against the cliff, curls into a wave, and descends toward me. I grab my other tennie, nearly drop it, scale the wall to my ledge, and stand, riveted, watching the bumping, grinding spectacle below me.

Again, time evades me.

The flood does not rise above four or five feet—nothing really, compared to debris left much higher on these walls from previous deluges—nor continue more than what seems like half an hour before it subsides. I learn it has voices all its own. First it bellows with anger; then follows snarling resentment at whatever momentarily bars its way. Having ridden over, slammed aside, or gouged out whatever obstructs it, the flood rolls along, hissing arrogantly, proud of itself. Finally it gurgles away, chortling over the mess it has left behind. Such a loudmouth.

I hope it's happy with my soap and wash rag.

❧❧❧

WHEN I LEAVE THE CANYON two days later, I try to assess the main difference between my solo and my trips with others. I've always thought my senses were alert to living outside. I grew up in the desert and spent most of my youth under the sun excoriating my skin, preferring that to covering it up. But I have learned that alertness is not enough. One must control one's fear, channel it like a hot arrow toward reason—a thing that's hard to do when you're alone, especially if you're the skittish type like me. Or else, you could ride panic over the edge. I tap the gray matter to analyze fear's many venues, conscious and subconscious, its velocity, recurrence, intensity, and endurance.

Does survival depend on our *reading* of the adrenaline rush?

At the beginning, my state of "joyous apprehension" could have been a disguised fear that came in quick and went out fast with "*To hell with it, I'm not about to kick off here!*" When the "horror syndrome" rolled in, it felt like vapor, lifting and falling. When did it leave for good? The heart quickens when we crawl into unknown, spooky places. This is natural behavior, subconscious, a welling up from some dark cavern of the mind. We don't really think about it; it just happens. The hair rising—fear of the unseen or unexpected, the bobcat—not a propelling fear. It told me "*Be still, look, listen, don't move.*" Depending on the velocity of the event, hair can rise *after* a sudden encounter with danger that has passed us by. Fear relief. Check that one; it's more a skin-prickle than rising hair.

Nature and her tricks! *Relax not in stone hammocks of excruciating beauty.* The trickle, rather than honing my senses toward possible catastrophe, lulled me into complacency. Ah, so. Then came the fear that definitely does propel: the rock tipping, the flash flood coming down. Adrenaline rushes from the heart to all muscles of the body if we must swim, to wings if we must fly; and some say they actually have, otherwise they would not be among us. Nor would others who've lifted the whole front end of a truck by themselves when adrenaline invaded their whole body, making them superhuman.

I discover why there'd been a dribble, then a flash, as I walk up and out on the last day of my hike, stumbling over the belch of desert flora and fauna until I come to the junction that explains it all. The big flood entered a side canyon's drainage far to the west of the main branch, which received only a trickle.

I feel a great sense of peace and accomplishment as I exit the canyon and walk calmly, happily, tiredly down the short remaining trail to my car.

It isn't there!

Someone's stolen my car. I know exactly where I parked it. It's gone! Fear of walking miles in the hot sun where no one will pick me up. Fear of having no water left in my bottle. Fear of not being able to get home in time for my next gig. Pity: *Why me? What did I do to deserve this?* Fear of—

You dumb twit. You left your car at the *getting-in* place, two miles down the road. This is the *getting-out* place!

Credits

"Juan for the Road," part of the *Tucson Trilogy*, was first published in *City Magazine*, Tucson, AZ, January 1989. Poetry excerpts are from Henry Herbert Knibbs: *Make Me No Grave*, and Charles Badger Clark: *The Old Cowman*. The songs include "The Lineman's Lament," a parody of "The Cowboy's Lament," and Nick and Charles Kenny: "Leaning on the Old Top Rail."

"His Heart to the Hawks" was published in slightly different form in *Earth First Journal, Edward Abbey—A Tribute,* by Dave Foreman, Spring 1989.

"When Rivers Sing" was published in *The Canyon Zephyr*, Moab, UT, Vol. 11, No. 4, October/November 1999.

"My Friend Tad" was originally the Introduction to Tad Nichols's book, *Glen Canyon: Images of a Lost World*, Museum of New Mexico Press, 1999.

"Reentry from the Wild Out Yonder" was published in the *Journal of the American Whitewater*, Vol. XL, No. 2, March/April 2000.

"The Lesson" was published in the *Mountain Gazette*, April 2004.

"Sandstone Seduction" was published in the *Mountain Gazette*, No. 82, September/October 2001.

"The Ride" was published in the *Mountain Gazette*, No. 78, December 2000.

"The Cottonwood Leaf" was published in the *Mountain Gazette*, No. 80, May/June 2001.

About the Author

Katie Lee was a prominent singer, songwriter, Western historian, river runner, actress, environmentalist, filmmaker, explorer, and author. She was born in Aledo, Illinois on October 23, 1919. However, she referred to herself as a native of Arizona as her family moved to Tucson before she was a year old. Lee worked her way through the University of Arizona by singing at a local hotel, foreshadowing her future singing career. After earning her Bachelor of Fine Arts in drama from the University of Arizona, she embarked upon a Hollywood career working in films, television, and on the radio, while also singing in lounges.

After a decade in Hollywood, making films and signing, Katie Lee returned to Arizona, where she began establishing herself as a folk and Western singer, working with many top artists like Josh White, Ramblin' Jack Elliot, and Harry Belafonte during her long career.

Perhaps the most significant chapter in Lee's life began in 1953 when she first ran the Colorado River in the Grand Canyon. Later that year, she took her first trip through Glen Canyon, falling deeply in love with the Glen Canyon area. Over the following years, Lee and two companions, Frank Wright and Tad Nichols, made 15 more trips through the canyon. We Three, as they referred to themselves, named 25 of Glen Canyon's side canyons during their trips. Lee fought long and hard against the damming of the Colorado River to create Lake Powell, joining other prominent figures and friends like David Brower, Martin Litton, and Edward Abbey in standing against the Glen Canyon Dam. Lee was a prominent member of the Glen Canyon Institute, which today (2020) continues the movement to restore Glen Canyon. She settled in Jerome, Arizona in 1971, where she ran Katydid Books and Music, her publishing company.

Katie Lee had a distinguished publication and recording list. She recorded nine albums during her career, including *Folk Songs and Poems of the Colorado River* (1964), *Songs of Couch and Consultation* (1958), *Life is Just a Bed of Neuroses* (1960), *Saucy Songs for Cool Knights* (1960), *Ten Thousand Goddam Cattle* (to accompany her book, 1976), *Fenced!* (1983), *Colorado River Songs* (1988), *The Best of Katie Lee* (1990s) and *His Knibbs and the Badger* (with Ed Stabler, 1992). She wrote articles about cowboy poetry for *Arizona Highways* and the *Journal of Arizona History*. Her documentary, The Last Wagon, won the 1972 CINE Golden Eagle Award. Interviews with cowboys Gail Gardner and Billy Simon were preserved in her short film *The Last Wagon* which won the Golden Eagle Award in 1972. *Ten Thousand Goddam Cattle* was published by Northland Press in 1976, and *All My Rivers Are Gone: A Journey of Discovery Through Glen Canyon* (1998) and *Sandstone Seduction: River and Lovers, Canyon and Friends* (2004) were originally published by Johnson Books and republished by Bower House (2023).

Lee died peacefully in her home in Jerome, Arizona on November 1, 2017, shortly after her 98th birthday.